ABOUT THE AUTHOR

ANTHONY TELFORD wrote *The Kitchen Think* out of frustration at trying to find quick answers to questions raised by his own cookbook collection. He has worked in professional kitchens as a chef since the age of 15. Telford has written about food for Melbourne's *Herald Sun*, *Bean Scene magazine*, *Melbourne Palate* and other publications. He was co-presenter for three years on Monday mornings food segment on Melbourne radio *3RRR*, and is a regular guest on *ABC radio*.

Telford was chef–presenter on Australian television, including the *Channel 9* series *'Guess Who's Coming to Dinner?'*, *Channel 10's* series *'Ready, Steady Cook'* and *Channel 10's* live morning show *'9am with David & Kim'* for 3 years. He has also been a regular demonstrator at food events and festivals and was the emcee for three years at *The Good Food and Wine Show* in Sydney, Brisbane and Melbourne. He also sat as a committee member for the Australian Culinary Federation. Telford has seven children and three Grand children and currently resides in Sydney, Australia where he continues cooking, eating, cooking, writing and cooking.

THE KITCHEN THINK

KITCHEN
WISDOM
BY
ANTHONY
TELFORD

sporr

First published in 2021

SPORR
12 Marsden Street
Camperdown NSW 2050
Australia

Book design: by Anthony Telford
Cover design: by Amy Kirchhoff
Cover artwork: by Luke Liu

"If you don't know, now you know"

The Notorious B.I.G

CONTENTS

INTRODUCTION

What separates the great or even good cook from the common being? It is the ability to see food and cooking as something beyond simple sustenance, see it as more than haute cuisine, so much more than junk food. Good cooks follows the seasons, becoming excited at the arrival of the first tray of local mangoes. They reprimand the local butcher, gives thanks to the fishmonger, smells the oil upon first opening it, stores tomatoes on the window ledge not in the fridge and drinks the wine with which they cook. A good cook will at least try the stinkiest of stinky cheeses. They will eat take-away, they will dine out in great restaurants and grace the tables of several bad ones. Most importantly, good cooks will talk about and share food with passion and with sincerity.

Stress is still rife in both the domestic and commercial kitchen: angry professional chefs abusing the waitstaff, young commis chefs screaming at kitchen hands, cooks attacking fellow cooks, and stressed domestic cooks brought to tears as the soufflé deflates faster than a chef's ego on the release of yet another food guide. Both the common cook and the high priests of cooking - Chefs - will inevitably, burn, under-prove, overcook, curdle, cut too thin, dice too chunky, toughen, crack, collapse, explode, wilt, mush, dry out, over-spiced and under salt.

One of my purposes in writing *The Kitchen Think* is to take this stress out of the kitchen by providing quick, easy access to problem-solving ideas and quick answers to irritating questions and ingredients. This book does not spoon feed, but rather gets you started on a culinary journey, and pushes you to continue by asking questions of suppliers and producers, of industry people, bookstore owners or fellow cooks. Along the way you will make mistakes, learn and rectify – the natural path of any good cook.

At a time when it seems everyone has something to say about food, when so many cooks want to share their slice of food wisdom through the written word, there is inevitably confusion.

Cooks and cookbooks have become a commodity in the global marketplace. The downside to this boom is that home cooks are left labouring through unfamiliar jargon, measurements and ingredients in books published in other parts of the world. *The Kitchen Think* aims to solve some of these mysteries by providing alternative names and explanations of products that may not be available where you live.

Of course, there are many, many questions on food left unanswered here, but this is a seemingly endless topic. I can only hope that my book answers the more common conundrums.

HOW TO USE THIS BOOK

Entries are arranged in strict alphabetical order (ignoring hyphens, apostrophes and word spaces). Headwords are printed in **BOLD-FACE TYPE** with alternative names in **lower-case bold**.

Cross references are printed in SMALL CAPITALS. Alternative names are listed alphabetically and cross referenced, unless they include the headword within their name (for example, 'rock melon' is not listed under 'r' because it includes the word 'melon' in its name).

All tables appear at the back of the book (see the contents list for table subjects).

A.

ABALONE belongs to the family Haliotidae, a marine gastropod mollusc or better easily described as a marine snail. Available fresh, tinned, frozen and dried, each requiring different treatment. To shuck fresh abalone from the shell, cut the connector muscle then pry out the flesh. Trim and discard the viscera (soft organs), remove the dark skin from the foot muscle (the actual edible part) and scrub the muscle to remove the black coating. The cleaned abalone can now be cut into thick steaks against the grain of the meat, then tenderised. (Note that pounding fresh abalone flesh to within an inch of disintegration is frowned upon by Asian cooks, who take immense pride in serving this expensive product; one does not need to treat abalone like OCTOPUS to guarantee tenderness.)

Fresh abalone need only be sliced very thinly and cooked very quickly, whether poached (steamboat style) or stir-fried. In a restaurant, fresh abalone should be presented to you in the shell, with the wriggling flesh exposed, before being taken away and cooked. Frozen abalone is not a substitute for the fresh product. It is better suited to soups or stewed in rich sauces and is the least exciting of the abalone styles available. Dried abalone resembles a rock, both in appearance and in texture, but the drying process, considered an art form in Japan, actually enhances the flavour. Experienced Chinese chefs cook dried abalone whole, in a sauce that is considered just as important as the abalone itself. The recipe is a well-kept secret, but involves a rich stock of chicken, pork and ham, and up to 13 hours of slow cooking. Also known as **paua** in New Zealand.

ABBREVIATIONS see page 254.

ACHIOTE see ANNATTO

ACIDULATED WATER is water with lemon or lime juice added, used to prevent cut fruit or vegetables from browning.

ADDITIVES see page 268.

AFRICAN HORNED CUCUMBER see KIWAN

AGAR-AGAR is used to set liquids into a jelly-like texture. It derives from the gelidium species of red sea vegetables, and the best known variety is Japanese isinglass (not to be confused with plain ISINGLASS). It is available powdered, flaked, in strands or in bars/sheets known also as **kanten bars**. Although more expensive, flakes, strands or bars of agar-agar are better than powdered, which bleaches and sulphuric acid. Some foods will not set with agar-agar (or gelatine) because of how acid or alkaline they are. These include kiwifruit, pineapple, fresh figs and pawpaw. Citrus fruit and berries require a higher than usual quantity of agar-agar, and chocolate and spinach do not set easily. Agar-agar is used by vegans as a substitute for animal-based gelatine.

HOW TO USE AGAR-AGAR
Soak in the cold liquid for 10 minutes. Bring to the boil gently and stir until dissolved (5 minutes for powder, 10–15 minutes for flakes/bars). Leave to set at room temperature for about an hour, then refrigerate (it should be refrigerated as it is high in proteins

1 teaspoon agar powder = 1 tablespoon agar flakes = 1/2 agar bar
The ratios below are a guide only – I recommend that you experiment a little as the amount of agar you need for a recipe can vary:
- for a hard set: 1 tsp agar powder per cup of liquid
- for a soft set/wobbly: ½ – ¾ tsp agar per cup
- for a 'jam-like' effect: 1/3 – ½ tsp agar per cup
- for dressing-like effect: ¼ tsp agar per cup

A jelly made with agar may 'sweat' when in humid weather. To prevent this, you may dissolve 1 teaspoon of corn starch (corn flour) with the agar into the liquid that you are cooking it in.

For other similar thickeners see also CARRAGEEN; GELATINE; GELOZONE.

AGAVE NECTAR see 'alternatives to sugar' in SUGAR

AJOWAN, also known as *ajwain, ajowan caraway, thymol seeds, bishop's weed,* or *carom* is a member of the family Apiaceae. The dried seed is reasonably hot with a strong thyme-like flavour. Bothe the leaves and the seeds of the 'herb' plant are edible. Harvested in the North of India and therefore used mostly in Indian cuisine.

ALARIA see SEAWEED

AL DENTE translates as 'to the tooth'. When a recipe asks for something to be cooked al dente, that doesn't mean the food is as hard as a tooth, but that it is cooked through while still firm to the bite – it gives the teeth a feeling or sensation of biting into that food. Usually refers to cooking pasta or rice, but can be used to describe other cooked foods.

ALLERGIES A food allergy should not be mistaken for a food intolerance. A food allergy is often caused by the immune system responding to proteins within the food and overloading on chemicals such as histamine, which in turn brings about the allergic reaction such as swelling, On the other hand, an intolerance or a sensitivity to a food or an ingredient within food is often linked too ther health problems. It has more to do with digestion and has less defined symptoms. Food allergies in adults are rarely curable, while food sensitivities will often improve or disappear over a period of time.

Allergy symptoms range from localised hives and swelling to the life-threatening anaphylaxis, which causes difficulty in breathing or a drop in blood pressure (shock). Vomiting, diarrhoea, blocked or runny nose, an intense sense of fear, dizziness, swelling of the face and throat (extreme swelling and immediate facial disfigurement are not uncommon), difficulty in thinking and tightness in the chest are also signs to beware of.

Allergies from food occur in around 1 in 20 children and 1 in 100 adults. In up to 80% of cases, children grow out of these, but allergies to nuts, seeds and seafood often continue into adult life and must be monitored. The most severe allergies, which can cause anaphylaxis, are o peanuts, tree nuts (such as pistachios, walnuts, almonds, pecans, brazil nuts and macadamias) and shellfish. Other common allergies are cow's milk, soy, eggs, fish and gluten.

Seek immediate advice from a medical practitioner if you have any adverse reaction to any food or drink. Alternatives to allergy-causing foods can often be successfully replaced with alternative ingredients, but some alternatives will change the flavour and or texture of a recipe. Milk, eggs, wheat and gluten have alternatives, for example, but it's hard to replace nuts and seafood without changing the nature of the recipe entirely. See specific foods for suggested substitutes.

Beware of cross-contamination when preparing food for a guest with an allergy. Even the tiniest particle can trigger a nasty reaction. Food should be prepared on completely different chopping boards and benches and in different pans. Do not deep-fry the food someone is allergic to with food they intend to eat.

ALLSPICE also known as **English spice** and **Jamaica pepper** (and in some countries, **pimento**) is the dried, unripe berry from an evergreen tree of the myrtle family, native to the island of Jamaica. Not to be confused with MIXED SPICE, although the name suggests a mix of different spices, in fact it derives from the aroma's likeness to a mix of cloves, cinnamon, pepper and nutmeg. If necessary, you can replace allspice with equal parts of those four spices. For really fresh allspice, buy the whole berry and pound or grind your own powder. See also SPICE MIXES AND PASTES.

ANCHOVY is a common, small saltwater forage fish and member of the herring (Engraulidae) family. Anchovies are sold fresh (hard to find), packed in salt, tinned in oil, as a paste (a concentrate, so take care with quantities) or even as a sauce.
Anchovies are great as a salt substitute in some dishes or sauces. Instead of seasoning with salt, drop two or more fillets into the sauce. They dissolve as they heat, adding a distinctive but not strong anchovy / fish flavour to the sauce. (For cold sauces, blend in the anchovies.) If you find them too salty, soak the fillets in cold water for 10–15 minutes then drain before use.
To prepare fresh anchovies, remove head, backbone and innards, rinse inside and out, dry with paper towels, then either pan-fry or

marinate (in olive oil, fresh herbs, and either lemon juice or white wine vinegar and lemon juice). Salted anchovies are considered by many professionals to be superior quality to tinned anchovies, which tend to be over-processed and mushy. To prepare, wash off the salt and remove the backbone. For a sauce or flavouring they are now ready for use. For salads or starter dishes, they must now be soaked in cold water until softened – change the water several times, it will take 30 minutes to an hour. If you don't plan to use immediately, pat them dry with a paper towel and store in oil (for up to a week), as they deteriorate quickly once removed from their salt-packed tin.

ANISE is similar in appearance to dill seed. Although often used in in cakes and biscuits, it is mainly harvested for use in alcohol (pernot, ouzo and raki). Not to be confused with STAR ANISE.
ANNISE PEPPER see SICHUAN PEPPER

ANNATTO is a small, triangular, brick-red spice with only the slightest sweet and peppery flavour. It is used more often as a colouring, in cheese, butter and confectionery and in Filipino, Latin American and Caribbean cuisine (described in *Food* by *Waverly Root* as a spice 'with which red Americans coloured their bodies and white Americans colour their butter'). There is no real substitute for annatto, as few other foods can provide this natural food colouring without also imparting their stronger individual flavour, thus the similarly coloured saffron, turmeric or paprika will alter the nature of the dish. A small quantity of cochineal will impart a deep-red hue similar to annatto (but then vegans would miss out, as cochineal is made from crushed and dried beetles). Also known as **achiote**, annatto can be bought in Asian and Indian grocers.

ANTI-CAKING AGENTS are added to salt in very small percentages to keep it free-flowing in all weather conditions. These are alumine-calcium silicate, ferro-cyanide, sodium aluminosilicate and yellow prussiate of soda. The allergy and health conscious will opt for a more natural, unrefined salt such as Celtic sea salt (high in minerals) to avoid the anti-caking agents.

APPLE It is suggested that there are up to 10 000 varieties of apple, yet the 5 to 10 varieties at the local supermarket are still too confusing for some, who buy based on price per kilogram rather than quality and what a particular variety can offer. While all apples can be eaten raw, some are better suited to cooking, and these fall into two groups: those that fall apart to create a mash or sauce (Bramley, McIntosh, Cortland, Melba), and those that retain their shape making them great for pies, compotes or for baking whole (Golden Delicious, Granny Smith, Winesap, Rome, Baldwin, Rhode Island). The **crab apple** is no bigger than 5 cm in diameter. And although this fruit may be eaten fresh, it is often too sour so is usually reserved for pickling, in jams and for CANDYING.

The ROSE APPLE is not of the apple family, and is also known as **java apple, wax apple** and **watery rose apple.**

 **Top tips for apples**

~ Leaving apples at room temperature for too long can retard the flavour, so keep chilled.
If chilled, leave the apples to reach room temperature before eating - this to maximise the apples natural flavour.

~ Peeled apples can be placed in ACIDULATED WATER (water mixed with lemon juice) to avoid browning, although rather than have them absorb water a better method is to toss them in a bowl with a good squeeze of lemon juice. No lemons? Use another citrus: orange, grapefruit, lime or mandarin, or even bottled pineapple juice.

~ Use leftover apples for an apple puree that can be frozen for later use: cook the peeled and diced apples over a slow heat with as little water as possible (preferably no water). This allows them to break down naturally, without adding excess water. Never sweeten this mix; it is best to add sugar just before using. As a vegan alternative, apple puree can be used in recipes where egg is used to add moisture as well as bind ingredients together (for example, muffins, cookies and dense cakes).

APPLE PIE SPICE Other than the obvious use, this spice mix is also used in biscuits, sweet breads and other desserts. By making your own spice blends, you can tweak the amounts and customise the blend to meet your own taste. Try the following recipe:

HOME-MADE APPLE PIE SPICE
Mix together:
1 tsp cloves
1 tsp nutmeg
3 tsp cinnamon
OR
3 tsp cinnamon
1 1/2 tsp nutmeg
3/4 tsp cardamom

AQUAFABA see CHICKPEA

ARTICHOKE see GLOBE ARTICHOKE; JERUSALEM ARTICHOKE

ARUGULA see LEAFY GREENS

ASAFOETIDA is sometimes called **giant fennel**, although it smells nothing like fennel and comes from the sap of the stem or roots of the asafoetida plant (a member of the parsley family). What it does smell like is more in tune with its colloquial names, **stinking gum** or **devil's dung**. The name comes from the Persian word 'aza' meaning 'resin' and the Latin word 'fetida' meaning 'stinking'. The unpleasant smell mellows when cooked however, leaving an aroma more like onion. Important in any authentic Indian or Middle Eastern cooking, it is used in place of garlic and as a flavour enhancer and a digestive aid.

ASPARAGUS means spring - figuratively speaking, of course: the time to use this vegetable when in its prime. Use as soon as possible after purchase or store well chilled for no more than 3–5 days. Before cooking, snap off any fibrous ends with your fingers – it's said that asparagus breaks naturally in just the right place. Do this by holding the asparagus three quarters of the way down the stem (from the tip), and hold the very end with the other hand, snap. **Purple asparagus** turns green when cooked as the purple pigment is destroyed by heat. **White asparagus** is produced from either variety by excluding light during the growing.
Soil is mounded over the row of asparagus and the spears are

cut while still under the surface (when they push the soil upward or when a wet spot is noted on the surface of the soil just before the spear breaks through). Spears must be handled in the absence of light during cutting and packing to keep them white. Incidentally, the reason why asparagus causes smelly urine is that the body makes a substance called methanethiol when processing asparagus which passes through the bladder as little as 15–20 minutes after consumption - Asparagus anosmia (as it is known) affects about 60% of the population.

ATEMOYA see CUSTARD APPLE

AUBERGINE see EGGPLANT

AVOCADO There are close to 30 varieties of cultivated avocado, from the Anaheim to the Zutano, each with specific qualities, tastes and oil content (from 12–25%). Haas (the best quality), with its dark, pebbly-green skin, and Fuerte, with a smooth green skin, are the most common; the many others from around the world tend to have short seasons, but are worth sourcing when available. Avocado leaves can be toasted slightly in a pan, cooled then ground with a mortar and pestle to release their subtle fragrance of anise and hazelnuts. Use in stews, chicken or fish dishes and salads made with avocado.

 Top tips for avocados
~ **To check ripeness,** gently press at the narrow, stalk end of the fruit. (This is where the fruit is most dense; if it is ripe it should give when pressed at this end, not at the bulbous, seed-filled end.
~ **To hasten ripening**, place in a paper bag with a ripe apple (the slow release of ethylene from the apple will initiate ethylene production from the avocado).
~ **Store** ripe avocados in the fridge for 4–10 days – how long they last will depend on the variety. As a general rule, the smooth, green-skinned varieties bruise more easily and do not store as long as rougher, dark-skinned avocados.
~ **To remove the seed** or stone, cut the avocado in half, give the seed a firm (not aggressive) hit with the heel of the knife blade,

twist and pull. Peel or use a large spoon to scoop out the flesh in one go.

~ The flesh of an avocado will inevitably brown after you've cut into it. To help prevent browning, brush with citrus juice, mash and mix with lemon or lime juice, or leave the seed in the half not being used, cover and refrigerate. Pre-mashing avocado flesh and storing back in the skin will also help to lessen the browning effect.

~ **To freeze** - Avocado flesh can be stored in the freezer for up to 2 months.

B.

BABACO is related to PAPAYA but keeps better. Babaco has no seeds and the thin skin is also edible. The slightly acidic flavour resembles that of strawberries or even pineapple, with hints of papaya. Use as you would a papaya. For ripeness look for well-yellowed fruit. Store in the fridge for up to 6 weeks or at room temperature for 3–4 weeks.

BACALAO is dried salted cod, popular in Italy, Spain and France. The best bacalao is said to come from Norway as it is less salty and softer. To prepare bacalao for cooking, soak for 2–3 days in cold water, changing the water 2–3 times a day. It can now be served with rice, and cooked in casseroles, stews and risottos, among many other dishes – the Portuguese claim over 300 uses for this salty fish. *Baccalà* is one of the many alternative spellings.

BACON is the salt cured and sometimes smoked pork belly, rib eye and in some cases, the shoulder or leg. Most countries have a version based on regulations. Bacon from the US is considered the bench mark for serious bacon eaters. Similar cuts of meat from other animals is also treated the same way and referred to as 'bacon'- for non pig eaters.

BAIN-MARIE, also known as a **water bath**, is a method of cooking food such as custards and other delicate egg or meat dishes. The food is placed in a dish that is in turn placed in a container of water (usually filled to halfway up the dish) then cooked in an oven or in some cases on the stove top at a low temperature. The idea is that the water prevents dry heat from scorching the outer parts of the food and produces steam which gently cooks the food evenly through to the centre. A cloth or towel is often placed at the base of the tray before water is added – as insulation to help maintain an even temperature. Bain-marie can also refer to the device used to keep food hot at (hopefully) safe temperatures for long periods of time. Seen anywhere from cheap snack bars and chicken shops to dubious all-you-can-eat smorgasbords and the more controlled hotel buffets.

BAKE To cook food in the dry heat of an oven. Note that the degree of dryness in the oven is determined by the food that is being baked. This means that if a batch of biscuits is in the oven, and then a roast is thrown in as well, the moisture or steam produced from the roast can and most probably will affect the outcome of the biscuits, both in texture and flavour.

BAKING This entry deals with baking cakes, biscuits, etc. See BREAD and YEAST for baking bread. See also BAKING POWDER, BICARBONATE SODA, EGGS, MEASUREMENTS and OVENS for more tips.

 Top tips for baking
~ Always sift flour to aerate it, making for a lighter, fluffier result. It can help to sift flour two or three times. If you do not own a sieve or sifter, take to the dry ingredients with a whisk.
~ When measuring in cups, moist or dense ingredients should be firmly packed into the cup. This isn't always an exact science so I favour weight measurements which tend to be more accurate.
~ Ingredients such as syrup, MOLASSES and HONEY can be a mess to measure: rub the spoon or cup with a thin layer of oil to avoid sticking.
~ When measuring several different ingredients on a set of scales, use a layer of cling wrap or paper each time. It saves wiping

the scales between measurements and provides a pouring device as well.

~ Solid and liquid fat cannot be substituted for one another in baking. Liquid fats can be replaced with other liquid fats and solid with solid. Note that melted butter is a solid fat, as the milk solids set when baked.

~ Beware of over beating egg whites. Many recipes call for egg whites to be 'beaten until peaks form', but these should be soft peaks, not stiff and dry. Whipping by hand, although the best results.

~ When baking with any flour other than wheat flour, use a lower temperature for a longer time. This is especially important if baking without milk and egg.

~ Always toss chopped fruit, dried fruit or nuts in the flour before adding liquid to the mix. This will help them stay evenly dispersed throughout the mixture and not sink to the bottom.

~ Accurate oven temperatures are important which is why it is vital to preheat the oven. See OVENS for more information.

~ Bake cakes and biscuits in a clean oven to ensure that no leftovers from roasts or other savoury dishes splatter or drop crusty bits into your delicate sweets.

✅ Top tips for cakes

~ Use the 'spring back' to see if your cake is ready, as sticking skewers and knives into the cake can mark the surface. Gently press the cake with a finger and watch it spring back to its original shape. If it stays indented, give it another 5 minutes in the oven.

~ Cakes made with a flour other than wheat flour tend to be drier. Try adding a small percentage of soy flour to the recipe (1 tablespoon per cup of flour), as it contains more moisture than other flours. Store the cake in an airtight container.

~ Tea cakes (not mousse or dense cream cakes) are best served at least 12 hours after they have been made (good luck) and at room temperature.

~ When making chocolate cake, dust the inside of the tin with cocoa or carob powder instead of flour. For other flavoured cakes, dust the tin with some of the dry cake mix. This helps to prevent flour build-up on the outside of a cake.

~ Many cakes can be successfully frozen (tea cakes, chocolate, flourless, lemon, fruitcake, marble cakes). They should be frozen immediately after cooling for the best taste and texture.

~ Frozen cakes should be left to defrost for 12 hours in the fridge, then left at room temperature for 12 hours before decoration and consumption.

~ De-chill icy cold mixing bowls – run them under warm tap water then dry before using (not hot tap water – just warm). Why? Eggs aerate faster and better when slightly warm. A cold bowl will lower temperature of eggs. This is a general useful baking tip – eg softened butter creamed in an icy cold bowl will make it firm up.

~ Eggs at room temperature – these will fluff better and faster. It's easy to warm up fridge cold eggs – just leave in warm water for 5 minutes.

Problem solving

~ **Burnt?** Remove the burnt bits with a knife or grater. Cover with icing or slice into layers, brush with melted jam or liqueur and stick back together before icing or covering with cream.

~ **Curdled batter?** If the cake, muffin or biscuit mix starts to separate as you add the eggs, the eggs are too cold. This causes the fat (butter) to harden, which prevents the mix from emulsifying. The best thing is to use room temperature eggs and incorporate one at a time until completely mixed. If the mixture has already separated, it will make very little if any difference to the final product, so simply carry on, mixing in the dry ingredients as if nothing happened.

~ **Lopsided?** If cakes constantly come from your oven lopsided, you have a problem with your oven. Rotate the cake 180 degrees in the oven while cooking to even things up. If it's too far gone, cool the cake then slice off the top to even it up, turn it over and ice the bottom.

~ **Some parts of the cake burning as it cooks?** If the cake is burning around the rim, yet the centre is still runny, turn the oven temperature down immediately (to about 140°C) until the cake is cooked. Check the oven temperature against a thermometer: the thermostat may be broken.

~ **Cracked surface?** Cover with a clean, dry towel: the heat and moisture should help reduce the size of the crack. To avoid this happening next time, try undercooking the cake by several minutes, then remove from the oven and cover with a bowl. This allows the cake to steam slightly, holding in the heat and gently finishing the cooking process.

~ **Collapsed cake?** Allow the cake to cool a stiff drink or four to calm the nerves. Then set about layering the cake to make up for lost height in baking. Slice horizontally into two or three layers. Brush each layer with melted jam or alcohol, with fruit (strawberries, bananas, cherries), whipped cream, custard (extra-thick packet custard or crème patissière), chocolate ganache or any combination of these. The flat base of the cake will end up on top, so it looks perfect every time.

✅ **Top tips for biscuits, cookies and slices**

~ The best flour for making biscuits is plain or all-purpose flour, but try replacing about 10% of the flour with cornflour or rice flour to soften the texture.

~ **Chill your biscuit/cookie dough** - Chilling cookie dough in the refrigerator firms it up, which decreases the possibility of over-spreading. It not only ensures a thicker, more solid cookie but an enhanced flavour as well.

~ Make 3 or 4 times the recipe. Cook only what you need, then roll the remainder of the biscuit
dough in foil. Keep it in the freezer for a rainy day.

~ **One batch at a time** - Only if you're able and time allows it, baking one batch at a time on the centre rack. *Why?* You get the best possible results when the oven only concentrates on one single batch. If you absolutely need to bake more than one batch at a time for an event, holiday baking, bottom rack once halfway through the baking process. Ovens have hot spots!

~ **For slice** - Leave the slice overnight to set properly before slicing. Remember to wipe the knife clean between each cut.~

~ **For chocolate topped slice** - Leave out of the fridge for 30 minutes before cutting. Score / mark where you plan to cut before cutting all the way through.

 Problem solving

~ **Burnt cookies?** How burnt are they? If only very dark (overcooked but not charcoaled), save them to use for the base of a cheesecake or use as part of a crumble mix. If you feel they are too dark to serve, wait until the are cold, then use the finest side of a grater or Microplane and gently grate the burnt side off.

BAKING POWDER is a leavening agent for baked goods made up of a phosphate aerator (sodium pyro-phosphate, a slow-reacting acid or occasionally tartaric acid), bicarbonate of soda (baking soda) and a starch (usually CORNFLOUR). The starch is added to absorb any moisture which may make the other two ingredients react. Baking powder should be used within a few months of purchase, as it degrades over time. Baking powder can be added to plain flour to replace self-raising flour (1½ teaspoons salt for every cup of flour). See GLUTEN for a recipe for gluten-free baking powder.

BAKING SODA see BICARBONATE OF SODA

BALMAIN BUGS see ROCK LOBSTER LOBSTER

BALSAMIC VINEGAR see VINEGAR

BAMBOO is of the grass family and some of the fastest growing plants in the world. For all the non-culinary uses of bamboo available, it is the new shoots or culms, that are of interest to cooks. Prepared properly to avoid the toxicity of the shoots (cyanide), Bamboo shoots are a wonderful addition to Asian stir-fry and curries.

BANANA is technically a berry and the tree on which it grows technically a herb. To hasten the ripening of bananas, place in the sun or in a paper bag with a ripe apple (the slow release of ethylene from the apple will initiate ethylene production from the banana). If they're ripening too quickly, remove the skin and freeze. A small store of frozen bananas is handy for cakes, muffins or smoothies, or they can simply be blended while still frozen for instant dairy-free banana ice-cream. Bananas can be kept in the fridge; the skin will go brown/black, but the flesh will retain its creamy-yellow colour.

Long-term storage in the fridge can mean the flesh will begin to break down or decay from the inside. Beer made from bananas is enjoyed in East African countries. Banana leaves are quite fibrous and are used in cooking, for baking and steaming fish and rice in particular. They are also used as a decorative addition to plates or as table covers, to make bags, baskets and for the roofs of houses.

A few types of bananas:

Cavendish banana is the common grocery variety found the world over. (Includes the giant, red and dwarf Cavendish and is also known as Grand
Naine, Williams and Mons Mari.)

The ice-cream banana or **blue java banana** is so named because it is said to melt in the mouth like ice-cream – try it if you can.

Lady finger bananas also known as **apple bananas, sugar bananas** or **dwarf bananas are smaller** (8–10 cm), ripen quickly and are quite sweet, although very starchy if not completely ripe. This also applies to baby bananas, which are smaller again at 6–8 cm.

PLANTAIN or **baking bananas** are not eaten raw but are boiled, stewed or fried, like a vegetable or potato.

Praying hands bananas also look like a baseball mitt when in bunches. They are sweet with a slight vanilla flavour.

Red bananas have pink flesh with more vitamin C than a standard banana but the same taste.

BARD is a technique similar to LARDING, designed to add fat to an otherwise lean meat. Fat (bacon rashers or pork fat) is draped, wrapped or tied around a piece of meat. Poultry and terrines are often barded as a means of self-basting; a terrine mould would be lined with bacon, filled and then cooked in a BAIN-MARIE in the oven. Game birds like pheasant and quail (see GAME) do well covered with fat in this way; the fat should be removed a few minutes before the bird is taken from the oven so as to brown the skin. A simple meat loaf can also benefit from being wrapped in bacon, keeping the contents moist and tasty.

BASIL This fragrant herb (fresh) doesn't like to be heated for long periods, so add at the end of cooking. Use fresh in salads, or blend with cream cheese and use as a spread in sandwiches. Basil (and other leafy herbs) should be torn rather than cut to avoid bruising and loss of flavour. There are some amazing varieties of basil that are worth trying: look for **holy basil,** excellent with fish and seafood dishes of Asian inspiration; **cinnamon basil**, for use in biscuits and desserts; **lemon basil,** for curries, seafood, poultry, veal and salads; **purple basil** for flair; and **Thai basil** or **horapa basil,** with its strong aniseed aroma, for stir-fries, soups, curries and salads.

Leftover basil? Make pesto, basil oil or basil butter. **To freeze -** puree the basil with a small amount of water: it will keep in the freezer for a couple of years, until the next world basil shortage. See also HERBS.

BASTARD CINNAMON see CASSIA

BEANS So many beans, so little space. Beans are usually divided into two groups: those with edible pods and those where only the seeds are eaten (see BEANS, DRIED for dried beans). Beans grow either in a bush or trained on a pole: bush beans grow close to the ground and need no support while pole beans are a climbing, vine-like plant.
Fresh beans are also known as **shelling beans** in the US.
Well known types;

Broad beans, like asparagus, are best in the spring; out of season they tend to be mealy and dry, good only for soups and purees. Once the beans are shelled, their outer skin can be removed. This skin toughens as the bean matures (sometimes becoming grey or even pink-tinged) so the older and larger the bean the more likely you will want to remove it before eating. Cook first (approximately 3 minutes) then pop the beans out of their skins. Young, tender, fresh beans can also be eaten raw. Mature beans (also known as **foules)** are often best pureed or dried. Also known as **fava beans** in the US (although in many other countries **fava** refers exclusively to the dried bean), **Windsor beans** or **horse beans.**

Edible soy beans, known in Japan as EDAMAME, are harvested as young green-shelled beans, before they mature into soy beans. In Japan, edamame soy beans are eaten as snacks and appetisers; the pods are boiled for 10 minutes before the bean is shelled. In China and other countries, the shelled beans are cooked with meat and vegetables in various dishes. The pods can be frozen (cooked or uncooked) for later use.

Green beans are many and varied, the most common being the **string** or **French bean** and the flat green bean. **String beans** are now bred with little or no sign of the chewy string, while flat green beans are tougher, larger and less palatable. The **yellow bean**, also known as *wax bean* or *butter bean* (not to be confused with **lima bean)**, is a varietal of the green with a delicate, tasty flavour, although it deteriorates faster than green beans. The **purple bean** which cooks green.

Snake beans, also known as **Chinese long beans, asparagus beans, bodi beans** and **yard-long beans**, can be cut into lengths and cooked like normal green beans.

Wing beans are used in stir-fries and in soups and can be found at Asian grocers. They have four wings running the length of the bean. Always buy them fully green and crisp; older ones bend too easily and the wings turn brown and decay.

BEANS, DRIED also known as **shell-outs** are pulses (see LEGUMES for a definition). They should be soaked for some hours, usually overnight, before cooking. Beans are soaked for two reasons: firstly, to speed up the cooking time, and secondly, because the flatulence often associated with eating beans can be attributed to the sugars in the bean that are water-soluble, so by soaking the beans and diluting the sugars, potent gases are reduced. Most dried beans take 1–2 hours to cook once they are soaked, or 15–30 minutes in a pressure cooker. The variance is dependent on the size of the dried bean as well as the intended use. For example, if you needed the beans firm for a salad or to cook in a sauce then 'AL DENTE' would be ideal. If making a dip, then cooking until very soft is ideal.

All beans can be cooked in the water they have soaked in, except soy beans, kidney beans and chickpeas which should be drained and cooked in fresh water as the soaking water retains bitterness from the beans. When cooking dried beans it is recommended to add a dash of oil to reduce the amount of foaming.

If a recipe calls for cooked or canned beans when all you have are dried beans, or vice versa, here is a rule of thumb for replacing one with the other: dried beans swell to three times their original volume after soaking and cooking.

HOW TO SOAK DRIED BEANS

For long soaking, cover dried beans with 4 times their volume of water and let stand in the refrigerator for overnight. Drain.

For quick soaking, place beans in a saucepan, cover with 3 times their volume of water and bring to the boil. Boil for two minutes. Remove from heat, cover and let stand for one hour. Drain.

1 cup dried beans = about 3 cups cooked beans

500 g dried beans = 21/2 cups dried beans = about 71/2 cups cooked beans

398 ml / 14 oz can beans = about 11/2 cups drained beans

540 ml / 19 oz can beans = about 2 cups drained beans = approximately 3/4 cup dried beans

Azuki /adzuki beans are primarily grown for the bean seeds, which in turn are used for soups, desserts and cake pastes and are the main ingredients in red bean paste and sweet bean paste. However the young fresh bean pods can be eaten like snow peas.

Black beans, also known as **turtle beans**, are a small black-skinned bean used in stews, soups and salads. Not to be confused with fermented black beans which are a type of soy bean (see below).

Black-eye beans are also known as **black-eyed peas, cornfield, turtle beans, Mexican beans** and **valentines**. These earthy-tasting beans cook in an hour and are a popular addition to dishes from the Caribbean, Mexico and the southern states of the US.

Borlotti beans have a distinct marking of pink or red streaks. They are available fresh but more often used dried. With their hammy, nutty flavour, the dried beans are a great salad and soup bean, while the fresh beans are wonderful in pasta. Sometimes called **cranberry beans** or **Roman** or **Romano beans**.

Lima beans or **butter beans** are the favourites of Rabbit from Winnie the Pooh and a must-have ingredient for the side dish SUCCOTASH. This flat, kidney-shaped bean has a buttery texture and flavour.

Marrow beans are a plump, white bean that are said to taste of bacon (I can neither confirm nor deny this claim). Once very popular in baked dishes. They swell considerably after cooking so make a great salad bean. Also good as a puree or in soups.

Red kidney beans are so named for their shape. They have a full flavour and mealy texture and are often used in salads.

Runner beans are available fresh or dried. They are quite large (although may take less than an hour to cook) so can be served braised or stewed as a dish on their own, where a slow-cooking method suits.

Soy beans have a higher protein content (35%-55% dry weight) than all other beans. Soy beans are one of the few known plant foods to contain all the essential amino acids, like those found in meat. Dried soy beans contain an enzyme inhibitor that can make them indigestible so they should be soaked for 24 hours (change the water every 8 hours) then cooked in fresh water for 3–4 hours. Once cooked they have a silky-smooth texture but little flavour, although they can be enhanced by adding flavours such as onions, tomato, rosemary, soy sauce, garlic or thyme in the last hour of cooking. I personally prefer eating soy beans in their many other forms (fresh, sprouts, bean curds, sauces) to avoid this long drawn-out process of cooking the dried bean. **Fermented black beans** (also known as **salted black beans, Chinese black beans** or **ginger black beans)** are black soy beans that have been cooked and then inoculated with a mould and fermented in their cooking brine for about 6 months and then partially dried. The better quality brands are then flavoured with Chinese five spice, orange peel and ginger. The beans now have a salty soy taste and a firm, pliable texture and will last indefinitely in the cupboard. Once opened they can be stored for months in an airtight container in the refrigerator. Although some recipes recommend soaking and/or rinsing the beans to reduce their saltiness, this is frowned on by Chinese chefs.

White beans is a general term that describes **cannellini**, **great northern beans**, **haricot beans** (also known as **navy beans** or **Boston beans**). Any of these can be interchanged in recipes.

BEAN FLAKES are similar to instant rolled oats in that they cook very quickly into a paste. They are ideal in soups or as a side dish or puree.

BEEF

 Top tips for beef
~ I recommend the personal experience of buying beef from a butcher, who, if you're loyal, will source, cut, hang (age) or put aside meat just for you. It beats peering for colour and marbling through the plastic wrap in the supermarket, and has the advantage that they can help choose the best cut for the dish you are planning.

~ Remove 'silver skin' from beef (and other meats) with a sharp knife to prevent the meat from contorting when cooked. Better still, ask your butcher to remove it for you to save time and wastage of precious meat.

~ **Grass-fed versus grain-fed -** The majority of the world's population wouldn't know the difference, nor would the majority of the world's professional cooks. Keep in mind that many things will determine the outcome of the final product, from stress and drought experienced by the animal while still alive, through to ageing and cooking technique. Most of the beef in Australia is grass-fed, and is generally favoured for its flavour.

~ **Bone-in versus bone-out -** Cooking meat on the bone does contribute to flavour, and the bone can also act as a mild heat conductor to help in the cooking process. However, if you are in a hurry and lack carving skills, buy it boned and rolled; the loss in flavour is not significant.

~ **Dry aged beef** is beef that is hung in the butcher's cool room for as little 5 days or as long as 30 days (any longer and the meat is thought to deteriorate, but it can be done). Hanging the beef (which can be done by several methods) allows enzymes within the meat to start breaking down muscle fibres, rendering it tender and tasty. Some muscle groups age at different rates, depending on the hanging method, and generally only the best cuts are reserved for hanging. Due to the significant loss of weight during the ageing process (as much as a third or more is lost in moisture), dry aged beef is rarely sold in the supermarket. Often prepared for the higher end restaurant industry where it attracts a much higher price. There is little advantage in hanging stewing beef or beef ready for mincing.

~ **Wet aged beef** simply refers to beef that has typically been aged in a vacuum-sealed bag to retain its moisture. The most common mode of ageing beef in most western countries. Popular because ageing takes place over a few days and typically lasts up to ten days without any moisture loss.

See also MEAT.

BEETROOT is also known as **beet, garden beet** and **red beet**. **Beetroot leaves** (also known as **baby chard, red chard, golden chard** and **beet tops**) can be eaten raw in a salad or cooked like spinach. The stems can also be washed and cooked. So when buying whole baby beets do not throw away the stalks and leaves; their earthy flavour works well with red meat dishes.

 Top tips for beetroot
~ Leave a couple of centimetres of the stalk intact when cooking to stop the beetroot from 'bleeding'.
~ Either boil in water (leave to cool in the hot liquid and the skins will slide right off) or roast at 170°C for 1½ –2 hours, depending on size (for best results, wrap each beetroot individually in foil).
~ Use an egg slice if you need to cut the beetroot evenly.
~ Avoid exceptionally large beetroot or you'll be chewing on woody cores with little sweetness.
~ If making a soup, the colour can change to rusty red: add some raw or cooked diced beetroot as a garnish which will bleed and improve the colour.

BEGONIA are a perennial plant adorned with very attractive edible flowers for about 4-5months of the year only. Ranging in colours, red, yellow, white, orange and pink. The flowers lend a sour flavour that marries well with seafood, especially raw seafood dishes such as fish carpaccio. Recommended to use as a garnish only and in small amounts due to the presence of oxalic acid.

BELL PEPPER see CAPSICUM

BENGALI FIVE SPICE or **panch phora** is used in curries and for fried vegetable and seafood dishes. It contains cumin seed, fennel seed, fenugreek seed, mustard seeds and nigella seeds.

BENNISEED are from he the same family as **sesame**. A flowering species originating in Africa, the harvested seeds are also known as **black benniseed, vegetable seed** and **black sesame.** Being a close relative of the sesame plant, benniseed can be used in much the same manner as sesame seeds.

BERGAMOT is both a fruit and a herb of the mint family that has edible flowers and leaves. The herb is similar to **eau de cologne mint**, which is also known as **orange mint**. Dried bergamot is popular in the US for tea infusions (similar to lemon balm). Its aroma is not dissimilar to the bergamot orange, but the herb and fruit are not related. Sour and pear-shaped, with a yellow rind when ripe, the fruit is prized for its oil but the pulp and juice are considered too sour to be edible. Bergamot oil, made from the rind of the fruit, is used in Earl Grey tea, and the PECTIN extracted from its rind is widely used in the production of marmalades.

BERRIES

 Top tips for berries

~ When buying berries, look at the base of the punnet or tray to detect any excess juices (rotting) or mould. Check the size of the berries too; some sneaky packers put the small, bruised fruit at the bottom and the plump, larger, unblemished berries on the top.

~ Do not wash berries if it can be helped. If they do carry a bit of dirt, wash briefly just before use, without soaking or agitating the fruit in the water. Drain in a colander or the punnet they came in. Do not store after washing, as degradation will be quick. Wash strawberries with the hull intact to avoid water absorption.

~ For maximum flavour, bring the berries to room temperature before eating.

~ Freeze berries before the rot sets in, if they are not being consumed fast enough. They can be used for baking straight from the freezer.

~ When baking with frozen or fresh berries, toss them in the flour mix, coating them evenly, which in turn prevents the berries form sinking to the bottom of the mix.

~ If need be, one type of berry can be replaced in a recipe with another similar berry – see the list below for a guide. There may be slightly differing results in flavour.

Bilberry are a very close relative of the blueberry and are easily interchangeable in recipes. Bilberries originate from Europe whereas blueberries are from America. A noticeable difference is the inner flesh - being medium green colour in blueberries, whilst the bilberry is filled with anthocyanins, giving it a distinct (and staining) red/purple colour.

Blackberries are also known as **brambleberries**. Similar berries are the **loganberry** (red, sharper tasting), **youngberry, olallieberry** (a sweet hybrid of the youngberry and loganberry) and **dewberry**, along with some 2000 other varieties.

Blueberry is to the USA what **bilberry** is to Europe. The bilberry is smaller and sharper in flavour. Related berries are the **huckleberry** (larger seeds and more tart) and the **juneberry** (also known as **saskatoon, shadberry, serviceberry**).

Boysenberry is a hybrid mix of blackberry, loganberry and raspberry, any of which could be used as a replacement if necessary. Another hybrid of the blackberry and raspberry is the **tayberry**.

Cranberry is also known as **bounceberry** (which is to do with the technique of sorting the good berries from the damaged ones before storage – dropped down a flight of stairs, damaged berries remain stuck to the stairs while the in-form ones bounce on to see further action). A related species is the **lingonberry**, although it is more tart.

Elderberries are often used in preserves as they are too tart to eat fresh. May be replaced with blackcurrants (see CURRANT) or even cranberries.

Mulberries look like blackberries, only slightly bigger and are far more fragile, both physically and in flavour. Hence they are best eaten from the tree (which for some reason favour being grown in a yard full of chickens – well, that's my experience of them as a kid).

Raspberry – name your colour: red, yellow, white, orange, pink, purple or black (wild raspberries). A close member of the blackberry family. Orange raspberries are salmonberries (not named for the colour, but because Native Americans would eat them with salmon roe). Black raspberries are keriberries. A related berry is the cloudberry, also known as baked-apple berry (which is the taste it may resemble when made into a tart).

Strawberry is the only fruit to wear its seeds on the outside. The perennial plant is related to the rose family with the fruit not technically classed as a berry but considered an 'aggregate fruit'...a fruit made up of many fruits - basically each seed (some 200 per strawberry) is considered a fruit in itself. Madness. Wild strawberries (also known as wood berries) are a delight when found. It is sinful to do anything other than eat wild strawberries fresh.

BEURRE MANIÉ is an uncooked ROUX. Made from a paste of equal parts softened butter and soup towards the end of the cooking stage to thicken. An antiquated technique at best. Definitely not the most favoured thickening method, as many cooks fail to cook the sauce long enough after adding the beurre manié which leaves a grainy texture and a taste of uncooked flour. Only add small amounts of this thickener to the sauce, stew or soup, usually a teaspoon at a time.

BICARBONATE OF SODA, or baking soda or sodium bicarbonate is used as a leavening agent in baking. It releases carbon dioxide when mixed with an acid such as lemon juice or cream of tartar, and this causes the mixture to rise. Too much baking soda, though, and the product will first rise then collapse while cooking (not to mention, taste horrible). And if you don't have enough acid in your mixture to react with the baking soda, the carbon dioxide is not released and the cake or muffins will have a bitter or soapy taste because of the nonreacted bicarbonate. Recipes that use baking soda always contain an acid – it might be an obvious source, such as vinegar or buttermilk – or less obvious such as honey or molasses which are acidic. Sometimes CREAM OF TARTAR is used. This is a dry acid that won't react with the baking soda until liquid is added.

BIRD'S NEST SOUP An expensive Chinese delicacy made from the nest of the swiftlet. The nest itself, made form solidified saliva. Often white in colour and priced around US$2000 per kilogram. Although there is the more rare red type named the "blood nest" with an asking price of US$10,000 per kilogram. After soaking for 2 hours in cold water, the nests are cleaned of all impurities, blanched for 5 minutes and then dropped into simmering stock for 45 minutes where they disintegrate, producing the gloopiness they are renowned for. The harvesting of bird nests is viewed as unethical and potentially violates the Migratory Bird Treaty Act (MBTA).

BISCUITS see BAKING

BITTER GOURD, also known as **bitter melon** or **bitter cucumber**, is an acquired taste, and is best suited to stir-fries, curries, soups or being stuffed with curried potato or meat. To remove some of the bitterness, slice and salt the pieces then rest for half an hour and rinse before using. Of the many varieties available, the hybrid white bitter melons are valued for their tenderness and only mild bitterness. Bitter gourd is from the cucumber family, Cucurbitaceae. See also LUFFA, LOOFAH.

BLACKJACK see PARISIAN ESSENCE

BLACK ONION SEEDS see NIGELLA

BLACK PERSIMMON see SAPOTE

BLADDERWRACK see SEAWEED

BLANCH To plunge food into boiling or simmering water for a very short period of time, so it is only partly cooked. The food is then drained and REFRESHED in iced water. Blanching enhances the natural properties of that food and is sometimes done in preparation for further cooking. The time it takes to blanch food will depend on the size and type of food it is.

BLINI or **bliny** and **blin** (singular) are a traditional Russian yeast pancake often associated with caviar.

BLINTZ from the Yiddish word **blintse** which comes from Slavic for pancake. In some ways related to blini (itself a pancake), just a different recipe and use. Blintz are usually filled with a mild cheese like farm cheese, cream cheese, cottage cheese etc, perhaps some dried fruits, then rolled and topped with sauce or berries.

BLOOM is the name given to the grey/white spots that appear on the surface of chocolate. There are two types, fat bloom and sugar bloom. Fat bloom (the most common) on chocolate occurs when when the cocoa butter (fat particles) separates from the solids, and mostly happens due to improper storage or age. Sugar bloom is less common and occurs due to moistness on or around the chocolate, when the moisture on the chocolate evaporates it leaves microscopic sugar crystals.
See also CHOCOLATE.

BOIL To cook food in boiling liquid (at a temperature no less than 100°C). For a rolling boil, the surface of the liquid must continuously rise and break.

BOMBAY DUCK is an Indian condiment made from the small lizard fish, cleaned, boned, salted and sun-dried.

BONIATO see '**sweet potato**' in POTATO

BONITO (dried mackerel) is something Japanese cooks would never be without. A primary ingredient in DASHI, it is also used in sauce for tempura and much more. Bonito is sold in blocks (to be shaved), as flakes and most often in powder or liquid form.

BORAGE is rarely used in cooking outside Europe, although it grows wild in many countries. The plant has small blue flowers and both the leaves and flowers are edible – often added to salads and soups – and have a flavour reminiscent of cucumbers. It is best to blanch or shred the leaves finely as they are covered with very fine, soft prickles that can irritate the throat.

BOUQUET GARNI (French meaning - garnished bouquet) is the classic French herb mix used to flavour stocks, soups and stews. A bundle of herbs is tied in a muslin cloth and then attached by a long thread to the handle of the pot so the bouquet can be removed easily from the stock at any point. The mix commonly consists of thyme, a bay leaf and a few parsley stalks. Sometimes a stick of celery is also included, and less traditionally other herbs and spices such as black peppercorns, garlic, fennel seeds, tarragon and chervil can also be added. You can now find prepared bouquet garni in the spice section of supermarket shelves in the style of teabags.

BRAISE is a method of cooking meat in liquid. The term braising is usually reserved for larger cuts of meat, while STEWING is used for smaller cuts of meat. As a general rule, add enough liquid to reach halfway up the item being braised. Although a recipe may specify the cooking time, my advice is to start checking the meat with an hour to go and possibly every 15 minutes after that, so as not to overcook it. Braised vegetables take 45 minutes, never longer. In short, braise does not mean to add liquid, cover and leave in an oven for the best part of a year hoping the item will become tender. When braising meat, remember that there is a difference between 'falling off the bone' and 'mush with a bone on the side'. **White braising** is a method seldom used today because of the time it takes. It is designed for meat such as veal, lamb, kid and other young animals. The meat is cooked on the stove top in a brown stock which is reduced to a glaze and topped up three times. It is then packed snugly into a baking tray and more brown stock is added (to cover about half the meat). The tray is covered and the meat cooked in the oven until tender.

BRASSICA are a genus of plant from the family of vegetables that includes **broccoli, brussels sprouts, cabbage, cauliflower, choy sum,**

collard, daikon, kale, mustard, radish, rape, rutabaga, swede, rocket, turnip, upland cress and watercress.

BREAD

 Top tips for baking bread
~ All flours differ from country to country and even brand to brand. They may contain more or less gluten and have been processed differently. The key to success with bread is to try the recipe and adjust as required.

~ Sieve the flour at least three times. This is not to sieve out lumps as most people think but to incorporate air and to evenly distribute the gluten. The latter will help the dough to rise evenly.

~ Try warming the flour before use; the heat will help in the initial stage of proving the bread. Place the flour in a stainless-steel bowl in a warm oven (no more than 50°C) until warmed through.

~ Do not add salt directly to yeast: salt inhibits its growth and can kill it.

~ Don't cheat with the kneading time: kneading the dough distributes the yeast evenly and develops (stretches out and elongates) the gluten strands. The less curled and the longer the gluten strands are, the better the texture of the bread will be. Short gluten strands will result in a texture more like biscuits or scones

~ Do not be tempted to add too much extra flour to the work bench when you are kneading. A light sprinkling is all that is required to prevent it sticking to the bench. As you knead, the dough will become less and less sticky as the starch and gluten absorb more of the liquid. Too much flour will change the recipe and dry it out, and you will end up with a very stiff, unworkable dough.

~ The process of proving or fermenting produces carbon dioxide which causes the dough to rise. (Alcohol is also produced but mostly evaporates during the baking process.) Prove the dough until it doubles in size. Any more than this and the bread can end up with a sour taste, will not hold a good form and will be heavy (see *over proving*).

~ **Over proving** can be as detrimental as under proving. (NB: Proving and proofing mean the same thing depending on which country you are from). Eventually the dough will sink back again as the carbon dioxide generated from the yeast will dissipate over time. Rising times vary according to the recipe and the temperature of the room, but 1-1.5 hours is typical.

~ For best results, prove dough at least twice or even a third time. You can prove dough in a warm area of the kitchen, in the sun, on the open oven door with the oven on a low temperature, or by placing the bowl containing the dough on top of a pot of water that has been brought to the boil, removed from the heat and covered with a cloth or dish towel.

~ Check the date on yeast. Dried yeast should keep for a few months, but really old yeast won't work and your hard work will have been in vain. Fresh yeast needs to be kept in the fridge and will only last a week or two, though you can freeze it for up to three months.

~ **To freeze bread dough** Make and knead the dough according to the recipe up to the point of the first rise. Freeze it as a slab in an airtight container or bag. Defrost when required (8 hours or overnight in the fridge) – a time which will count as the first rise. Or freeze the dough after you have allowed it to rise, knocked it back and moulded it into the shape required. In this case, freeze on a flat tray so as not to wreck the shape, then transfer to an airtight container or bag once frozen. As the dough defrosts it will also rise a second time and will be ready to bake. Don't freeze dough that includes a lot of fresh ingredients as it will become watery when the dough defrosts.

~ **Sourdough** is made with a yeast strain (see 'wild yeast' in YEAST) that will tolerate the lactic and acetic acids which give the bread its sour flavour. A **sourdough starter** is added to the main dough mix which is then usually left to ferment over 5 days. This is often a simple mix of flour and water and resembles a thick pancake batter. A **sponge starter** is flour and water with the addition of packet yeast or a little sour dough. This type of starter dough is often preferred domestically and by chefs (not bakers) as it is ready to use as soon as 2–3 hours after making, although leaving it overnight gives more sourness. It will, however, produce a much milder tasting and finer textured bread than a sour dough starter, which is characterised by irregular air pockets, chewy texture and tangy flavour. See also YEAST.

BREADFRUIT is the size of a melon with bumpy green scales but is prepared as a vegetable. The taste varies depending on its ripeness. The green firmer fruit should be cooked like potato. The slightly over-ripe fruit can be used for sweeter dishes. It is never eaten raw. When buying breadfruit it should feel dense, not spongy. As it ripens, the skin is adorned with brown speckles. It is generally kept in drums of water in the shop. It does not store well, so buy at the desired ripeness and use immediately. To prepare, cut a hard breadfruit into quarters lengthwise. Remove the dark core and discard. Pare the skin off and put the cut pieces into water.Breadfruit can be roasted in the peel for an hour at 190°C and then served as a side dish in a coconut-based curry sauce.

BRINE refers to the method of subjecting food to a liquid solution made up of salt and water. It is used as both a method of preservation or to season. ratios of salt to water vary according to density of the food as well as the intention. For example, fish can be brined for as little as 10 minutes, whereas a shoulder of pork will stay submerged in brine for 12-24 hours. Brining meat (not intended for preserving or drying i.e pork belly to be used for bacon) is done to extract water weight and increase flavour and juiciness once cooked. Adding whole dried spice to a brine solution is also common. Bay leaf, pepper corns, mustard seeds, chilli, fennel, cloves and caraway are just some of the spices well suited to adding to a brining solution.

Adding dry salt to a product is not considered brining. Dry salt mixes are used to extract moisture and ferment or preserve the ingredient. Fermenting fresh mushrooms, for example, will only require 1-3% of salt (to raw weight), left in an airtight bag with air removed in a warm area for a few days. Preserved lemons use ROCK SALT and water, packed into a jar and left to brine for at least three months.

Unlike preserved lemons, which is simply a layering method and then topped up with water, brine solutions need to be brought to the boil to dissolve the salt (and to properly infuse the dried spices) and then cooled thoroughly, before having meat or vegetables added. A brine solution is used once only due to it being contaminated and diluted.

BROAD BEANS see **BEANS, fresh**

BROAST is not a cooking technique but a trademarked application from the US-based *Broaster Company*, available only to the food service industry (hence the description 'broasted' will only ever be seen on a restaurant menu). It is a system that pressure cooks chicken while frying it and includes a marinating process. This method locks in the juices while locking out the oil.

BROCCOFLOWER is a relatively new vegetable, no doubt developed by bored agricultural scientists. A cross between BROCCOLI and CAULIFLOWER, it has a bright, light-green colour and a milder flavour than either of its parents.

BROCCOLI is a member of the BRASSICA family, harvested for the immature flower head. Unfortunately it is the stem that holds the flavour and it is often banished to the compost heap.
The stem should be trimmed or peeled and used as a vegetable in its own right. When buying broccoli, look for tight flower heads, any that are starting to unfold or blossom can be bitter. **Chinese broccoli** is also known as **Chinese kale** or **gai lan**.

BROCCOLINI – another one from the thumb-twiddling scientists – is a cross between Chinese broccoli and BROCCOLI. I've always campaigned in vain for the stems of broccoli to be eaten with as much enthusiasm as the head, and now along comes broccolini with its baby broccoli style head and nifty, asparagus-like stalk that even the kids don't mind gnawing on.

BROIL is a US term meaning to expose food to a high heat, either on a hotplate or under an oven broiler or grill. An oven broiler is the toaster section in an oven with the heat source directly above but not touching the food. In the restaurant industry these overhead broilers are called SALAMANDERS.

BROILER see POULTRY

BROTH often refers to meat broth (see also STOCKS). In broader terms, broth can mean any liquid (often water) extraction of an ingredient or ingredients mineral, vitamin and flavour content through cooking.

Vegetable broth (often root vegetables) will only need 30-40 minutes to exhaust them of their nutrients. Fish broth is ready in 20 minutes. Chicken takes four hours and bones from larger beasts (beef. veal), 8 to 12 hours. A simple broth made from bones or vegetables is considered nourishing for the human body.

BRUSSELS SPROUTS grow on a long stem, not a small bushy cluster as you might expect. A good way to cook them is to remove as many of the outer leaves as possible, cover the leaves with boiling water from the kettle and let stand for 30seconds, then drain and REFRESH. These leaves are now ready for sautéing in brown butter or tossing in a stir-fry. The pale heart that remains can be sliced raw and mixed into a salad, or steamed whole and served with a powerful sauce. I once heard of a kid who liked Brussels sprouts.

BUCKWHEAT is a fruit, harvested from a plant related to the rhubarb family, that is full of nutrients, particularly protein. It is ground to produce a dark, grainy flour (used in pancakes and soba noodles) or crushed and roasted (used fried in savoury dishes, breads and stuffings or toasted in cereals). **Buckwheat groats** are the seed with its inedible hull removed (the hulls are used in bedding products – that's right, pillows). They are bitter when raw, but can be toasted or roasted in oil to create **kasha**, which is sold whole or ground coarse, medium or fine. Raw groats are also finely ground (into **grits**) for use in cereals.

BUDDHA'S HAND CITRON is a most awkward-looking citrus fruit used for its zest, as the inside contains no useable fruit. If a recipe calls for a lot of lemon zest, try Buddha's hand instead. Also known as **fingered citron.**

BULGAR see BURGHUL

BUNYA BUNYA is a native ingredient from Australia, from the Bunya pine (but not of the pine family of trees). Bunya nuts - as they are more commonly known - are the kernel which is collected from the "cone" which is gathered form the ground when it is ripe and falls form the tree. Said to taste like chestnuts.

BURDOCK ROOT, also known as **gobo**, is an edible root used as a vegetable. It can be fried or stir-fried, combined with other vegetables. Peel the rind from this root as it tends to be bitter. Can be used in place of black salsify.

BURGHUL also known as **bulgur**, is wheat that has been soaked, cooked and dried. It can be bought whole or in small broken pieces (**groats**) of varying size, which is used for dishes like pilav (pilaf) and tabouli. Burghul does not require cooking, although it can be included in cooked dishes; soaking in water is all that is needed. Burghul should not be confused with **cracked wheat** which is the uncooked whole wheat kernel that has been, well, cracked and takes longer to cook and has less flavour than burghul.

BURGOO is a traditional Irish stew and can wrongly be known as a porridge. Based on a meat and seasonal vegetables, burgoo is very serious business for some folk. In the state of Illinois, US, some parts hold yearly festivals with claims of having the worlds best burgoo.

BURNT CARAMEL see PARISIAN ESSENCE

BUTTER is made up of 80–85% fat, 12–16% water and 0–2% salt. It is sold either salted or unsalted. Generally speaking, salted butter is used for savoury cooking, unsalted for baking and desserts, and clarified butter as a substitute for cooking oils. Unsalted butter is favoured by professional cooks, as it allows them to control the amount of salt added to the dish. And as salt is the preservative in salted butter, unsalted butter is considered a fresher product. It is known as **sweet butter** in the US (and **reduced salt butter** is known as **sweet cream butter**).

    Clarified butter has had the milk solids removed, leaving only the fat content. **Ghee** is clarified butter that is further simmered until all the moisture evaporates and the milk solids begin to brown. The resulting product has a nutty, caramel-like flavour and aroma and a longer life and higher smoking point than clarified butter. Although originating in India, the best ghee now comes from Holland, Scandinavia and Australia. Well-sealed, it can last up to six months in the fridge and a year in the freezer.

Cultured butter (also known as *Danish-style butter* and *sour cream butter*) is made from cultured cream and is popular in European countries. Terms for butter also vary.

Melted butter is known as **drawn butter** in the US.

A **stick of butter** is a US term, equivalent to 125 g, 4 oz, ½ cup, 8 tablespoons.

A **pat of butter** has a number of meanings depending on how it is used. It can be a shallow dish in which butter is served; an imprecise dollop of butter; a precise teaspoon of butter; or a 250 g block.

Like all dairy products, butter should be used as soon as possible after purchase. Store in the fridge (at 4°C) or freeze it if necessary. It can take on fridge smells if not wrapped properly and will become rancid with age. If you use stale or rancid butter in cooking, its flavour will permeate the food.

 Alternatives to butter

˜ As a spread, use avocado, nut butters, tofu spreads, olive oil spreads or any number of dairy-free dips. In cooking, use oil. In baking, use margarine, nut butter or olive oil spread.

BUTTER BEANS see BEANS

BUTTERMILK is made from cream. It is the residual liquid remaining from when cream is churned to produce butter. The butter milk often seen on supermarket shelves is a manufactured concoction of water, the milk sugar lactose and the milk protein casein which is pasteurised and homogenised, with the addition of a lactic-acid-producing bacteria cultures.

BUTTERNUT also known as **white walnut** from the butternut tree native to North Eastern states of America and South East Canada.

BUTTERSCOTCH is a confectionary or candy made with brown sugar and butter. See also ˍ for temperatures relating to butterscotch recipes. **Butterscotch sauce** is based on brown sugar, butter and cream. See SUGAR page 34, for table of caramel temperatures.

BUTTERNUT SQUASH see SQUASH

C.

CACAO is the fruit from which the cacao bean is extracted. Although the words 'cacoa' and 'cocoa' are often used interchangeably to describe products derived from the cacao tree, 'cacao' ought only to refer to the tree and the bean it produces, while 'cocoa' refers to the products derived from them – butter, powder, liquor etc. The cacao bean is made up of 54% cacao butter, 11.5%protein, 9% starch, 5% water and hundreds of other elements like theobromine, caffeine and aromatic oils. Cacao beans are processed in a similar way to coffee beans. See also CHOCOLATE; COCOA POWDER.

CACTUS FRUIT see DRAGONFRUIT

CAKES see BAKING

CALAMARI see SQUID

CALAMONDIN is a citrus fruit from the Philippines which is very similar to the KALAMANSI. Both fruit are acidic in flavour with great 'pucker power' and are interchangeable in recipes. This small, orange fruit can be used like a lime, and is great for marmalade.

CALORIE is a measure of the amount of heat energy it takes to heat one gram of pure water to 1°C. In relation to food, the word 'Calorie' (with a capital C) is in fact equivalent to 1000 calories or a KILOCALORIE. However, it is still a measurement of energy, as food contains energy for the human body to burn. The average adult needs 2000 Calories per day, although obviously height, weight, gender, age and activity level all affect your requirements; some (active people and athletes) may need more while others (obese and inactive people) require less. Excess Calories will be converted to body fat and stored for a rainy day. For many people it doesn't rain too often and this stored energy or body fat continues to deposit while waiting to be used. To determine the amount of Calories in food, check the labels or the source of food to work out how many grams of fat, each into approximate Calories with the following formula (remembering that a dietary Calorie is 1000 calories or 1 kilocalorie): fat contains 9 kilocalories of energy per gram, carbohydrates contain 4 kilocalories of energy per gram and protein contains 4 kilocalories of energy per gram. For example, if you eat a health bar that contains 9 grams of fat, 30 grams of carbohydrates and 6 grams of protein, your intake will be 81 kilocalories of fat, 120 kilocalories of carbohydrates and 24 kilocalories of protein. Therefore this one bar has added 225 kilocalories (dietary Calories) to your daily intake.

A final note: very few people possess the tenacity to count food energy, especially when it comes to nutrition, working out if one needs to be calorie deficient (for weight loss) or understanding their 'Macros' and 'Micros'. For the novice, as a method of judging nutritional quality it is not exact, often confusing, and in some cases completely worthless (for example, nuts, which are highly nutritious, have an extremely high Calorie count, yet diet soft drinks have a very low count and provide no nutrition at all.) The choice is yours.

CANDY is a US term that refers to cooking foods in sugar for preservation and flavour. It can also simply mean to coat in sugar. Or simply the US term for what other countries refer to as **sweets, bon bons, confectionary, lollies** or **treats.** Candy is also somewhat of an ironic paragraph to follow calories.

CANTALOUPE also known as **rock melon,** a alternative name used particularly in the UK and in parts of Australia. See also MELON.

CAPE GOOSEBERRY is not related to the gooseberry. The fruit, roughly the size of a cherry and housed in a straw-coloured husk, is golden-yellow to orange when ripe. It is sweet with a grape-like tang, but the bitter husk is deemed inedible. The high pectin levels mean cape gooseberries are ideal for making jams and preserves. They are also good in desserts (especially dipped in chocolate then chilled) as well as savoury dishes and salads, and the dried fruit can be used like a raisin in puddings. **Goldenberry** and **husk cherry** are the two most common of many alternative names. See also TOMATILLO.

CAPON see POULTRY

CAPRETTO see KID

CAPSICUM is also known as **bell pepper** or **sweet bell pepper**, particularly in the US. Colours range through green, yellow, orange, red to dark purple. Some varieties of green capsicums are unripe red capsicums which change colour as they ripen, so the final colour is determined by when the capsicum is picked. Red capsicums are the ripest and therefore sweetest. Other common varieties of capsicum are the **banana capsicum** (sometimes called **banana chilli**) which is bright yellow and banana-shaped but lacks the sweetness of the bell capsicum, the **bull horn**, which is elongated, thin and curved with a pale green colour and a very mild chilli flavour, and the **pimento**, a small, juicy, aromatic, heart-shaped capsicum that is popular in Spain, particularly stuffed. Pimentos are best when fully mature and scarlet. See also CHILLI.

 Top tips for capsicum
   ~ **Buy capsicums** that are firm, with hard stems, shiny skins, rich colours and no blemishes; avoid those that are limp and damaged.
   ~ **When slicing** raw capsicum, place it skin side down on the cutting board. (Knives slip easily off the outer surface of capsicum a cutting into the inner membrane is much easier.)
   ~ **To roast** (usually red capsicum), smear with oil (optional) and place in a hot oven for 20–25 minutes, turning occasionally. Remove from the oven, place in a bowl and cover with plastic wrap to make the skins sweat. Peel off the outer skin when cooled, and store in the fridge for up to a week. Roasting on a grill plate or barbecue works equally well. Some recipes suggest cooking until skin is charred black (done to produce a smoky flavour) but bear in mind that, the more burnt the less flesh is usable as its moisture is cooked out.~ Keep the

juices from roasting and cooling, too: this sweet, brown liquid can be used in sauces or dressings.

CARAMBOLA is a subtropical fruit which also goes by the name **star fruit**. This star-shaped fruit is light- to dark-yellow, even orange, when ripe and light-green when unripe. The green darker edges can be bitter so should be trimmed back. The flavour can vary from tart to very sweet depending on which of the dozen varieties it is (the king star is tart). It makes an excellent addition to a fruit plate for dessert or for snacks. Keep refrigerated when ripe.

CARAMELISE To cook sugar or the natural sugars within food to a light brown or caramel colour. White sugar caramelises at 170°C (340°F). See page

CARAWAY is from the same family as parsley. Its fresh leaves and roots can also be eaten but most often the caraway seed is eaten (technically the fruit of the plant). Caraway seeds taste of a combination of dill and anise with a tangy, almost nutty flavour and are popular in the cuisines of Austria, Southern Germany and North Africa. When a recipe calls for you to grind your own caraway seeds, you will find it hard going unless you dry roast them first. The roasted seeds are much easier to crush.

CARDAMOM is sold as powder, seeds or pods. The pods can be green or off-white. The more common green cardamom is the Indian variety; white cardamom, the size of a pea, is less common and less pungent than the green. Black or brown cardamom is a different spice which has a camphorous taste, and cannot be interchanged with green cardamom. If the recipe calls for seeds or powder, it is best to buy cardamom in pods and remove or grind the seeds yourself. (Roast the pods whole before removing the seeds.) Often the pod is simply bruised (crushed with the flat of a knife) and added whole to the dish.

CARDOON is a member of the thistle family and is closely related to the GLOBE ARTICHOKE. The young tender-leafed mid-ribs (petioles) and immature flower stalks are eaten, after being carefully and thoroughly blanched to bring out the true flavour. The plant hearts are sometimes blanched like celery stalks, and the roots can also be eaten, cooked as you would a parsnip. In Italy, strips of cardoon stem are eaten raw, dipped in good olive oil, although many will find them bitter. There are spineless and spiny cardoons available but the spineless are better.

CAROB refers to the fruiting body of the evergreen carob tree. The pod is technically a legume which humans have been harvesting for some 5000 years. The pod is made up of pulp (90%) and seed (10%). It is very high in sucrose (40%) and other sugars (up to 70%). Carob is ground into a cocoa-like powder, roasted or raw, used for drinks and in baking. Carob bars and chips are used for cooking, and the pod can be boiled in water to produce a thick, syrup-like molasses. Carob is used as an alternative to CHOCOLATE, as it contains a third of the calories, is almost fat-free (chocolate is half fat), is high in PECTIN, and it doesn't interfere with the absorption of calcium (as chocolate does). It is also caffeine-free so the seeds can be roasted and made into a coffee substitute. Carob can be substituted measure for measure with chocolate, but it has a milder flavour so play with the recipe, perhaps adding more carob to compensate.The seed is separated from the pulp and pod, where the endosperm is extracted to produce **locust bean gum**, a thickening agent and stabiliser used in the food production industry.

CARRAGEEN is a seaweed that is red/purple when harvested, then is sun-bleached and sold as a yellow/brown-coloured thickening agent. Carrageen is similar to AGAR-AGAR but produces a softer gel. Rinse thoroughly, soak (it will swell) and then cook in the liquid it is to set. Even after cooking carrageen will not completely dissolve, so keep a strainer handy and discard the remains. Ideal for vegans and vegetarians, and available at health food shops. Also known as **carrageen moss** or **Irish moss**. For other similar thickeners see also GELATINE; GELOZONE; ISINGLASS.

CASSIA is related botanically and in flavour to CINNAMON, although it is not as delicate a flavour, hence its alternative name **bastard cinnamon**. It looks more like tree bark, compared to the neatly curled quills of cinnamon bark, and is the stronger of the two. It can be added whole to meat dishes, fruit compotes and marinades, or the dried, ground powder can be used in cakes and desserts or to enhance the flavour of chocolate.

CAULIFLOWER is a member of the cabbage family, grown for its white flowering head. Look for tight, white and unblemished heads of cauliflower. Once cooked, cauliflower tends to lose whiteness over a period of time, especially in soup. The addition of lemon juice will not help.

CEDRO see YUZU

CELERIAC, an ugly tuberous root of the celery family, is becoming increasingly popular outside Europe and Asia. Celeriac has a very mild celery flavour. It can be cooked and mashed with potatoes or on its own, or it can be trimmed and thinly sliced or shaved raw in a salad with celery and lovage. Also know as **celery root, knob celery, German celery** and **turnip-rooted vegetable.**

CELERY is a member of the aromatic flowering plant family which includes carrots, fennel, parsnip and parsley. The stalk, leaves and seeds are all edible. The inner pale leaves of celery are delicious raw when added to salads. Celery seeds are full of flavour and often used to make celery salt which in turn is a must add ingredient to the cocktail, 'Bloody Mary' as well as essential in 'Old Bay seasoning' mix. Celery juice was trending momentarily as a detox hero based on no real scientific evidence. Allergic reactions to celery is very real and life threatening.

CERVENA is meat from New Zealand farmed deer that is all natural, grass-fed, without hormones or steroids, and less than three years old. It has changed the reputation of VENISON from that of an often tough and strong gamey meat into one with a consistently tender texture and mild yet distinctive flavour. The name is a compound of 'cervae', the Latin word for deer, 'venison', from the Latin word for hunted game and 'A', for premium quality.

CHALAZA is the white strand-like substance found in a raw EGG. The purpose of the chalaza is to anchor the egg yolk in the centre of the egg white. The more prominent the chalaza, the fresher the egg.

CHARD see BEETROOT (**baby chard, red chard, golden chard**); SILVERBEET (**Swiss chard**).

CHAR-GRILL is short for '*charcoal grill*': to cook over the high heat produced by burning coals. The smoky characteristics that define char-grilling are as prominent as the grill lines left on the food being cooked. A ribbed grill plate leaves the same markings as a char-grill but without the flavour. Both methods are considered an excellent method to cook meat due to the fats rendering and basting the meat as they drain to leave a succulent piece of meat. Also known as *char-broil*.

CHAYOTE see CHOKO

CHE is a remarkable little fruit which when ripe has a sweetness akin to figs and a flavour reminiscent of watermelon. The fruit is ready to eat when the skin is red with some darkened blotches (it has little if any flavour when immature). Store covered in the fridge. Pureeing the flesh and straining out the seeds produces a sweet nectar ready for further use in desserts and ices. Adding a touch of lime juice balances the sweetness perfectly.

CHEESE

 Top tips for buying and storing cheese
    ~ Don't be afraid to ask for a sample of cheese before buying (although a supermarket is the last place this service would be offered). If you are unable to sample the cheese, look carefully before buying: avoid any wrapped cheeses that show weeping or shrinkage and any unwrapped cheeses that show signs of drying around the edges or cracking in harder cheese.
    ~ Stored in its original wrapper, unopened, in the coldest part of the refrigerator, cheese (especially hard cheese) can live a grand life, often beyond its 'use by' date. However, cheese is a living food and needs to breathe to develop. The best way to store it is wrapped in a

calico cloth or wax paper. (Don't use plastic wrap or foil.) Ideally, keep cheese in a cool, moist cave, with good ventilation and a stable air temperature from 8–12°C. As most houses lack a good cave, the refrigerator will have to suffice.

~ Mould spores from blue cheese can spread to other cheese and other foods in the same storage area, so make sure blue cheese in particular is thoroughly wrapped.

~ Freezing cheese is not recommended, although leftover grated cheese and some semi-hard cheeses keep well in the freezer. Soft cheeses like brie and camembert do not appreciate this treatment.

~ Remove cheese from the fridge and let stand at room temperature for 1–2 hours before serving. This allows flavour and aroma to develop.

✅ Top tips for a cheese board

~ Don't feel the need to always serve a vast array of different cheese at a dinner party. Choose two or three, ranging in texture from hard to semi-hard to semi-soft, allowing 80–100 g of cheese per person, less if cheese is to be served before or after a dessert.

~ Make sure your guests enjoy a particular cheese before spending your money – blue cheese is not for everyone.

~ Serving cut fruit on the same plate as the cheese is an insult; cheese should be simply served on its own. Any fruit to be enjoyed with the cheese, whether fresh, dried or as a paste, can be served on a separate plate. Offer bread as well as dried biscuits with cheese. Fruit breads, nut breads and wine breads are all suitable.

See also COTTAGE CHEESE; FETTA; FROMAGE FRAIS; HALOUMI; LABNA; MASCARPONE; RICOTTA CHEESE.

CHEMPEDAK is a smaller version of its close relative the JACKFRUIT. Chempedaks have a 'waist' – a slight indentation around the middle of the fruit – and a thinner dark-yellow or even orange skin and juicier, sweeter flesh than the jackfruit. The smell of the uncut fruit is second only to DURIAN, and the flavour is one of durian and mango. It can be used like jackfruit, but is better suited to desserts. Also known as

champada (Thailand).

CHERIMOYA see CUSTARD APPLE

CHERRY is the stone fruit from the plant species *Prunus*. Sweet cherry's and sour cherry's are commercially grown from several cultivars and differ from wild cherries and the ornamental 'cherry blossom'. In the northern hemisphere, cherry's peak in summer June/ July. Whilst in the southern hemisphere, they peak in summer also, being December which means cherry's are often associated with Christmas celebrations. Sweet cherries are best eaten fresh out of hand but can be used in cooking. Whilst **sour cherries** are almost always used in cooking. Dried sour cherries are particularly sought after in baking and savoury meat recipes.

CHERVIL is a delicate herb with a very gentle anise flavour, usually used to garnish a dish or in raw in a salad. Chervil is a component in the classic herb blend fines herbes and is one of three herbs used in the classic French cold egg sauce, sauce gribiche. See also HERBS.

CHICKPEA or GARBANZO BEAN most commonly refers to the creamy-coloured, thin-skinned legume from the Middle East and Mediterranean region – the kabuli variety. A less common variety of chickpea is the *desi* (from the Indian region), which is smaller and darker-skinned than the garbanzo but yellow within. Chickpeas are high in soluble fibre, and sold dried, canned and vacuum-packed. Dried chickpeas should be soaked before cookingIf you want to peel cooked chickpeas, submerge them in a bowl of cold water and rub gently between your fingers; the skins will rise to the top. Canned or vacuum-packed chickpeas need to be drained and rinsed well before use to remove the sodium before using. The liquid drained from canned chickpeas is known as AQUAFABA, and is a very useful alternative for vegan cooks. Aquafaba mimics the functioning properties of egg whites making its use in meringues style dessert making a blessing for vegans and for those with egg allergies. The use of aquafaba is a relatively new culinary discovery by a musician on or around December 2014.
See BEANS, DRIED for equivalents of dried to cooked chickpeas.

Chickpeas are also made into FLOUR, known as BESAN FLOUR.

CHICORY is a name used for two related types of green leafy vegetable. See WITLOF (**chicory, chicory heads**); LEAFY GREENS (*curly chicory, red chicory*).

CHILI PEPPER (also **chilli, chili, chile, chilli pepper)** are the berry from is the genus CAPSICUM which is a member of the NIGHTSHADE family (*Solanaceae*). Originating in Mexico, chili pepper derives the name "pepper" from Christopher Columbus and crew, as the heat from eating them reminded them of black pepper. Chili pepper is one of the oldest cultivated crops in the *Americas,* and Chilli heat is determined by a substance called capsaicin, found mainly in the white ribs that the seeds are attached to, then to a lesser extent in the fine veins of the inner flesh, and even less again in the seeds. The stem end of the chilli is the hottest portion. As a rule, larger, blunt-tipped chillis are usually milder, while smaller dark-green chillis with pointed tips are often very hot. However, individual pods from the same plant can have varying degrees of heat. Removing the seeds and veins, and soaking chillis in cold salted water for at least an hour will help reduce heat. When handling chillis, take great care not to touch your eyes afterwards. Plastic gloves are recommended.

Some chillis (jalapeños, anchos and long green and red chillis) are best peeled to remove the tough transparent skin. One of the best ways to do this is to pierce the stem end with a knife and then drop the chilli into hot oil until the skin begins to dull and blister slightly. Peel under cold running water. Or they can be roasted like capsicum.

Chilli heat is measured in Scoville heat units. The capsaicin is chemically extracted from the chilli and subjected to high performance liquid chromatography. Basically, these units represent the number of times the extracted capsaicin dissolved in alcohol can be diluted with a quantity of sugar water before the capsaicin can no longer be tasted.

CHILLI HEAT RATINGS

1–10   SCOVILLE UNITS   EXAMPLE

0	0 - 100	capsicum (bell pepper), banana pepper, pimento
1	100 - 500	cherry, pepperoncini, NuMex, R-Nak, Mexibel, aji flor
2	500 - 1000	Santa Fe Grande, anaheim, sandia, Big Jim
3	1000 - 1500	Española, poblano, mulato, ancho, Española improved, pasilla, chilaca, hot cherry, NuMex 64
4	1500 - 2500	rocotillo, cascabel, poblano
5	2500-5000	TAM jalapeño, mirasol, cayenne (large, thick), guajillo, cascabella, Hungarian wax, Peter pepper, Turkish, Espelette pepper
6	5000 - 15 000	aji amarillo, romesco, jalapeño, serrano, yellow wax, wax, aleppo pepper, cheongyang chilli pepper
7	15 000 - 30 000	de arbol, catarina, japones, guntur chilli
8	30 000 - 50 000	aji, cayenne, cayenne long thin, prik khee nu, dundicut, tabasco, costeno, rocoto, piquin

1–10	SCOVILLE UNITS	EXAMPLES
9	50 000 - 100 000	yatsafusa, chipotle, santaka, Thai, chiltepin, aji limon, aji or, cusqueno, datil, malagueta pepper
10	100 000 - 350 000	habanero, Bahamian, Jamaican hot, bird, bird's-eye, Scotch bonnet
11	350 000 - 750 000	Red Caribbean, Red savina habanero
12	750 000 - 1 500 000	Ghost pepper, Infinity chilli, Napa viper chilli, Trinidad moruga scorpion
13	1 500 000 - 3 000 000+	Carolina reaper, dragon's breath, pepper X, law enforcement spray (pepper spray)
	15 000 000+	pure capsaicin

CHINESE APPLE see POMEGRANATE

CHINESE BARBECUE SAUCE see HOI SIN SAUCE

CHINESE DATE see JUJUBE

CHINESE FIVE SPICE is used as a seasoning in sauces, marinades and cooked red meat dishes. It contains equal parts of cinnamon, cloves, fennel seeds, star anise and Sichuan pepper.

CHINESE GOOSEBERRY see KIWIFRUIT

CHINESE GRAPEFRUIT see POMELO

CHINESE LEEK FLOWERS see CHIVES

CHINESE OKRA see LUFFA

CHINESE PARSLEY see CORIANDER

CHINESE PEPPER see SICHUAN PEPPER

CHINESE RESTAURANT SYNDROME is a collection of symptoms that some people claim to experience after eating Chinese food. A food additive called MONOSODIUM GLUTAMATE (MSG) has been implicated but has never been proven to cause this condition. Also known as **hot-dog headache, glutamate-induced asthma** and **MSG syndrome.**

CHIPOLATA is a small PORK sausage.

CHIVES, although from the onion family, are treated as a herb. Never freeze or dry chives. (Although you can buy them dried, what's the point? Dried chives look sad and they hate it.) Fresh chives are good mixed in butter, scrambled eggs, salad, mayonnaise, cream or cottage cheese (for sandwiches). **Chinese flowering chives,** also called **Chinese leek flowers**, make a great decorative addition to stir-fry, salads and Vietnamese rice paper rolls. Fresh chives are a delicacy in Asian cuisine, and have a stronger onion flavour over regular chives. Garlic chives smell more than taste like garlic. They are used in salads and stir-fries. See also HERBS.

CHLORELLA see SEAWEED

CHOCOLATE has a long history as a glamour food, the food of the gods. The very best chocolate fetches top dollar for its smooth texture and pure flavour, which unfortunately means that much of the chocolate we consume is a sad, milk-laden version of the good stuff, often churned into cheap confectionery and crude compound cooking blocks. The good stuff displays its cocoa butter content proudly (from 33%), and is a real treat to use and eat.

Store chocolate at room temperature (ideally at 20°C) in a cool, dry place, in its original wrapper or in foil. Dark chocolate has a shelf life of several years, while milk chocolate should be used within 12 months. Don't store chocolate in the fridge or freezer, as it will have a greater tendency to **bloom** once thawed. (Bloom is the name given to the grey/white spots that appear on the surface of chocolate when the cocoa butter separates from the solids.) See also BLOOM. Why would you freeze it anyway? Eat it!

Chocolate is made from the CACAO bean. The rarest cacao tree, whose bean is the most expensive and sought by the world's best chocolate makers, is the criollo (which means 'native'), although 90% of the world's production of cacao beans comes from the forastero (translated as 'foreigner'); trinitario ('third') is a hybrid of the two.

The cacao bean is fermented then dried before being roasted and ground to form cocoa liquor or chocolate liquor. Chocolate liquor is bitter and can be put aside to set then sold as bitter chocolate. It is about 50/50 cocoa solids and cocoa butter; the solids provide the chocolatey taste in the final product and the butter provides smoothness and 'mouthfeel'. Next the chocolate liquor goes through a hydraulic press that separates the cocoa butter and solids, and this is the stage when the chocolate maker applies recipes and techniques that will ultimately define their brand. Commonly added are sugar, milk solids and flavours such as vanilla. The next step in the process is conching, when the chocolate liquid mass is stirred and mixed at 55–75°C to give it a smooth texture. This process causes friction between added sugars and the cocoa particles, leaving a polished cocoa particle. Invented by chocolate manufacturer Rudholf Lindt, conching gets its name from the shell-like shape of the machine's rollers. Lower-quality chocolates may not have been through the conching stage, resulting in a grainy, average-tasting chocolate. Others are conched for hours, even days, for a more luxurious texture. Valrhona, one of the best chocolate makers in the world, conches its chocolate for five days. The final stage in making more luxurious texture. Valrhona, one of the best chocolate makers in the world, conches its chocolate for five days. The final stage in making chocolate is slowly heated then slowly cooled. Tempering allows the chocolate to harden properly and prevents the cocoa butter from separating. Adding flavours, conching and tempering are fine arts with idiosyncratic results. The two things to look for when you're choosing chocolate are the percentage of cocoa liquor compared to other additives, and the percentage of cocoa butter to cocoa solids (the latter is often hard to determine from the label). **Adding liquid to melted chocolate:** Heat the liquid first. If you add cold liquid, the chocolate will solidify or seize. Even the moisture from a wet spoon is enough to tamper with melting chocolate. Alternatively, you can add liquid before you start melting the chocolate and heat them both together.

HOW TO MELT CHOCOLATE

Put the uninitiated cook around chocolate and they quickly become the painter's apprentice, slopping it around and coating everything, including the inside of the cutlery drawer. There are two methods for melting chocolate effectively:

IN THE MICROWAVE: melt at 50% power for 20–30 second intervals, stirring each time. Don't omit the step of stirring, as warmed chocolate keeps its shape, looking like it needs more time when in fact it has begun to melt.

IN THE DOUBLE BOILER: Bring water to the boil, then turn off the heat source, place the chocolate in a bowl over the boiled water and let the residual heat from the water slowly melt the chocolate. Rush this process and you run the risk of scorching the chocolate, making it stiff, lumpy and grainy.

Problem solving

~ **Seized?** Once chocolate has seized, it is unlikely to remelt (although you can try adding a spoonful of vegetable oil which can soften the chocolate enough to continue). The best use for it then is chocolate sauce or a GANACHE.

~ **Bloomed?** Blooming often occurs when chocolate is chilled and then returned to room temperature. Chocolate that blooms is still edible with only the slightest difference in flavour and texture. You can melt it to regain its original texture.

Bittersweet chocolate is the chef's choice for desserts because of its stronger flavour. It contains more cocoa liquor than semi-sweet and sweet chocolate (at least 35%, whereas semi-sweet contains 15–35% and unsweetened chocolate is pure cocoa liquor) and less added sugar.

Compound chocolate, manufactured as a cheap alternative to chocolate, is made with vegetable oil and cocoa powder instead of cocoa liquor. It melts at a higher temperature, making it manageable for the novice cook. It is sometimes **confectioner's chocolate**.

Couverture means 'covering', which is its intent. Couverture chocolate is made to coat truffles, cakes and sweets, but is used by anyone who knows their chocolate for all manner of dipping, coating, molding and garnishing. Its high cocoa butter content gives couverture its characteristic viscosity (the cocoa butter thins the chocolate to a smooth, glossy and quite runny texture compared with poorly made or cheaper styles of chocolate which when melted stay quite firm). It can be replaced with dark chocolate or compound chocolate, but neither will guarantee the excellent results gained from couverture chocolate. Available in specialty food shops and high end food halls, as well as online.

Dark chocolate is sweetened but has no added milk solids. (This is the chocolate you might have stolen from your dad's private stash as a child, only to decide that, if it isn't milk chocolate, it isn't chocolate at all.) Dark chocolates range from bittersweet and semi-sweet to sweet.

German chocolate has nothing to do with Germany. It was formulated in 1852 by Samuel German, to make life easier for bakers by adding more sugar to the chocolate, and is seen as the predecessor to bittersweet chocolate.

Mexican chocolate has added cinnamon, sugar and sometimes nuts and is used for hot drinks and MOLE SAUCE.

HOME-MADE MEXICAN CHOCOLATE
1 tablespoon cocoa powder
1/2 teaspoon castor sugar
1/4 teaspoon cinnamon
Combine to make the equivalent of 30 g Mexican chocolate.

Milk chocolate or **sweet chocolate** is rarely used in cooking, as the added milk solids can interfere with baked goods. However, it can be used successfully in a mousse.

Semi-sweet chocolate is similar to bittersweet chocolate, but contains less cocoa liquor (15–35%). An excellent cooking chocolate for good domestic cooks in the know. (Sweet chocolate has more sugar again),

Unsweetened chocolate or **bitter chocolate** is made with 100% cocoa liquor. It is bitter and not to be eaten straight from the pantry. Favoured by professional bakers, as they have more control over the quantities of sugar, etc in the final product.

HOME-MADE UNSWEETENED CHOCOLATE
If necessary, unsweetened chocolate can be replaced with cocoa (not drinking chocolate).
1 tablespoon vegetable oil
3 tablespoons cocoa powder

Mix together to make the equivalent of 30 g unsweetened chocolate

White chocolate is made from what's left over after the cocoa liquor has been removed, so contains only cocoa butter, sugar, milk solids and vanilla. Different brands contain varying amounts of cocoa butter, and some contain none at all – as a rule of thumb, those made with cocoa butter are ivory-coloured, while those with little or none are a brighter white. All white chocolate must be melted at very low temperatures to keep it from scorching and turning lumpy.

⭐ Alternatives to chocolate
~ Interchange different styles of chocolate with caution, as the properties of each chocolate will react differently. CAROB is the most commonly used alternative.

CHOCOLATE (PUDDING) FRUIT see SAPOTE

CHOKO is the bland, old person's food served to an eight-year-old as punishment for misbehaviour. The whole vegetable is edible, including the seed. Peel chokos with rubber gloves on or, under water to avoid the sticky build-up of sap that dries on the hands. Chokos can be used or served with many things besides cheese sauce – in chutneys (India), in cakes and tarts (Mexico), or parboiled then served with blue cheese or goat's cheese melted over the top. The young choko can be shaved and used raw in a salad, like celeriac, cucumber or fennel. Grated or julienned choko is delicious added raw to a vegetable spring roll mix. Also known as **chayote, christophine, custard marrow, miriton, pepinella** and **vegetable pear.**

CHOY SUM also known as **Chinese flowering cabbage** has yellow flowers which can be eaten along with the dark green leaves and stems. A mild spinach-like flavour, with no bitterness. Popular in stir fry and soups.

CHRISTOPHINE see CHOKO

CILANTRO see CORIANDER

CINNAMON The best quality cinnamon is Ceylon cinnamon. Indonesian cinnamon is a medium quality option and Vietnamese cinnamon is of poor quality, resembling CASSIA in appearance and flavour.

CIPOLLINI ONIONS see ONIONS

CITRON see BUDDHA'S HAND CITRON; YUZU

CLABBER is a curdled or soured MILK (the name derives from the word's use as an archaic word for pantry). Unpasteurised milk is left to sit for two or three days until it curdles. The cream is removed to produce clabber cream or crème fraîche (see CREAM). Clabber is eaten as is or with a little black pepper or nutmeg, cinnamon and brown sugar and a splash of fresh cream. It can also be strained overnight in cheesecloth to produce a kind of COTTAGE CHEESE.

CLAM is a bivalve mollusc that can range in size from 3–14 cm. Other names are **vongole** (Italian) and **quahog** (Native American). Frozen or canned clams are useful for soup, but nothing beats fresh clams. When purchasing fresh clams, look for shells that are tightly closed already or shut close when you tap them (this shows that the clams are still alive and fresh). Store fresh live clams at 0–4°C and consume within two days. Some people like to 'purge' clams by storing in a container of fresh water in the fridge (the clams filter the water, eliminating sand and other impurities) but this is usually only necessary if you have collected your own.

CLAMBAKE is surprisingly not limited to clams. Usually at the beach, in a pit with hot rocks, covered in seaweed, seafood (including clams) are steamed. Also known as a **New England clambake,** the meal is usually accompanied by vegetables, especially corn, potatoes and onions. Non-beach versions also exist and usually cooked in a pot.

CLING WRAP is also known as **glad wrap, cling film, plastic wrap** or **saran wrap**. Developed in 1949, Dow Chemical refined the spray and developed saran plastic wrap. Plastic wrap is commonly made out of PVC (Polyvinylidene Chloride). The irony is not lost that plastic wrap is in everyones kitchen where burns are most likely to happen - being that hospitals use it for burns victims. It helps maintain burn wound moisture and helps to protect exposed nerve endings which can assist in multimodal pain management. Avoid wrapping affected area circumferentially with plastic film wrap as this can have a tourniquet effect as oedema worsens.

✔ **Top tips for cling wrap**
    ~ If the cling wrap won't stick, wipe the surface you want it to stick to with a damp cloth.
    ~ Tuck a small piece of paper into the edge of the roll and you'll find the end of the roll every time.
    ~ Some people find cling wrap easier to handle when it's kept in the fridge.
    ~ Cover the top of your fridge with cling wrap, never having to wipe the top of the fridge again!
    ~ Wrap unused crockery and cutlery in cling wrap before storage.

CLOVES tend to lose volatile oils through evaporation, so shouldn't be stored for long periods or stored in the fridge to preserve the natural oils. To check freshness, drop some in water: if they sink or float upright, all is well, but if they lie on their side, they are stale. I have seen fresh cloves on the stem in markets, looking evocative with their pink and light-green buds, but have found no references to using them in cooking. These unopened buds from the clove tree can be picked from the stem, laid on a mat and dried in the sun (about four days, weather permitting) leaving you with the dark-brown, tack-like spice we all know. This freshly dried clove will be pungent, high in volatile oils and ready to use. See also SPICE.

COBBLER also known as **fruit cobbler,** is a pie made of fruit with rich biscuit dough usually dropped only on top of the fruit before baking.

COBNUT which is **hazelnut,** also known as **filbert.**

COCKSCOMB see POULTRY

COCOA BUTTER also known as **theobroma oil**, is created during the chocolate-making process.   Extracted form the cocoa nibs, cocoa butter determines the viscosity of chocolate (the best chocolates have a higher percentage, 33–40%, of cocoa butter). Chocolate cannot be called chocolate without the 100% use of cocoa butter. It can be bought separately and used to thin chocolate. Cocoa butter is also an important

COCOA POWDER is a product derived from the CACAO bean during the CHOCOLATE-making process. Cocoa liquor and cocoa butter are extracted from the cacao bean, and the dry cake that remains after pressing is ground into cocoa powder. Cocoa powder is mildly acidic and can be bought as low-fat and medium-fat. Drinking cocoa or drinking chocolate contains cocoa powder, sugar, malt extracts, milk powder, LECITHIN and vanilla. It is used in sweetened chocolate drink mixes. Dutch cocoa was invented by Coenraad Johannes van Houten in the Netherlands. It is cocoa powder that has been alkalised to leave a darker, smoother, less bitter and more soluble powder. If a recipe calls for Dutch cocoa and all you have is ordinary cocoa, add a very small amount of baking powder when sifting the cocoa. This will help alkalise the mix.

COCONUT An unripe coconut contains a clear, watery liquid known as coconut water or coconut juice, which diminishes as the coconut matures and the meat forms. Coconut cream and coconut milk are both made from pressing coconut meat: cream from the first pressing and milk from the second pressing (so the milk is more watered-down). Although one can be substituted for the other with only minor differences in taste and texture, I recommend a combination of both cream and milk when making curries: try 2 parts milk to 1 part cream.

COCOZIELLI or **cocozelle** is a type of SQUASH which can grow to ridiculous heights (1.5 metres or more). There is really nothing to say about a vegetable this big, except make sure you invite many friends and family over for dinner if you ever cook it.

COD refers to both the **Atlantic cod** and the **Pacific cod**. A firm, white fleshed fish that over history was an important commodity both economically and politically, as is well documented in the book *Cod* by *Mark Kurlansky* detailing the cod wars of the late 20th and early 21st century.

CODDLE To cook eggs gently in water at just below boiling point or by covering them with boiling water long enough for the whites to barely set. Cooking eggs with the use of a water circulator set at 63°C for 63 minutes produces a textured egg where both the yolk and whites are soft. Known as *onsen tomago* in Japan, this style of egg is nit for everyone. The term can also apply to cooking fruit.

COFFEE a most important trade commodity crop of berries from which the seed (bean) is roasted and brewed.

COLLARD or collard greens are similar to KALE but with smooth leaves and a much sweeter, softer texture.

COLOSTRUM, particularly bovine colostrum, has been used in India and Scandinavian countries for centuries either dried or in celebratory desserts and puddings. The health benefits of bovine colostrum have been well documented. This 'pre-milk' is available in capsule form, as a powder or a liquid.

CONFIT To cook food in its own fat or juices, then preserve it in the very same fat or liquid. (Although you can make confit of garlic, lemon or other fruits by cooking the food slowly in oils, fruit juices and/or with salt.) Confit of duck, goose and pork is a specialty of the region of Gascony in France where the meat is first rubbed with salt – to extract juices and partially cure the meat – before it is slowly cooked then sealed and preserved in its own fat.

CONTROLLED-ATMOSPHERE STORAGE permits the year-round sale of fruit and vegetables. Fruit and vegetables require oxygen for continued respiration after being harvested. If the air is depleted of this oxygen, and is enriched with carbon dioxide, respiration is slowed and storage life prolonged.

COOK DOWN see REDUCE

COPHA is solidified coconut oil, used in chocolate crackles and White Christmas (both iconic Australian recipes). It is classed as vegetable SHORTENING, so can be replaced in recipes with other types of shortening or another brand of solidified coconut oil.

CORIANDER leaves and seeds taste very different so cannot be substituted for one another. Coriander leaf, also known as **cilantro** in the US or **Chinese parsley,** is my favourite herb, with its enticing aroma and bold, refreshing and incomparable flavour. Having said that, it is also the most polarising of herbs, as approximately 14% -21% of certain ethnical backgrounds like caucasians and Africans, have a chemical aversion to the flavour where "enticing, bold & refreshing" is replaced with words like "soap, gym socks, dishwater, dirt & stink beetles". What causes this flavour affliction?The aroma and flavour compound *S-Linalool*, a naturally occurring chemical in scented plants, with the compound also contained in about 60% of cleaning agents. Coriander also has some aldehydes that are found in soaps, detergents, and lotions as well as the bug family of insects.

It is definitely one that should only be used fresh – when cooked or dried the flavour diminishes greatly. The root is used extensively in Thai cuisine where it is pounded into pastes and dressings. Unfortunately, coriander root can be hard to come across, especially in supermarkets. If a recipe calls for root when none is available try doubling the quantity of finely chopped stem, butdifferent texture (slimier) and will not match the depth of flavour the root can provide. Coriander sold with its root intact can be stored in a small amount of water(1–2 cm only) and covered with a plastic bag – it will last for one or two weeks and longer if you change the water.

Coriander seeds are technically the fruit of the plant. As with most whole spices, the powder is best made by lightly roasting and then grinding whole seeds in a mortar and pestle. This freshly ground coriander is far superior to the ground coriander found on supermarket shelves.

Problem solving
~ **Leftover coriander?** Make a coriander pesto or store in oil in the fridge or freezer (see HERBS for method). Another good option is to mix it with a bit of chilli and add to the last stage of a chutney (mango chutney is ideal).

Alternatives to coriander
A close member of the coriander family, **pak chi farang** (also known as **saw-leaf coriander, long coriander** and **Mexican coriander**), makes an excellent substitute, although the leaves are hardier and stronger in flavour.

CORM is another name for tubers: bulbous underground edible plant stems, such as potato, carrot, celeriac and parsnip.

CORN, as in **sweetcorn, whole-kernel corn, corn on the cob** or **maize**, is best cooked and eaten immediately after harvesting. As corn ages, the sugars rapidly break down into starches and flavour is lost. Only buy corn with a full husk; corn that is presented with the tops cut off or packaged with no husk at all will be old and starchy.

If you intend to grill corn, first soak the ears, husk and all, in water for a couple of hours. Cook on the grill with the husk still on, turning regularly, then remove the husk (shuck) when it's done. Corn can be boiled with its husk on or off, then either eaten immediately or cooled and stripped of the juicy kernels for salads, fritters or . An edible fungus that grows on corn stalks (a strange, purplish growth) is considered a delicacy by some.

Corn is also ground into different types and grades of flour. The degree to which it is milled determines its use and name. The kernel stripped of the hull and the germ is called **hominy. Hominy grits** is a Southern American soul food term for **cracked hominy** (also called *samp*), which closely resembles polenta. **Polenta** is an Italian style of **cracked maize. Cornmeal** is milled more finely than polenta and used to make many dishes including corn bread. (**Cornmeal** is known in the US as **cornflour,** although the US product is a little finer.) The most finely milled product is cornflour (see FLOUR), endosperm of the kernel, the innermost layer of the grain.

Baby corn is not young sweetcorn but a different variety.

For **corn syrup** see 'alternatives to sugar' in SUGAR.

COTTAGE CHEESE is the fresh curd scooped from low-fat pasteurised milk. Draining cottage cheese further creates **pot cheese,** and if you squeeze the remaining liquid from this, you'll produce **farmer's cheese.** Drained cottage cheese can be used in place of RICOTTA in some instances, although it is not ideal as it has a lower fat content and is best served chilled, while ricotta likes to be cooked.

COURGETTE is another word for ZUCCHINI.

COUVERTURE see CHOCOLATE

CRAB should be bought either alive or precooked. When buying live, look for a creature that has a bit of kick in it. Crabs are usually tied with twine to prevent them from latching onto stray fingers. When buying precooked crustaceans, the outer shell should be bright orange to red in colour, free from any disagreeable odours, with white, firm flesh on the inside. Also take note of the joints of the cooked crab, they should be white not brown. Soft, pasty flesh indicates an animal that was stressed before being cooked.

450 g crab in the shell will yield 1 cup of flaked crab meat.

HOW TO COOK LIVE CRAB

The *RSPCA* recommends crabs be placed in the freezer for 4–5 hours before cooking to 'put them to sleep'. Alternatively, place in a bowl of iced water 30 minutes to an hour to sleep them. If cooked alive, crabs will shed their limbs. Bring seawater or salted water (1 litre water to 100g rock salt, allow 5litres water per kg of crab) to a vigorous boil, then add the crab and cook for 1 minute for every 100g (plus 2minutes overall). The shell will turn a bright orange when the crab is cooked. Lift out of the water and place on a tray to pick over. Previous techniques suggest to place the hot crabs into a tub of chilled water or under cold running water (to halt the cooking process). Part of the issue here is the cold immersion does two things - **1**. it dilutes the natural flavour in the meat and **2**. it makes the crab meat harder to lift from the shell. Therefore, best practice is to pick the meat from the shells while the crab is still hot. You may need gloves and tea towels to do this job. If you plan to sauté the crab, it should merely be blanched in boiling water first: use the method above but remove from the water and cool after 5 minutes.

CRAB STICK is also known as **sea legs** or **surimi**. There's not even a whiff of crab in a crab stick. It is made from white fish, usually **Alaskan pollock** (also used to make other imitation seafood products such as imitation scallops or prawns or fish patties). Real Californian rolls should be made with the leg meat of crab, kept whole, not thin strips of this faux crab.

CRACKLING see PORK

CRAYFISH is a freshwater crustacean (although usage of the word varies – see ROCK LOBSTER). Crayfish species are abundant in North America and Australasia (100 or so species in Australia and 250 in North America) but less common in most other parts of the world.

Crayfish are generally much smaller than **rock lobsters**, with many species considered too small to eat. The Tasmanian crayfish (endangered) is the largest in the world, followed by the Murray River crayfish (hard to find). **Yabbies, redclaw** and **marron** are three well-known crayfish in Australia. Marron is the third largest freshwater crayfish in the world, and is indigenous to Western Australia. Its meat is considered to be the finest of all crayfish. About 31% of its total body weight is meat (compared to 15–20% for yabbies). Redclaw, a native of Queensland, is best eaten in that region, as it does not travel well. The American **crawfish** is a smaller version of the Australian yabby.

All of the species of crayfish have many edible parts: the tail, the claws, the 'mustard' and the 'coral', and the shell can also be used to flavour soups and sauces. The tail and claws represent about 40% of total body weight. The 'mustard' is the orange-brown liver or *hepatopancreas* found in the carapace (main shell) also known as *tomalley* and which connoisseurs enjoy spread over the tail meat. The 'coral' is the developing egg sac found in the carapace of the female, which can be eaten on its own or whisked. Crayfish and lobster should be bought either alive or precooked, not dead and raw. When buying them live, look for a lively creature. The tail of a lobster should tuck underneath and not hang down when the lobster is picked up. When buying precooked crustaceans, all of the outer shell should be bright orange to red in colour, free from any disagreeable odours, with white firm flesh on the inside. Soft, pasty flesh indicates an animal that was stressed before being cooked.

HOW TO COOK LIVE CRAYFISH

Place in the freezer for 2–3 hours before cooking to avoid stressing the animals by cooking them while still alive. Alternatively, place in a bowl of iced water 30 minutes to an hour to sleep them. If they are still lively before putting in the boiling water, place them back in the ice water for another 15minutes. Drop into boiling salted water, bring the water back to the boil and set timer for 1 minute for every 100g - until they have turned a bright orange/red. Remove and REFRESH in iced water.

CREAM The different types of cream sold in different countries and used in recipe books from around the world can be one of the more frustrating things to deal with as a cook (or a tourist). Essentially it is the fat content in cream that affects the final outcome of a dish. As the European, American, South African, Australian and New Zealand dairy fraternities continue to churn creams with differing fat contents and use different marketing names, it can be decidedly challenging to guarantee a perfect result. The list below attempts an explanation of the main types of cream. My advice is to understand the recipe that the cream is used in to work out whether it needs a cream with a low, medium or high fat content, and whether it's required for whipping, pouring, cooking or for use as is.

 tips for whipped cream
    ~ Chill the bowl you plan to use in the refrigerator. This will ensure the cream stays chilled and thus reduce the chance of it separating.
    ~ Expect cream to increase in volume by 2–2½ times when whipped. To gain maximum volume, begin the whipping process at a slower speed, and increase the speed as the cream begins to thicken.
    ~ If the cream begins to turn yellow, it has begun to over-whip and separate. Try mixing in more cream with a spatula until combined. If the cream is too far gone, however, your only hope is to turn it into butter and buttermilk – continue whipping until the milk solids are separated from the milk fat.
    ~ Add sugar to whipped cream when tracks begin to form. This helps to maximise its volume
    ~ To make cream lighter add a dash of milk to the final stages of whipping. This mixture will not stand as long.

    Clotted cream is made from rich, unpasteurised milk that is heated to 85°C for about one hour. In this time yellow clots of coagulated cream form on top of the milk. This rich cream with a fat content of 55% is also known as **Devonshire cream**. Can be used as a substitute for **quaimaaq**.
    Crème fraîche is a naturally soured cream, also known as **racreme,** and **clabber/clabbered cream**. It doesn't curdle when

heated, which is why it is used for cream-based sauces. It is easy to make at home.

HOME-MADE CRÈME FRAÎCHE

1 cup whipping cream
1/2 cup sour cream OR 2 Tablespoons buttermilk
Mix together and pour into a glass bowl. Cover with cling wrap and leave on the kitchen bench for 8–14 hours (until set). Stir and refrigerate. It will last 7–10 days in the fridge.

Double cream, generally speaking, has a fat content of 45–48%. (Note that some UK cookbooks ask for double cream when they want is a pure cream of 30–35% fat content: you'll just have to see whether the recipe works and if not try a different cream next time).

Extra thick single cream is an English product made from single cream (18% fat) which has been homogenised, pasteurised and then cooled. This cream cannot be whipped, but instead produces a thick spooning cream similar to Australian double cream.

Half and half is half milk and half cream. It is an American product that is not readily available elsewhere (except for Canada), but you can make your own by using equal parts milk and pouring cream. It cannot be whipped as it contains only 10-12% fat.

Pouring cream is an Australian product, the equivalent of **single cream** (with a minimum of 18% fat) in the UK and **light cream** (18–30% fat) in the US. It can also be called **coffee cream** (in many European countries) and **table cream** (US & Canada).

Qaimaaq is a type of cream, also known as **breakfast cream**. If necessary, substitute with CLOTTED CREAM.

Sour cream is cream that has been soured with lactic acid bacteria. The degree of sourness varies between countries – if you're from Ireland you may like it very sour, if from the US, quite mild. Sour cream is about 12%-16% fat content. In Norway, **Rjome** or **rømme** is a sour cream with 35% fat content and is wonderful as sour cream porridge (Rømmegrøt). The Icelandic **sýrður rjómi** also contains 35% fat.

Traditionally, sour cream was made by letting cream that was skimmed off the top of milk ferment at a moderate temperature. Sour cream can easily be made at home, using buttermilk or yoghurt as the starter. The recipe can be varied, but try the following.

HOME-MADE SOUR CREAM
250 ml cream (18–36% fat, no additives)
Approx. 2 tablespoons or 50 ml yoghurt or buttermilk
Mix together and leave in the bowl overnight or for 24 hours in a warm area while the mix sets. Depending on how thick you like it, use immediately or strain through muslin cloth (cheesecloth) for several hours until the thickness is agreeable.

Sterilised cream (23–28% fat), also known as **manufacturer's cream** or **ultra sterilised cream**, is heat-treated which results in a caramelised flavour. This European product, sold in tins or Tetra Paks, cannot be whipped but is spoonable enough to accompany desserts. If unavailable, use pouring cream instead.

Thickened cream as it's known in Australia and NewZealand, with 35% fat which contains a thickener such as halal GELATINE or vegetable gum. With added thickeners it is also known as In **whipping cream** in Canada, Germany and Sweden. These thickeners are added to stabilise the cream when whipped. Sometimes mineral salts are also added. Use when your British cookbooks call for whipping cream (35–38% fat) and American cookbooks call for heavy cream or heavy whipping cream (35–42%fat), both the UK and he US version contains no thickeners.

Whipping cream may or may not contain additives or thickeners depending on the country.

CREAM OF TARTAR or **tartaric acid** is a white powder made from argol, the crude tartaric acid build-up left on the sides of casks when grape juice is made into wine. It is used to stiffen egg whites when making meringues, soufflés and cakes, and in sweet-making. It is combined with BICARBONATE OF SODA in baking – if your recipe calls for cream of tartar and baking soda it is probably an old recipe, as BAKING POWDER has superseded this combination in more recent times.

HOW TO REPLACE CREAM OF TARTAR

If you have no cream of tartar, omit the baking soda component as well and replace with baking powder.

1 teaspoon baking powder = ¼ teaspoon baking soda plus 5/8 teaspoon cream of tartar

If the recipe contains additional baking soda that does not fit into this equation, add the additional amount along with the baking powder.

CRÈME ANGLAISE is fresh egg custard.

CRÈME FRAÎCHE see CREAM

CRÈME PATISSIÈRE is best described by Michel and Albert Roux: 'crème patissière is to patisserie what veal stock is to cooking' (*The Roux Brothers on Patisserie*). It is a custard made from egg yolks, sugar, flour, milk and fresh vanilla; a simple staple that can be flavoured with chocolate or coffee among other flavours, used in éclairs, profiteroles and fruit flans, as a soufflé base and in innumerable other recipes.

CROCKERY

 Top tips for crockery

~ Three methods of warming plates for a dinner party:

    1. Leave in a very low oven for an hour.

    2. Wipe each plate with a damp cloth and microwave until warmed through.

    3. Cover the plates in hot water in the sink, then put them on the draining rack and dry when you're ready to use them.

Problem solving

    ~ **Cracked bowl?** A hairline crack in a plate or bowl can be temporarily mended by simmering in milk. Heat over low for an hour. Allow to cool in milk and then remove and rinse.

CUBEB is a hollow black spice from the PEPPER family and hard to source in the West. Used in Indonesian curries, cubeb can be replaced with black pepper mixed with a little allspice.

CUCUMBER is as much as 96% water. This is why they are salted when used for dips or relishes – to extract some of the water so it doesn't dilute the other ingredients or affect the texture of the final dish. There are two main types of cucumber:slicing cucumbers and pickling cucumbers. Slicing cucumbers are longer, smoother and tougher-skinned than those designed for pickling which are stumpier with bumpy, soft skins. Most of the flavour is in the seeds but the jellylike flesh surrounding the seeds is very watery (and the seeds are sometimes said to cause indigestion). This is why some recipes ask for the seeds to be removed: it reduces the water content but at the expense of the taste. Whether you remove the skin is also a matter of taste – or should I say texture, as the tougher skins on larger cucumbers are not pleasant eating.

HOW TO SALT CUCUMBER
Slice and sprinkle with cooking salt and leave stand for 30 minutes, rinse under cold water and squeeze dry, then mix in the other ingredients.

Common cucumbers are the tough-skinned, dark green, white-fleshed variety that when mature contain large seeds that tend to be bitter. I recommend peeling and removing seeds before eating fresh, and as much as they are considered a slicing cucumber, I prefer to pickle them.

Continental cucumbers, also known as **telegraph cucumbers, burpless cucumbers, English cucumbers, seedless cucumbers** or **hothouse cucumbers,** barely have any seeds. They are a slicing cucumber with near-white flesh thin, dark-green skin. At 20–30 cm they are one of the longest cucumbers and are often sold individually wrapped in plastic (choose carefully as this can hide blemishes).

Japanese cucumbers have a slender body, and a deep-green, bumpy skin with a mild flavour. They are equally good for pickling and slicing.

Kirby cucumbers range in colour from yellow to dark-green with white or black dots. These are an ideal pickling cucumber.

Lebanese cucumbers (also known as **Persian cucumbers**) are similar in colour, flavour and texture to Continental cucumbers but are much smaller. Considered a pickling style of cucumber, they eat just as well raw.

CUMQUAT I first stumbled upon this little citrus fruit in my dad's orchard as a nine-year-old. An ornamental plant growing to about 1 metre, the cumquat tree bears fruit that resembles an orange the size of a cherry tomato. The fully mature fruit can be eaten whole: the soft rind is tangy, while the flesh tastes sharp and almost like sherbet. However it is more often used in marmalades and conserves, CANDIED or in sauces and stuffing. The fresh ripe fruit will keep in the fridge for up to 10 days.

CURE is a method of preserving food. Cured meat is meat that has been preserved through ageing, drying, canning, salting, brining or smoking. The goal of curing is to slow spoilage and prevent the growth of microorganisms. The most common method is salt-curing, where salt is added to meat which is then left to stand for a period of time to draw off the water content. What remains is a semi-dried piece of meat, of salty taste, with the flavour depending on the quantity of salt, time and type of meat. Salted beef and corned beef are examples of cured meat. Meat is dry-cured when the salt mix is applied to the meat, which is refrigerated, then washed before being cooked. Hams and bacon are examples of dry-cured meat. Sugar-curing is when sugar is added to the salt mix to sweeten the food. **Gravlax** is the well known cured salmon brought to us via our Nordic friends. Known also as *Gravadlax, gravad laks* and *graved salmon,* cured in salt, sugar and fresh dill. The Italians give us *prosciutto*, lardo, *bresaola* and *salami* to name a few. Every country offers up their signature cured meat steeped in centuries of traditional recipes and methods. From *biltong* to *jamon, smoked salmon* to *salt cod and caviar to duck eggs,* the list is as interesting as it is tasty.

CURRANT (not to be confused with **dried currants**, which are made from a small seedless grape). The fruit comes in 4 colours:

Blackcurrants are used in cooking only and made into a liqueur (cassis) and a syrup ('Ribena' is one brand, the name comes from the botanical term for currants, 'ribes'). **Redcurrants** are mostly used for cooking in jams, jellies and sauces. **White currants** can be used in cooking, and are less sour than the red, and can therefore be eaten fresh; the more translucent the berry the better variety it is. **Pink currants** are simply a cross between red and white.

CURRY LEAF, a delicate herb with a pungency that resembles curry, can be found fresh in Asian grocers (sold in bags of small stems of soft, dark-green leaves), although dried leaves are more readily available. The fresh leaves are vibrant, while the pre-packed dried leaves have little flavour. Fresh leaves can be toasted or oven-dried just before use to release the essential oils, then added to soups, sauces and curries. They are also delicious finely shredded in a spring roll or samosa mix. Packets of leaves can be frozen (as you would kaffir lime leaves, see LIME) then added to the dish straight from the freezer. And if you really like the flavour, it might even be worth planting one of these decorative leafy trees in the garden.

CUSTARD APPLE, also known as **atemoya**, a close relative of **cherimoya** which is common in the US. **Pond apple, sweetsop, soursop, sugar apple** and **bullock's heart** are names interchanged between many related cultivars with differing skin colour, flesh colour, flavour and size, but often these are all simply marketed as **moya.** The inedible skin may be a yellowish to dark-green, the flesh white to yellow, and the size may range from that of a softball to a football. Custard apples mature and ripen like avocados, and once mature, deterioration is rapid, so keep your eye on this fruit. When ripe, chill, cut in half and eat with a spoon, spitting out the rather large bean-like seeds. Or freeze the flesh and simply eat like ice-cream. Also great in milkshakes, sorbets or poached very lightly in coconut milk and served warm.

CUSTARD MARROW see CHOKO

CUTTING BOARDS Wooden or plastic? If you're like me, you're getting a little tired of this argument; every few years there seems to be new evidence as to why we should buy either one.

The issue with chopping boards is that bacteria (and strong flavours) from food can remain on the board and contaminate other foods, for example if you chop vegetables for a salad on the same board as you previously chopped raw chicken, the salad may pick up dangerous bacteria. And if you've ever eaten fruit that has been prepared on a board that's been used to chop garlic or onions, you'll kill food bacteria, but it's also said that wooden boards hold bacteria for dangerous periods of time which could lead to cross-contamination.

Some believe that bacteria can be washed more effectively from plastic (or non-porous acrylic), and to avoid cross-contamination plastic boards are sold in a range of colours to help you remember to use a different board for different types of food.

HOW TO CLEAN A CUTTING BOARD

Invest in a metal scraper which will help remove layers of food matter that even a scourer won't budge. (If you need convincing, scrape the back of a knife down one of your clean cutting boards and see how clean it really is.) Always rinse food from a cutting board in cold, soapy water first. This will neutralise food and smells before it is washed in hot soapy water, which tends to 'cook' food particles and odours into the board. Rinse and air dry or pat dry with paper towels. Non-porous acrylic, plastic, glass and solid wood boards can be washed in an automatic dishwasher (although water will break down the oils in a wooden board so it will dry and crack over time). Boiling a plastic chopping board is recommended, if only a domestic pot could fit one. After boiling, use a metal scraper to remove the dead layer, then wash in soapy water. Discard excessively worn cutting boards. Remember, cold, soapy water first - always.

I recommend that whatever material you choose, have at least two boards, more if budget and storage permit. You can use each side of each board for a different food. Engrave a mark in the corner to show what food that side is used for. For example, "F" for fruit, "V" for vegetables, "S" for seafood and "M" for meat. If you have more than two boards then add cooked meats and dairy to.

CUTTLEFISH see SQUID

D.

DAIKON is a type of radish of the BRASSICA family. Daikon can be eaten raw, pickled or cooked. Raw, it has a pleasant, mild bite and almost sweet flavour. Also known as **Japanese mooli, white radish, Japanese radish, icicle radish, Chinese radish** and **lo bak/loh baak**.

DANDELION is a vegetable as well as a common weed. It contains more potassium than bananas. Every part of the dandelion is edible: the roots can be steamed as a vegetable or dried for tea, the crown is used in salads or as a vegetable, the leaves (best in spring when they are less bitter) are good in salads or soups or tossed with boiled potatoes, the flower buds can be used to make wine or (if they're very young) sautéed in butter for a flavour resembling mushrooms, and the petals of flowers in salads (use sparingly, as they can be over-powering). The leaves of older plants are steeped in boiling water (5–10 minutes) to make a bitter tea, which can be served with honey. A less bitter tea can be made from the root: dry in the oven for 1–2 hours at 180–200°C, then grind like coffee. Both types of tea are used as a digestive and diuretic.But here comes the warning: as with all flowers, only consume those that are organically grown or grown using organic pesticides. People who suffer allergies like hay fever and asthma should avoid eating flowers altogether.

DASHI is fundamental in Japanese cuisine as a soup stock and flavour base in many dishes. Generally made with dried fish (sardines or BONITO) and KOMBU, dashi can also be vegetarian, made with mushrooms. Instant dashi is a powder that simply needs boiling water added. Although quick and easy, it is frowned upon by purists. If you have a recipe for home-made dashi, have a go –there are after all only two or three ingredients involved and one of them is water, how hard can it be?

DAUN PANDAN see PANDANUS LEAF

DE-BEARD see MUSSEL

DEEP-FRY To cook in large quantities of fat, usually oil. The principle behind deep-frying is that the high temperature of the oil immediately seals the food so it cooks crisp on the outside without getting oily inside. Successful deep-frying requires careful monitoring of temperatures, choice of oil, straining or disposal of oils and cleaning of equipment. The temperature at which to fry food depends on size and quantity. As a very general rule temperatures of between 180°C and 195°C will do. Keep in mind that the oil temperature drops, in some cases significantly, when food is added. Don't overcrowd the pan as the temperature will drop too quickly and therefore won't seal the food which will become soggy and oily instead of crisp. There is no single 'best' oil for frying, but oils such as cottonseed, vegetable, soy, corn, safflower, peanut and canola are often recommended because they have a higher smoking point. Oil smokes at the point when it begins to decompose and create the nasty-smelling compound acreolein. Lard or animal fat has fallen out of trend over the last few decades for several unfounded reasons, only to be replaced with various seed and plant oils. Which is somewhat unfortunate as rendered animal fat which is other wise wasted does provide valuable nutrients to the human body. It's also very delicious. Think potatoes friend in duck fat.

DEGLAZE means not getting out another pan to make sauce in. Remove the food (usually meat) from the pan and set to one side to rest, covered with foil. Place the pan back on the heat and splash in wine, flavoured vinegar, stock or even water then stir to lift any cooked-on juices that browned in the bottom of the pan.

DILL or **dill weed** is a herb that traditionally accompanies fish and egg dishes, and is used in some Eastern European cuisines. Dill seed, like caraway and coriander, is technically the fruit of of the plant. It is best roasted and ground immediately before use.

Q Problem solving

~ **Leftover dill?** Unless you're planning to make a slab of gravad lax (fresh salmon cured in salt, sugar and dill), leftover dill can be hard to deal with: make a dill pesto, store in oil in the fridge, or freeze (it's best to freeze in small amounts, see HERBS for method). Dill is also great with potatoes, so toss potatoes with herb butter or make a dill vinegar to use in mayonnaise for salad. And don't forget the option of dill pickles.

DISASTERS The last word on all disasters is to prevent rather than cure. Read the recipe's method from start to finish before you start cooking, stir as asked, check oven temperatures (twice), turn things off before answering phones or doors, buy a kitchen timer with a loud alarm, taste, touch and smell things regularly, take your time and have patience. See individual foods for specific repair tips and remedies when things go wrong.

DOUBLE BOIL is a cooking method that avoids the direct fierceness of a naked flame or electric hotplate. This is a controlled way to melt or thicken food like chocolate, lemon curd, sabayon and hollandaise, to name a few. Bring water to the boil then place a bowl with the ingredients over the boiled water. Usually the heat source is turned very low or removed altogether after the water has boiled, allowing the residual heat to do the job. Patience is the key to success when double boiling.

DRAGONFRUIT These delicious fruit grow on a climbing cactus. The flesh inside can vary from white to red, depending on the species. Flecked with black seeds the size of sesame seeds, the flesh is reported to taste of kiwifruit, although I think it has a flavour that much more resembles a mellow mulberry flavour (the red fleshed variety. The white fleshed variety seems devoid of any and all flavour). Also known as **pitaya, pitahaya** or **cactus fruit**.

DRESSINGS The most common dressings, used to dress a salad or meat or to garnish a plate, are made with oil combined with either vinegar or lemon juice. A vinegar- and oil-based dressing is a vinaigrette. Generally the ratio is 3 (or even 4) parts oil to 1 part vinegar. This type of dressing can be kept at room temperature, but it is better refrigerated (oils with higher fat content, such as olive oil, tend to solidify in the fridge but will return to their former state when brought to room temperature). For dressings made with lemon juice the ratio is 1 to 1 or, at the most, 2 parts oil to 1 part juice. Lemon juice is an acid, so if using in a salad dressing, be sure to add the dressing just before the salad is to be served. If the dressing is added too soon, the lemon juice will burn the lettuce leaves, while the salt in the dressing will draw out moisture in the salad ingredients, leaving them wilted and flat.

Q **Problem solving**
~ **Separated vinaigrette or dressing?** Non-egg-based dressings and vinaigrettes tend to separate when left to stand. Simply shake well to homogenise the dressing before using it.

DRIPPING is the fat from roasted meat. Drain and keep in the fridge for another day and use instead of oil when next cooking meat or some vegetables.

DUCK in most Western countries is still the meat we go out for. Due to a high fat to meat ratio and the expense compared to chicken, duck has struggled to adorn domestic kitchen tables. Duck is processed from 6–15 weeks of age, depending on the breed. Most duck available to the public is the Pekin or Peking duck (this is the name of the breed as well as the famous dish). For a stronger game flavour, try to source the big-scented Muscovy duck. Duck's web (the membrane between its webbed toes) is up there with chicken feet and cockscomb when it comes to challenging ingredients.

Duck needs to be RENDERED during the cooking process. This is why Peking duck hangs in the window of Chinese restaurants, with heat lamps breaking down the fat, leaving crisp outer skin and moist tender meat. And this is all you really need to know about cooking duck: render, render, render. You can do this by simmering the whole duck for 40 minutes in water, then roasting for another 30–40 minutes at 220°C, or slow-roasting the bird for 11/4 hours, draining the fat from the tray every 15–20 minutes (keep the fat for frying other foods such as potato), or making a wicked mess in the kitchen and cooking it Peking Duck style. I recommend buying duck legs (one per person) instead of a whole duck in most cases, to save stress and drama over oven space. See POULTRY for general information and more cooking tips.

DUFF Not the beer favoured by Homer Simpson, but the name of an English pudding: plum duff is a type of steamed pudding with dried fruits, really another name for **plum pudding** or **Christmas pudding.**

DUKKAH, a North African (Egyptian) condiment, is delicious with bread dipped in olive oil or as a coating for meat and fish. It is made up principally of coriander seeds, cumin seeds, nuts (usually hazelnuts), brown sesame seeds, salt and pepper, all roasted and then coarsely ground together.

DURIAN is also known as **stinkyfruit,** for, like JACKFRUIT, it possesses a distinctive smell that Westerners struggle to comprehend and appreciate. The outer skin is very spiky and should be handled with care, which is why durians are often sold in netted carry bags. It can be made into ice-cream, drinks, salads, sweets, cakes, custards, desserts and TEMPOYAK. It was named the 'king of fruits' by 19th-century naturalist Alfred Russel Wallace for its thorns, strong aroma and heavenly flavour, but no two people who eat the fruit seem to agree on a description for its flavour. Wallace described it as a 'neither acid nor sweet, nor juicy, rich, glutinous, smooth, delicate custard highly flavoured with almonds, intermingled with onion-sauce, cream cheese, brown sherry and other flavours'. My personal experiences with this fruit come up with caramel, banana and vanilla with a slight onion tang – strange yet very likeable. Look for durian with no holes, splits or cracks in the surface, no wrinkling of the stem, no dirt or filth covering the skin, and that rattles slightly when shaken. It should have a definite aroma about it, but not an over-the-top fetid odour which suggests the fruit is over-ripe. A knife inserted into the fruit should come out sticky. Once you cut the durian open, you will find five or so segments, each carrying several seeds which in turn are surrounded by the custard-like aril (an extra seed covering). The seeds are also edible, usually roasted and served mixed with rice or as a sweetmeat.

E.

EAU DE COLOGNE MINT see BERGAMOT

EDAMAME see '**edible soy beans**' in BEAN

EDDO see TARO

EGGS

 Top tip for eggs
~ When I speak of eggs, I mean the freshest possible eggs you can get your hands on: their flavour is incomparable.
~ To set the record straight, a rooster is not needed for egg production in itself but for producing fertile eggs –that is, eggs that will hatch a chick after incubation. A rooster is good for waking people up at an ungodly hour, attacking the hand that feeds it, and mating with an entire yard full of hens. (Fertilised eggs can be eaten if they are collected as soon as they are laid – it takes 21 days of a hen sitting on an egg continuously to develop the embryo).
~ Fertile and infertile eggs are equally nutritious and will only vary in flavour according to the conditions the hens are kept in. ~ Brown eggs and white eggs are exactly the same in flavour, quality and nutrition – the pigmentation is genetic, not to do with a hen's diet, condition or the colour of the hen.
~ A blood spot on a yolk is not a sign that an egg has been fertilised; it simply shows that a blood vessel on the yolk's surface burst while the egg was forming.

~ Store eggs in the fridge in their cardboard box. (Eggs are porous and absorb odours from the fridge, which taints their natural flavour; the box will help protect them.)

~ Purchase eggs with a plan in mind. If baking a cake which may only use one or two eggs, plan on an omelette or other egg-based dishes within a day or two of purchase.

~ If, like me, you are an egg snob, the best place to buy eggs is at a local market, from the crusty-looking farmer with chicken poop and shell grit wedged under their fingernails.

~ For cake and pastry recipes, room temperature eggs are a must, so remove from the fridge and rest on the bench for half an hour before starting the recipe. A cold egg mixed with room temperature batter will seize or cool the mixture and won't mix in smoothly. Without a smooth, airy emulsion at this stage, a cake or pastry may tend to be grainy in texture, flat in appearance, become dry, cook unevenly or even sink slightly.

~ When whipping egg whites, a copper bowl helps hold the over-beating, while a glass bowl will cause the egg white foam to become grainy and dry. It's a chemical reaction thing; tests have been done, so trust me on this one.

~ Cream of tartar can also be used to stiffen egg whites: use 1/8 teaspoon cream of tartar for 2 egg whites.

EGG SIZES

Jumbo, very large or extra large	over 73g	0-1
Large	63g-73g	1-3
Medium	53g-63g	3-5
Small or pee wee	under 53g	5-7

Problem solving

~ **Leftover egg yolks?** Try hard not to break the yolks, placing them in a glass or bowl. Cover with a bit of cold water and refrigerate for up to 3 days. I suggest making a mayonnaise or fresh custard. Leftover egg yolks can be frozen but will be gummy and unusable unless you add a pinch of salt or sugar before freezing. Label your yolks 'savoury' or 'sweet', depending on which you added, then defrost in the refrigerator before using as you would a fresh yolk.

~ **Leftover egg whites?** Store in the freezer. Wash and thoroughly dry an empty plastic container with a screw top lid. Add leftover egg whites and freeze. Continue to add whites until two centimetres from the top. Don't forget to date the container, as whites will be at their best in the freezer for up to three months. Use egg whites for meringues and pavlovas. The problem then becomes one of volume, not numbers. Where a recipe asks for three egg whites, you now have a cupful at your disposal. As a guide, the white of one 55–65 g egg weighs 25–35 g. In other words, a little under half the weight of the entire egg is white.

~ **Dirty eggs?** Wipe with a dry cloth. If you wash an egg it will become even more vulnerable to absorbing fridge odours.

~ **Stuck to the carton?** Wet the carton and the egg will come out with ease.

~ **How do I tell if it's fresh?** A fresh egg will sink when placed in water (unless it has been damaged). An egg that floats has lost moisture, which has been replaced by air in the blunt, fat end of the egg. The white of a fresh egg clings to the yolk when the egg is cracked onto a plate and the CHALAZAE is prominent. Also, egg white becomes more transparent as the egg ages (caused by the slow escape of carbon dioxide); fresh eggs have a cloudier white.

~ **Separating eggs and there's eggshell shrapnel or egg yolk in the whites?** Remove with an empty half eggshell. If a lot of yolk has managed to infiltrate the white, keep it for scrambled egg and start again.

~ **Separating eggs and there's egg white in the yolk?** Don't worry. It is highly unlikely that the white will affect the further use of the yolk.

~ **Undercooked boiled eggs?** If they're still quite raw in the centre, peel all eggs, mash them together and quickly sauté in a bit of butter in a pan on the stove, just until the yolks have set. Cool immediately and use in sandwiches or eat while hot as a form of scrambled egg.

~ **Curdled fresh egg custard?** Take to it with a mixer. The sauce will now be fluffier and a little thinner than intended, but still useable.

~ **Collapsed soufflé?** A collapsing soufflé is known as the 'double deflation method' – as you helplessly watch the soufflé plunge below the rim of its receptacle, you witness too the deflation of your culinary ego. Turn the soufflé out of the mould and onto a tray. Place the turned out soufflé back in the hot oven for another minute or two and called it 'twice-baked soufflé'. Although it will not rise the second time around, this dense, eggy pudding will have a more concentrated flavour. Serve it on a plate garnished with sauce or ice-cream or both.

~ **Egg stuck to the dishes?** See WASHING UP.

Duck eggs (available from Asian grocers) can be used in many recipes that specify hens' eggs, but the flavour is stronger, oilier and richer, and not to everybody's taste. The flavour, naturally, is a cross between duck meat and egg. Duck eggs are also larger, so do not substitute one duck egg for one hen's egg. Duck egg whites cannot be whisked successfully as they lack globulin, a protein that, when whisked, holds air bubbles. From the Phillipines come **Balut.** Fertile duck eggs are incubated until the foetal stage then boiled for 15 minutes and eaten with ginger, Vietnamese mint and soy sauce. As a street food, popular in Vietnam, Cambodia and parts of China.

Quail eggs are readily available from poultry shops as well as some supermarkets. These delicately flavoured little eggs can be brutal on your patience if you have to boil and peel them, as the shell is delicate and somewhat elastic. If poaching or frying, always cut the top off them egg, and pour onto a shallow dish or saucer before placing in the pan. Quail eggs take about 2 minutes to poach. When boiling quail eggs, swirl the water for half the cooking time to centre the egg yolk. They will take 3–4 minutes to hard-boil.

Thousand-year eggs are not a thousand years old, because that would be just silly. There are three varieties: hulidan, dsaudan and pidan. For pidan eggs, duck's or hen's eggs are coated in a clay-like plaster of red earth, garden lime, salt, wood ash, and tea. Once coated in this alkaline mud, they are buried in soil for 100 days to cure. The eggs can be eaten raw – usually with soy and ginger – or cooked after the coating is removed (scrape off and wash under running water). The flavour resembles lime and pungent ammonia. As for the colour, the whites turn amber to black with a gelatinous texture and the yolk a dark-green with a creamy texture. Hulidan eggs are covered with a mix of salt and clay or ash and left in a cool, dark space for 1 month. When opened, the eggs have a partly solidified white and yolk with a salty flavour. Dsaudan eggs are packed in a mix of salt and cooked rice and then stored for a minimum of 6 months, in which time the shell will soften and the insides will coagulate, producing an egg that is mildly salty and winey tasting. Also known as **century eggs, hundred-year eggs, preserved eggs, fermented eggs, ancient eggs, skin eggs, black egg** or **Ming dynasty eggs.**

HOW TO COOK EGGS

Omelette is probably the only egg dish that should be cooked at a medium high heat for a very short period of time. All other egg dishes should be cooked at moderate to low temperatures so as not to make the white turn rubbery.

For the perfect **hard-boiled egg**, without the nasty grey rim around the yolk, try the method that follows. Note that egg protein is delicate and should be cooked delicately; rapid boiling eggs makes the yolks hard and the whites rubbery. Place room temperature eggs in a pot with just enough cold water to cover the eggs, top with a lid and bring to the boil, turn the heat down slightly to a simmer, set the timer for 8 minutes from the moment water begins to simmer. The water should never actually boil, just simmer. After 8minutes, pour off the water, and place in plenty of cold water to halt the cooking process. For easy peeling, tap the eggs all over o crack the shell and place back in the cold water. Fresh eggs will always be much harder to peel than older eggs, and chunks of the white will often come away.

To **coddle eggs** or prepare **soft-boiled eggs** for dipping toast soldiers, try this: Bring plenty of water to simmering point. You can add vinegar (5%) to help prevent eggs from cracking.
Use room temperature eggs, not eggs straight out the fridge (again to prevent cracking). Cook for 3, 4 or 5 minutes depending on how soft an egg you desire.

Scrambled eggs should be cooked over a gentle heat with a bit of patience, otherwise you'll end up with a hard, rubbery mass of weeping egg. Mix eggs with water, milk, cream or (if you're feeling decadent) MASCARPONE. Use a ratio of 1 egg to 1/2 tablespoon of liquid. Add herbs towards the end of cooking if desired.

Poached eggs - There's one true secret to producing the golf ball/comet-looking eggs found in the best breakfast joints around the world: freshness. The fresher the egg, the better the egg white will cling to the yolk. You can help this along by creating a whirlpool effect in the pot of simmering water before the egg goes in, then releasing the egg into the centre of the vortex. Adding salt or vinegar to the water may also help the whites to become firm. But at the end of the day, these tricks are irrelevant if the egg is not as fresh as possible. When you drop an egg into the water and you find the white floats and disperses on the top while the yolk sinks to the bottom with merely a tail of white intact, chances are this egg is reasonably old and better for boiled eggs. In the better cafes, chefs will have two simmering pots of water, one with a 5% vinegar solution and the other a "rinsing pot". Eggs are poached for 2 - 3 minutes and the vinegar solution and then transferred to the plain simmering water for 10seconds to rinse off the vinegar taste.

Fried eggs - For those who despise a crispy underside to fried eggs. Heat butter over a medium heat until it begins to bubble, then turn the heat down to low, break in the eggs and cover the pan. The lid will enclose steam which will slowly cook the whites on the surface.

(Heston Blumenthal, 'the alchemist of British cooking', separates the yolk from the white, gently fries the white, then adds the yolk towards the end of cooking – a great method that works well but isn't always practical).

 **Alternatives to eggs**

~ Eggs act as a binding agent in recipes which makes it hard to find an exact replacement with equal properties.

~ **Egg replacer** is a powdered leavening agent made from toasted soy flour, wheat starch, lecithin, dextrose and guar gum. Made to use measure for measure instead of whole eggs in baking.
10 g powder mixed with 40 g water = 1 egg

~ **For savoury dishes -** the tofu-based products, mock egg salad, imitation scrambled eggs and egg-free mayonnaise might be appropriate.

~ **Not enough eggs for baking?** Replace every third egg with one tablespoon cornflour. For recipes with three or more eggs, egg replacer is the best option. For recipes using only one egg, use egg replacer or one of the following:
* 1 tbsp soy flour mixed with 1 tbsp water
* 1/4 cup ripe mashed bananas OR apple or
* prune puree
* 3 tbsp mashed tofu
* 1 tsp ground flaxseed mixed with 3 tbsp water

EGG CREAM contains neither eggs nor cream, but rather milk, chocolate and seltzer water. It is a drink asked for in New York. When made with love, the froth on top resembles beaten egg whites.

EGGPLANT is also commonly known as **aubergine**, as well as **eggfruit** and **garden egg**. Buy firm eggplants that are heavy in relation to their size, free from scars or cuts. A wilted, shrivelled, soft or flabby eggplant will usually have a bitter flavour, while young, fresh eggplant is not bitter and can be used immediately. When recipes suggest you salt eggplant to remove bitterness, you can omit this step unless the eggplants are old or the recipe specifically requires the excess water to be extracted, although note that salting does remove much of the moisture and reduces the amount of oil the eggplant can absorb in cooking.

 Top tips for frying eggplants

~ The key is to take your time. The eggplants may absorb all the oil, but they will dispense excess oil when thoroughly cooked.

~ Most recipes for baked dishes containing eggplant, such as lasagne, call for the eggplant slices to be fried. If you are concerned about the amount of oil the slices will absorb, I suggest pricking the whole eggplant all over with a fork, then roasting whole in a hot oven (220°C) until soft. Remove, cool slightly, peel and drain the flesh in a colander or sieve. (The inner seeds can be removed if when you taste them they seem too bitter). Then use the roasted eggplant flesh as per the recipe.

HOW TO SALT EGGPLANT
Cut then sprinkle with cooking salt, stand for 30 minutes to 1 hour, then rinse and pat dry with paper towelling.

Several varieties of eggplant are listed below. In general most eggplants are interchangeable. The main groups are globe-shaped eggplants (common supermarket varieties, including the black beauty), Italian eggplants (the smaller globe-shaped variety), oblong-shaped Japanese and Lebanese eggplants and the small, striped Thai eggplants. White eggplants of all varieties are gaining popularity for being firmer, sweeter and moister.

Asian bride eggplants are very thin-skinned and cylindrical (15 cm long), white with lavender stripes along the length. Less bitter than purple-skinned varieties, they are excellent in curries.

Black beauty eggplants are the large, black-skinned variety common on market and supermarket shelves.

Black finger eggplants and black gnome eggplants are two Lebanese eggplant varieties. Elongated in shape, they require no salting but become leathery and tough the longer they are left in the fridge.

Japanese eggplants can be purple or white and are elongated.purple and the size of a walnut. Great for hors d'oeuvres and kebabs, steamed or whole in curries.

Long purple eggplants are thin-skinned, purple and crescent shaped. They are bitter and should be salted before cooking.

Pea eggplant also known as **turkey berry,**

devil's fig, platebrush or susumber. Available in well stocked Asian grocers, particularly Thai grocers. As the name suggests, pea eggplant are small but not as small as a pea. Excellent in Thai curries and soups , added whole and bursting with a mild bitterness that fully complements the hot, sweet sourness of a curry.

Purple rain eggplants are lavender with white streaks, larger and slightly tougher-skinned than the Asian bride.

Rosa bianca is possibly the best eating eggplant, with no bitterness whatsoever. A delicate, sweet flavour, with an almost pudding-like texture, this reasonably large eggplant has lavender streaking over white skin.

Thai apple eggplant, green stripe eggplant, Lao green stripe eggplant and **Thai eggplant** are names for the small green-and-yellow streaked eggplant found in Asian grocers. They can be Thai green curry.

Turkish orange eggplants look like little pumpkins when ripe, bright orange and the size of a tomato. They are sweet, thin-skinned and best eaten when still green.

White egg and **easter egg eggplants** are the shape and size of an egg and classed as an ornamental, with tough white skin which needs to be peeled. The white flesh, although somewhat watery and mildly sweet, holds well when cooked. Often used for pickling.

ENDIVE or **curly endive** is also known as **frisée** or in the US as **chicory** or **chicory endive**, see LEAFY GREENS. For Belgian endive see WITLOF.

ENGLISH SPICE see ALLSPICE

EPAZOTE is a pungent herb used especially in bean dishes in Central American countries, Mexico and New Mexico. It is said to make the beans more digestible. Also available as a powder.

ÉSCHALOT is a shocking derivative (word) of the true French spelling of shallot: 'échalote'. The word 'éschalot' is used to describe a true shallot in some regions, because they use 'shallot' for spring onion. See also ONION.

ESSENCE is a word not often used outside the professional kitchen, except to describe flavour enhancers such as almond or vanilla essence. An essence is a stock, only less diluted, the idea being to intensify the flavour of the ingredients being cooked. It is essentially a distillation of a vegetable (often mushrooms or celery) cooked in water. This essence is then used to enhance the flavour of other stocks, sauces or soups.

ESSENTIAL FATTY ACIDS (*EFA*) see FAT

F.

FARINA is a general term for flour, but can also refer to a flour by-product of potatoes, pulses and in some cases nuts, or the coarsely ground endosperm of a type of hard winter wheat which can be used as an alternative to semolina flour. See also FLOUR.

FAT types of fats:
    Essential fatty acids (*EFA*) are essential to human health but our bodies can't make them so they must be supplied through food or supplements. The two vital *EFAs* are **Omega 6** and **Omega 3** (see polyunsaturated and super-unsaturated fats, below). *EFAs* are highly perishable, deteriorating rapidly when exposed to light, air, heat and metals, so they cannot be dried, powdered or stored for long periods. To get the most out of *EFAs*, choose fresh products.
Monounsaturated fats are good for us and should be included in our diets. Foods rich in mono-unsaturated fatty acids are generally liquid at room temperature and semi-solid when refrigerated (for example, olive oil). Other foods high in mono-unsaturated fatty acids include peanuts, pecans, cashews, macadamias, avocados and canola oil.
    Polyunsaturated fats, also known as *Omega 6 EFAs*, are the good guys and are found in grapeseed, corn, cottonseed, pumpkin, sesame, soy, walnut oils, and in safflower, sunflower and hemp (which

have the highest *EFA r*eading). However polyunsaturated fats can be harmful when commercially processed.

Saturated fats were type cast as the bad guys because they clog your arteries. Found especially in butter, eggs, beef, lamb, chicken and pork, saturated fats are considered the new hero health foods. All oils and fats contain some saturated fatty acids (some other foods with high levels are palm kernels (88%), coconut, cocoa butter and shea nut butter). Of course, these fats also provide flavour which is why it's a good idea to cook the chicken with the skin on, or the steak with the fat left on, to keep the food moist and flavoursome. One should consider deeper research before dismissing animal fats as the enemy of those trying to lose weight. Look into the benefits of the carnivore lifestyle - which is not to say this way of eating is recommended for everybody.

Super-unsaturated fats are often referred to as *Omega 3 EFAs* and they're another of the good guys. They are harder to come by than *Omega 6,* but the richest source is flax seed. They are also found in tuna, salmon and trout and in blackcurrant seed oil. In land animals, the brain, eyeballs, adrenal glands, and testes are rich in super-unsaturated fatty acids.

Trans fatty acids are the really evil ones. They are the result of a chemical alteration, or transformation, that converts 'natural' unsaturated fats into 'unnatural' unsaturated fats that act like saturated fats. Stabilizing polyunsaturated oils to prevent them from becoming rancid and to keep them solid at room temperature. They may be particularly dangerous for heart health and may pose a risk for certain cancers. Trans fatty acids are worse for you than saturated fats because they interfere with the work that the natural essential fatty acids must do. Margarines, shortenings, shortening oils, and hydrogenated and partially hydrogenated vegetable oils contain a large amount of trans fat. Salad oils, butter, milk and meats generally have small amounts of trans fatty acids.

Vegetable shortening is a semisolid fat that is mostly solid at room temperature. It is named for the "short" or crumbly texture that it produces in cooking and baking applications, particularly in shortbread, pie crusts and puff pastry. Developed in the 1900's as a more economical and nutritional alternative to animal fat. Sold in a block form like butter, vegetable shortening is generally used to replace butter in baking (although some are produced as solid oils for frying) as it inhibits the formation of long, tough strands of gluten in dough and contributes a light texture. Its use varies depending on the brand. Trex (UK) is used to replace butter in vegan cooking, especially baking. (When replacing butter with Trex use 20% less than the specified amount of butter, as Trex contains no water).

See also LARD; OIL; SHORTENING; SUET.

FATBACK see PORK

FAVA BEAN see 'broad bean' in BEANS

FECULA is a name for different types of starch, including cornflour, arrowroot, tapioca, sago and ground rice. See also FLOUR.

FEIJOA is a native fruit from several South American countries including Brazil, Argentina, Columbia and Paraguay. A member of the myrtle family, feijoa is mostly eaten fresh but can also be used in puddings, ice-cream, pies, pastes, jams, syrups, and liqueurs. The flavour of this highly perfumed fruit resembles strawberries and sweet pineapples (which is why it is called **pineapple guava** in the US). Once the fruit is fully ripe, which means it gives a little when pressed, it should be stored in the fridge for up to a week. The flesh will turn brown once the feijoa is cut, but to avoid this you can juice it out and drop it in acidulated water (lemon and water). The skin of the feijoa is edible as too are the flower petals.

FENNEL is used as a herb and a vegetable and as fennel seed. **Florence fennel** (also known as **sweet fennel**) is a variety prized as a vegetable for its swollen base, which has a mild anise flavour, and is particularly popular in Italy and the Mediterranean. Often called **fennel bulb** (although it is not a bulb), it can be cooked or eaten raw – the longer it is cooked the more the flavour will dissipate. It is delicious quickly grilled or sautéed then served with yoghurt mixed with the finely chopped leaves from the stalk. For a salad, toss with a little lemon juice immediately after slicing to avoid discolouration. **Garden fennel** is generally used only for fennel seeds (see below), while the

fruit of bitter fennel is occasionally used to make liqueurs and in pickling or meat stews. **Wild fennel** – found on roadsides throughout the world – is edible but has no real vegetable end to speak of. The feathery leaves of any of these fennels can be added to salads or used as flavouring as a herb. Fennel seed (technically the fruit of the plant) has a pale-green tinge when dried; the greener the seed, the better the quality. The seed has a sweet
anise aroma and flavour, excellent in pickled vegetable mixes, in bread and with seafood. **Fennel pollen** is collected from the flower once the flower has reached peak bloom, and it's then dried and screened to separate most of the stems from the fennel plant. ... The harvesting of fennel pollen is labor-intensive, which in turn attracts a high price.

FENUGREEK is used as a spice although it is in fact a LEGUME plant (and used as one in Ethiopian cuisine). As many as 50 varieties exist, differing in colour from red-brown to yellowish-green. Dried fenugreek has no discernible smell, but once ground and cooked its true character is revealed: it has a strong, acrid curry smell with a slightly bitter taste that strangely resembles maple syrup which is why it is used in the production of imitation maple syrup. An indispensable addition to curries and chutneys in India and Pakistan. Fresh fenugreek leaves are sold in bunches (the stalks are discarded, as they are too bitter to eat).

FERMENTED BLACK BEANS see BEANS, DRIED

FETA or **Fetta** is a soft to medium-firm cheese with a mild to strong salty tang and crumbly texture. Often made commercially with pasteurised cow's milk and served in Greek salad (unless you live in Europe, where the same salad may be called Russian salad or Macedonian salad). Feta is also known as *Bulgarian cheese*, which is traditionally made from sheep's milk or even goat's milk. Best stored in the brine, whey or oil it is purchased in. Feta can be marinated in oil and herbs and stored in the fridge (rinse it and pat dry with a paper towel before marinating).

FIBRE is the part of a plant which cannot be broken down by the human body. There are two types of fibre, soluble and insoluble, both of which are essential to a healthy diet. Soluble fibre slows our absorption of glucose (sugar) and fats, which in turn helps make us feel fuller for longer. It is also attributed to the reduction of high cholesterol in the blood. It is found in barley, oats, rye, psyllium, potatoes, arrowroot, grapefruit, apples, oranges, green beans, cabbage and pulses (lentils, dried beans and peas). Insoluble fibre acts like a sponge when eaten, soaking up moisture, swelling in our stomachs (which gives a full feeling), and stimulating the digestive system so waste products pass quickly through the body. It is found in arrowroot, wheat and 100% wheat by-products like whole-wheat bread, pasta, certain breakfast cereals and bran. Other high and moderate fibre foods include nuts, brown rice, spring greens and muesli.

FIG is actually a flower, turned in on itself while the seeds within are the actual fruit. The skin of ripe figs ranges from green or yellow to brown, purple or even purplish-black, depending on the variety.Figs are the only fruit to fully ripen and then begin drying on the tree. They contain a natural humectant, a chemical that extends the freshness and moistness in baked goods. Figs also provide more soluble and insoluble fibre than any other fruit or vegetable.

Like all fruit, figs are best eaten from the tree, when the skin begins to split, exposing the pink flesh with its many edible seeds. When buying, look for shapely, plump figs with unbruised, unbroken skins and a mild fragrance; a sour smell indicates fermentation or rotting. The fruit should be just soft to the touch, but not mushy. If the figs seem somewhat shrivelled, as if they are beginning to dry, they will be particularly sweet. Size does not indicate quality, but you'll probably want to choose uniformly sized fruits if you are planning to serve them as individual portions for appetisers or dessert.

Fresh figs are delicate and can damage easily, so store in a container lined with paper towelling or, even better, fresh fig leaves. This helps them last longer by protecting the base of the fig which is where any spoiling will begin.

FILÉ POWDER is a thickening and flavouring agent used primarily in gumbo and other Creole dishes. Made from the dried and ground leaves of the sassafras tree, filé powder should only ever be added after the hot pot has been removed from the heat. Prolonged cooking of filé will make it slimy and stringy.

FINES HERBES is a mixture of chopped herbs, usually chervil, chives, parsley and tarragon.

FINGERED CITRON see BUDDHA'S HAND CITRON

FISH and other seafood have such a staggering variety of species that they would have to be at the top of the list when it comes to the confusion surrounding names. On an international level, it becomes far more confusing, as each country and their respective cookbook authors call on seafood native to that country. To supply a universal dictionary of the names of all fish caught globally would be a mammoth task: even fishing bodies struggle to standardise a market name for each of their own country's species, let alone collaborate to solve international naming frustrations.

So, although I have listed many of the more common alternative names for crustaceans and fish in this book, this general advice is probably the most useful: when using foreign cookbooks or travelling overseas, the key is to establish what kind of texture and flavour the recipe requires. Is it firm-fleshed or flaky, lean or oily, flat or round? (See below for a discussion of these categories.) Then ask for a fish with these specific qualities at the local market or fish shop rather than struggling with unfamiliar names.

The two main categories of fresh fish are flatfish and round fish.

Flatfish are bottom-dwellers which swim parallel to the ocean floor. The side that faces down is pale, while the upper side is dark and contains both eyes. Species include flounder, sole, brill, turbot (halibut) and plaice. You usually lose about 50% of a whole flatfish in cleaning, preparation and removal of inedible parts, while the waste ratio of round fish is higher (60%) due to the larger head. Flatfish are lean, and the best of them is probably the halibut (the largest flatfish in the world).

Round fish are, as the name suggests, rounder in shape, and have eyes on either side of the head. They are then divided into a further three categories of lean, moderate and high fat content. The higher the fat content, the darker, firmer and more distinctively flavoured the flesh becomes. 'High' fat means on average 12–14%, although in eel it can be as high as 30%. Fish in this category include butterfish, mackerel, tuna, salmon and sardines (pilchards). Fish species with lean fat content tend to carry their oil in the liver rather than the flesh. At about 2.5% fat, lean fish are mild in flavour and lightly coloured. Fish in this category include red fish, snapper, bream, garfish and perch.

Fish with moderate fat content (6% or less) include swordfish, whiting, ocean trout and barramundi.

HOW TO COOK FISH

Fish is a delicate protein that I associate with egg white. In their raw state, both fish and egg white are translucent protein. Apply heat and both react in the same way: they change colour (from translucent to opaque) and texture (becoming firm). However, there the similarities end, as egg white can be cooked for a lengthy period and will still be quite edible, while fish needs to be monitored closely so it doesn't become dry and tough. The proteins in fish need to only just set: the juices change from clear to white and the flesh has become opaque but remains moist. If you continue to cook beyond this point, the fish will begin to 'bleed': the juices are forced from the flesh, leaving blobs of white protein on the surface of the cooked fish. The more juices forced from the flesh, the drier the meat you are left with. Cooking fish in the microwave is asking for trouble, as the risk of overcooking is high. There are better ways. For the best results with defrosted fish, cook while it is still icy (before it starts to drip). Follow the recipe as if the fish were fresh but give it a longer cooking time – as much as 25% more – and allow for it having a little extra moisture.

 Tips for buying fish

~ Use your eyes – and nose. First, look at the fish: you want to see bright, clear and often protruding eyes and a shiny, bright-coloured skin. The gills should be red to bright pink (as a fish ages, its gills turn to a light pink, then grey and finally to a greenish or dull brown). The outer skin should be firm to press and, if it hasn't been scaled, it will have a natural film or slime. Your fish (and fish shop) should smell of the ocean, without any strong smell of overt fishiness or of ammonia.

~ Ask the fishmonger to gut (draw) and scale (dress) the fish for you. This can save not only time but an unbelievable mess. A fully dressed fish usually means gutted and scaled, with gills, head, fins and tail removed.

~ When buying fish fillets or cutlets, look for cleanly cut, firm, elastic, shiny, translucent flesh. Any fillets that appear dull and watery may well be old or defrosted. Fillets with drying or browned edges are not acceptable

~ Frozen fish should be bought tightly wrapped. If you notice freezer burns after unwrapping, take it back.

~ Frozen seafood can, in some cases, be superior in quality to fresh. After being caught, fish to be sold is held on fishing trawlers in ice slurries or in chilled seawater at 0°C. It could be days before it reaches the shop, while fish which is sold as frozen is 'snap' or 'fast' frozen on the ship so it doesn't run the same risk of being over-handled or bruised or deteriorating in quality.

⭐ Alternatives to fish and seafood

For those allergic to seafood, there is no substitute. Allergic reactions to seafood (which include fish and shellfish, the most common being prawns or shrimp) are the third most common food allergy after eggs and milk. The reaction is usually with that person for life, and if anything, becomes more aggressive with each exposure to seafood. In severe cases, even the vapours from cooked seafood can trigger a reaction.

Storage and preparation

Fresh fish is said to have a shelf life of 12 days from the moment it is caught, provided it is stored at 0°C, which should mean you have about 7 days with it. However, as most refrigerators sit on 4°C this cuts shelf life back to about 3–4 days after purchase. Be aware that the entrails of freshly caught or whole uncleaned fish decay faster than the flesh, which means you run the risk of spoiling your catch if you don't clean it before storing. When filleting flatfish at home, remove the fillets from the pale or white side first. This will make taking the fillets from the darker side easier.

Frozen raw fish will last about six months in the freezer. Defrost the fish, covered, in a refrigerator. This takes about 24 hours. Once defrosted, it does not have the tight, firm flesh characteristic of fresh fish and in some cases may be waterlogged or seem like a dish sponge, so take account of this when you are deciding what to cook with it. Never re-freeze fish: it will cause the flesh to break down, go watery and lose flavour, and it poses a greater risk of food poisoning when the fish is defrosted the second time.

Irony is this next, very important, point. The fact that fish live in water, once removed from water, try never to expose it to water again - especially in the scaling and filleting preparation. The less tap water the fish is exposed to the better shelf life and better cooking you will get from your fish. Bacteria and wetness are enemy number one for fresh fish preparation. Removing scales from a fish leaves tiny open 'pockets', where, if water is applied, collects where the scales were attached to the skin and becomes a breeding ground for bacteria, which is when fresh fish gets that ammonia, "fishy" smell. Instead, use a paper towel and wipe the skin of moisture once scaled.

New methods and techniques have come about in recent years thanks to one or two pioneering professional chefs. One such chef - who I was fortunate to share the kitchen with - is Joshua Niland, from Sydney Australia. Joshua's ground breaking techniques in ethical, nose to tail efficiency in the use of as much as 95% of the whole fish is astounding. His use of fish offal, the dry ageing methods and the charcuterie range is something else. If you are indeed serious about handling fish then I highly recommend viewing some of Josh's online videos or purchasing one of his award winning books.

FISH, SALTED see BACALAO

FISH SAUCE or **nam pla** is indispensable in Thai and Vietnamese cuisine. Made from small fish combined with salt that have been fermented, then the juice extracted and boiled. A good fish sauce is a clear brown colour with a pungent smell and imparts a rich salty flavour to soups, sauces and dressings. There is no significant

difference between this and Japanese fish sauce. There is no instant substitute for fish sauce, but in an emergency, several crushed anchovies in ½ cup hot water is a start. I have had some minor success using *Worcestershire sauce* - which contains fish. Or you could make your own GARUM. Which is a Roman fish sauce made by salting and fermenting fish in small clay jugs or vessels, used commonly throughout ancient Roman cooking.
Vegetarians could use a light soy sauce, or as a last resort, SALT.

FISH, SMOKED Cold-smoked fish is prepared over a slow-burning wood chip fire with an air temperature not exceeding 32°C. This prevents the proteins coagulating and the flesh cooking. All cold-smoked seafood then needs to be cooked before eating (with the exception of smoked salmon which is eaten raw). Hot-smoked fish is prepared at temperatures between 50°C and 85°C at which point the fish begins to cook. Hot-smoked seafood then requires no further cooking. (Note that this only applies to seafood – other types of meat may need further cooking after being hot-smoked). All fish to be smoked is first cured in a brine solution to help in the drying process, protect against harmful bacteria, and add flavour. The fish is then hung to allow a gloss to form on the skin before smoking begins. The type of wood used and the addition of teas or other flavours add character, but must be managed carefully so as not to overpower the fish with bitter smoky flavours.

FLAKE see SHARK

FLEUR DE SEL see SALT

FLOUR is classified by its extraction rate, which is the percentage of wheat grain present in the flour. At the top end, coming in at 100%, is wholemeal flour, with brown flour around 80–85%, followed by plain flour at 75–80%. The protein content determines how the flour will perform during baking, as it is the protein that forms gluten. Generally speaking, bread and pasta is made with flour with a high protein content or hard flour (11–14%) (in the case of pasta this is because pasta dough must be rolled very thin which is easier with the elasticity of high-gluten flour), while cake-making or soft flour has a low protein content (7–10%). Cakes or biscuits made with high-gluten flour will be chewier, especially if the dough or batter is mixed excessively. Vigorous mixing of any flour-based recipe (whether hard or soft) will work the gluten, which is why some recipes for scones, sponges, short pastry etc suggest mixing as lightly as possible. The protein content of flour is marked on the packet.

 Top tips for flour

~ Sift flour two or three times before mixing with other ingredients. This aerates the mixture, as well as removing any lumps or foreign matter. Aerating ensures that the final product is given every chance of being light and fluffy.

~ Add the sifted flour to the wet mix, not the other way around. Use a metal spoon (chef's spoon) or a rubber/plastic spatula to fold the flour into the mix. This cutting and folding will also ensure the final mixture retains as much of the air as possible.

~ If you find small brown insects (psocids or booklice, often mistaken for weevils) in your flour, dispose of it immediately. To avoid these little pests, buy smaller quantities of flour and store in an airtight container in a dry, cool place. Humidity can wreak havoc on dry goods in the tropics, so try storing flour products in the fridge, but remember that keeping them airtight is the key.

~ Plain flours have a shelf life of 6–9 months if stored correctly. Wholemeal or brown flour's shelf life is considerably less due to its fat content, so 2–3 months is recommended.

In the following list of flours, **w-f** indicates wheat-free and **g-f** gluten-free.

Amaranth flour (w-f, g-f) is made from the tiny seeds of amaranth, a plant that is related to spinach and beetroot (beets). (The leaves of the plant are also edible.) Amaranth flour is not designed for making leavened breads, as the result of it being too dense, but is great for flat breads, pasta, biscuits (cookies), pancakes and muffins.

Arrowroot flour (w-f, g-f) (also called **arrowroot starch** or simply **arrowroot***) is made from the arrowroot, Maranta arundinacea (although some varieties are made from plants such as bananas, potato or tropical roots). It is higher in fibres than all other starches, by as much as 25%, yet is still smooth, and has one and a half times the thickening power of plain flour. Great in baking and as a thickener, where it mixes clear, not cloudy (which is handy to know if thickening a clear liquid) and often better than CORNFLOUR (**cornstarch**) because it doesn't impart a chalky taste if undercooked. Like all starches, mix arrowroot with a little cold water first to make a wet paste before adding it to the hot liquid.

Barley flour (w-f) Although barley contains gluten, the gluten is quite weak, so mix it with wheat flour when baking. For bread, a good ratio is to make the barley flour 25% of the mix. For other baking, mix 50/50 with other flours.

Bean flour (w-f, g-f) can be used to make pasta, crepes and flat breads, and some traditional Middle Eastern dishes.

Besan flour (w-f, g-f) also known as **garbanzo flour, gram flour** and **chickpea flour** is made from finely milled chickpeas or **pigeon peas** (*chana dhal* or *bengal gram*). Used extensively in Indian cuisine as a batter, and also makes an excellent binding and thickening agent as well as panisses (chickpea fritters), breads, dips and desserts.

Bleached flour is whiter and contains less vitamin E than unbleached. Use it exactly as you do unbleached flour.

Buckwheat flour (w-f, g-f) or **Indian wheat**. Although the word 'wheat' appears in its name, buckwheat is totally wheat and gluten free. Buckwheat, also known as **beech wheat**, is from the family of plants that include rhubarb and sorrel and has nothing to do with the wheat family which is a grass. Pancakes and soba noodles are two well-known products made from buckwheat flour. See also BUCKWHEAT.

Cake flour is a US product not readily available on European and Australasian supermarket shelves. Cake flour is made from soft wheat with as little as 9% protein compared to the 10–12% in plain flour and 12–14% in strong flour. It is bleached with chlorine gas, which, besides whitening the flour, also makes it slightly acidic. This acidity makes cakes set faster and gives them a finer texture. If a recipe calls for the use of cake flour or soft wheat flour, use plain flour but substitute 10% of the quantity with cornflour (cornstarch) or potato flour. This will help soften the mix. **Cassava flour** (w-f, g-f) is made from the tuberous root of the cassava and is used to create tapioca products. For tapioca, a starch, the fibre element of cassava (approx.

12%) has been removed. Pearl tapioca and tapioca flour are used as thickeners in soups and sauces or used in desserts. Tapioca flour can be used to make gluten-free bread, where it imparts a chewy texture.

Chestnut flour (w-f, g-f) is a sweet flour used in desserts and batters. It should be fresh when it smells of chestnuts. Do not substitute with water chestnut flour, found in Asian grocers, which is used as a thickening and binding agent or to make water chestnut crackers.

Cornflour (w-f, g-f - although many brands are made with wheat, so check the labels before buying) has a very fine, squeaky texture and is used as a thickener, or in baking to lighten the texture of a product. It is known as **cornstarch** in the US, and should not be confused with **cornmeal** (see CORN).

Durum flour is a **hard wheat flour** used to make pasta and noodles. ('Hard' in this case doesn't refer to the level of gluten or protein but to the physical properties of the wheat which splinters when ground.) It is also referred to as **durum wheat semolina, fine ground semolina** or **continental flour**. See also semolina flour, below.

Gluten flour, made by the removal of the starch and the bran, can be added to plain flour to boost its gluten level so it resembles strong flour (see below).

Gluten-free flour is sold commercially. (This flour can be made from wheat with the gluten removed, so is often not suitable for people with wheat allergies). Or, it is a combination of several gluten free grain flours mixed together in various ratios. See also GLUTEN.

Graham flour is a US product similar to wholemeal flour (which can be used as substitute).

Jerusalem artichoke flour (w-f, g-f) is a useful alternative for people with hypoglycaemia and diabetes. It doesn't thicken as other flours do, so is suited to pasta, pie crusts and biscuits.

Kamut flour is an ancient grain, twice the size of wheat and with 30% more protein. It is used for baking (bread and biscuits) and pasta.

Kuzu / kudzu (w-f, g-f) is a starch (found in Asian grocers) made from the roots of the kudzu plant. It is used for thickening soups and sauces, and for coating food to be deep-fried.

Legume flour (w-f, g-f) can be made from any legume: yellow or green peas, red or green lentils, white, fava and lima beans. These flours can be mixed with other flours to add extra protein to gluten-free baking.

Lotus flour (w-f, g-f) has a moderate, pleasant taste that hints of sour, salt, bitter and – of all things – mild cheese. A truly unique taste (which can be neutralised with the addition of a little salt to the recipe). Used for baking (breads and biscuits) and pasta.

Malanga flour (w-f, g-f), from the taro family, is considered to be the most easily digested complex carbohydrate due to the grains in the starch being so fine. Also said to be the most hypoallergenic of all the flours. It is used in baking and as an excellent thickener.

Matzo is a Jewish unleavened bread made from flour and water and cooked very quickly so it doesn't ferment or rise (hence it is said it must be mixed and cooked within 18 minutes). The resulting thin crisp cracker is then eaten as is or cooled and processed further as **matzo flour** (finely ground, for cakes and biscuits), **matzo meal** (coarsely ground, as a replacement for breadcrumbs and for matzo balls or dumplings) or **matzo farfel** (little cubes used as a noodle or bread cube substitute).

Millet flour (w-f, g-f) Millet and millet by-products are considered animal fodder to many westerners but they are a staple in African, Indian and Asian countries. Can be mixed with plain flour in baking, in a proportion of up to 30% millet flour. Try mixing in some whole millet seeds for texture.

Nut flour (w-f, g-f) is derived from the ground 'cake' formed when oil is pressed from nuts such as almond, macadamia, walnut, chestnut and pecan to name a few. Store in the fridge or freezer and use soon after purchase. See also NUT MEAL.

Nut meal is ground from whole nuts, with the oil retained, to leave a coarse, oily mix which can turn rancid within weeks. Store in the fridge or freezer and use soon after purchase. See also NUT FLOUR.

Oat flour (w-f, g-f) is used for thickening stews and soups. It is great in biscuits, muffins, breads and desserts.

OO flour (double O flour) is an Italian wheat flour with a low protein content. If none is available, use plain flour.

Pastry flour is a US product used for making pastries (as its name suggests), and sits somewhere between cake flour and plain flour in the protein content. Great for pie dough if ever you find it.

Plain flour, or **all-purpose flour** in the US, is the most common of the white flours. Use within 9 months or, for a long duration, keep in the fridge or freezer and bring to room temperature before cooking.

Poi flour or **poi starch** (w-f, g-f) is made from dehydrated, fermented paste from taro stems. It is used extensively in Polynesian cuisine.

Potato flour (w-f, g-f) is used primarily as a thickener and in gluten-free baking. However, it makes a great addition to cake recipes because of its ability to absorb moisture. Experiment with replacing some plain flour with potato flour in baking for a moister or dryer final product. Try replacing 10% of the flour or you can replace 1 whole cup of wheat flour with 5/8 cup potato flour.

Quinoa flour (w-f, g-f) The flour from this fruit (a flake rather than a grain) is sometimes found in pre-made pasta.

Rice flour (w-f, g-f), both white and brown, has a very light and airy texture and a slightly sweet flavour. It is used in desserts, cakes and biscuits and as a gluten-free thickener.

Rye flour (w-f) is usually mixed with wheat flour to make bread; the lighter the bread the more wheat flour in the mix. Pumpernickel bread is high in rye, strong in flavour and deep in colour. Rye flour is low in gluten.

Sago flour (w-f, g-f), made from the stem of the sago palms, is used to make pearl sago for desserts and to thicken soups, sauces and stir-fries.

Self-raising flour (**self-rising flour** in the US) is plain flour that has baking powder added. I suggest making your own when needed, as the baking powder in packaged self-raising flour absorbs atmospheric moisture over time and loses its leavening ability, even if stored in an airtight container. Sometimes called **phosphated flour** (with mono-calcium phosphate added to improve the baking qualities) or pancake flour.

HOME-MADE SELF-RAISING FLOUR
Mix together:
1 cup plain flour
1½ teaspoons baking powder
pinch of cooking salt

Semolina flour is used for making cous cous and pasta. Semolina is made from the coarsely ground endosperm of durum wheat. It is sold as extra fine, fine, medium and coarse, each of which are suited to specific cooking methods. Extra fine is used in fresh pasta and specialty breads. Known as **creamed wheat** or **cream of wheat** in the US and sometimes **farina**, fine semolina is used as a porridge or in cakes and biscuits. Medium and coarse are often used in dessert or pudding recipes.

Sorghum flour (w-f, g-f) is nutritionally packed and adds a great flavour to gluten-free baking when combined with other flour products.

Soy flour (w-f, g-f) should be stored in the fridge or freezer, and must be mixed with another flour; by itself it is unappetising. It is rich in protein, so is used as a bread improver, and can help goods keep moist and last longer. Try replacing 2 tablespoons of every cup of flour with soy flour. Remember that baking will brown more quickly if it contains soy flour so use a temperature about 10°C lower than the recipe suggests. Soy flour can also be toasted before use to intensify its nutty flavour – do so in a dry pan over medium heat until the colour just begins to change.

Spelt flour (w-f) is very low in gluten, and makes an excellent substitute for wheat, with its delicious nutty flavour. If making bread with spelt flour, use only three-quarters of the water specified in the wheat flour recipe.

Stone ground flours are wholemeal, either plain or self-raising. The best are organic and milled in small batches by water-powered stone mills – this crushes and grinds the whole grains slowly so flavour and nutritional oils are distributed throughout. (In contrast, most flour milling is done by high-speed steel cylinders or hammer mills, which heats and oxidises the grain, killing healthy enzymes and allowing oils to become rancid.) They have slightly fresher flavour, a courser texture and slightly better nutrient value than regular wholemeal flour.

Strong flour, is also known as **bread flour, high gluten flour** or **hard wheat flour.** The high gluten content of this flour makes it the ideal product for making bread, giving the final loaf a better structure.

Teff flour (w-f, g-f), the world's smallest grain, is packed with nutrients (proteins and calcium) and has been enjoyed for centuries by highland Ethiopians. It is used to make the spongy, sour flatbread 'injera' which is used to scoop up meat and vegetable stews and to line the trays on which stews are served soaking up juices as the meal progresses – when this edible 'tablecloth' is eaten, the meal is officially over.

Wholemeal flour, or whole wheat flour in the US, is a more nutritious flour than plain, as it contains all the bran and wheat germ.

FOOL is a simple dessert of crushed or mashed fruit mixed with cream (usually whipped cream), the name said to derive from 'fouler', the French word to mash. The fruit can be fresh, poached or stewed. Fruit rich in acid, such as raspberry, rhubarb and passionfruit, are commonly associated with fool, yet mango, apricot and papaya also work.

FRICASSEE can be a confusing term as it has many interpretations; essentially it is a type of stew. It began life as a crude dish of meat boiled in broth, but now most often refers to small cuts of white meat cooked in a cream-based sauce.

FRISÉE see LEAFY GREENS

FROMAGE FRAIS is also known as **fromage blanc,** a soft, white, fresh cow's milk cheese that is lightly fermented. Its consistency is thin, like yoghurt, and it has a low fat content (4%) so is used in dishes that need creaminess without too much fat. A higher fat fromage frais (with added cream, 8% fat) and a very low-fat version (0.1%) are also available.

FRUCTOSE see '**alternatives to sugar**' in SUGAR

FRUIT See individual fruit names. Remember, the best fruit is that which is in season. Fruit that has travelled from another state or from overseas degrades and should be a last resort.

G.

GAI LAN see '**chinese broccoli**' in BROCCOLI

GAME refers to meat from wild (or once-wild) animals, most commonly HARE, KANGAROO, RABBIT and VENISON, all of which are very lean, so rubbing with olive oil will aid the cooking. Sourcing game meat from supermarkets is often difficult but many market stalls stock small amounts of game (plan ahead, and find a stall holder who can meet your needs).

Eating wild game (as opposed to farmed game) can be risky, as little is known about the many harmful parasites that these wild animals can harbour. So take great care when cooking or eating a possum stew or wild boar roast the next time you visit Jim Bob up in them thar hills. In other words, avoid backyard stall holders selling local game boasting fresh buckshot and the possibility of parasites.

Game bird is generally what you enjoy on your travels through Europe, and not quite the same elsewhere. These are wild birds such as grouse, woodcock, partridge, guinea fowl, snipe and pheasant. Some species, especially quail and pheasant, are farmed with success. When buying quality game birds look for these points: the beak should break easily, the breast plumage ought to be soft and the breast plump, and the quill feathers (those close to the body) should be pointed, not rounded.

Most game bird is hung before cooking to mature and tenderise the meat and develop its flavour. Hanging is a matter of taste, however, as some people find that hung or 'high' meat has an overly strong gamey smell and flavour.

Game meat sold in supermarkets usually has a milder flavour. Quail are too small and gain nothing from hanging, so consume immediately. When cooking game birds, follow a good recipe. Keep 'medium-rare' in mind and you're off to a good start: the lean meat from game birds (including flightless birds such as emus and ostrich) can be dry and nasty if overdone.

See POULTRY for general information and more cooking tips.

GANACHE is a chocolate coating for cakes. It's a useful way to use up chocolate that has seized (see CHOCOLATE) when you've been trying to melt it.

> **HOW TO MAKE GANACHE**
> Bring cream to simmering point using 11/2–2 times the amount of cream to seized chocolate - or COUVERTURE chocolate.
> (e.g. 150–200 ml cream to 100 g chocolate).
> Turn off the heat source, add the chocolate and stir until dissolved.

GARAM MASALA is a ground spice mix made from a base of cumin and coriander along with cardamom, cinnamon, black peppercorns and spices (such as nutmeg, mace, dried chilli, ground ginger and fenugreek). Garam masala is usually added towards the end of cooking a dish.

GARBANZO BEAN see CHICKPEA

GARLIC Look for firm garlic bulbs with large, juicy, easy-to-peel cloves and a strong, aromatic, compelling flavour. Loose cloves or broken bulbs means older, poorly handled specimens. If a clove shows a prominent centre (white or green), when sliced open it is not fresh. As much as I endorse organic anything, garlic would have to be at the top of the list, as most shop-bought garlic (often imported from China) is about 6 months old by the time we get it home.

Elephant garlic has very large bulbs and is closely related to leeks. It has a much milder, sweeter flavour than ordinary garlic and this makes it ideal to use for garlic soup or sliced raw into a salad. Roasted or sautéed whole cloves of elephant garlic make for a tasty appetiser. Also known as buffalo garlic.

Garlic shoots can be used like chives, snipped into a salad or sautéed as a vegetable side dish.

When frying garlic in European dishes, keep the heat low and cook without colouring to avoid the acrid flavour of burnt garlic. In Asian cooking, garlic is more often cooked in moderate to hot oil, until golden or browned (but never burnt or blackened) to give it a nutty flavour.

A head or bulb of garlic contains approximately 10 garlic cloves.

1 large clove =
1 tsp chopped garlic =
½ tsp minced garlic =
⅛ teaspoon garlic powder =
½ tsp garlic flakes =
¼ tsp granulated garlic =
½ tsp garlic juice

HOW TO ROAST GARLIC

Remove any loose papery skin from the whole bulb, cut off the top centimetre, rub with oil, wrap in foil and roast at 200°C for 35–45 minutes.

OR

for easier access to the squishy sweet golden garlic paste within, cut the whole bulb in half horizontally before wrapping. Individual cloves can be roasted in oil, unpeeled, for 25–30 minutes.

GARUM from the ancient Romans comes this fermented fish sauce. An excellent condiment, full of rich umami flavours. Good chefs will waste no part of the fish to make their own garum.

GELATINE derives from the collagen within animal parts, especially skin, hooves and bones. When boiled it becomes sticky then sets to a jelly-like texture. Commercial gelatine is available as granules or as sheets (known as leaf gelatine). Chefs tend to recommend leaf gelatine (common in European countries) rather than granules because it translates to a more precise measure. Gelatine granules are sometimes referred to as powdered gelatine (favoured in the US). For other similar thickeners, see also AGAR-AGAR; CARRAGEEN; GELOZONE; ISINGLASS.

HOW TO USE LEAF GELATINE
Soak in cold water for 4–5 minutes to soften before use. Squeeze out all excess water and stir into the heated liquid that is to be set and continue stirring until the gelatine has dissolved (1–2 minutes).
HOW TO USE GELATINE GRANULES
Mix with a little cold water or other liquid, then add to the hot liquid which is to be set.

4 leaves of leaf gelatine = 1 T of granules (1 sachet, 1/4 oz)

GELOZONE is a branded product but rates a mention as a vegan-friendly thickener, made up of three thickening agents: 407, 410 and 412 (see list of additives on page 284). Carrageenan (407) is a by-product of CARRAGEEN. For other similar thickeners, see also AGAR-AGAR; GELATINE; ISINGLASS.

GERMAN CELERY see CELERIAC

GIRELLO is an Italian term for a cut of meat (beef, veal or lamb), the 'eye of round' or 'eye of silverside'.

GLAZE refers to any stock that has been reduced to a gelatinous consistency. This sticky reduction can only be made from fresh stock; if you try to make it from commercial stock you'd be left with a small blob of dark salt. Glaze is used to strengthen the flavour of or thicken sauces, as a coating for meats or terrines, and as the base for a sauce which then has cream or butter added. Commercial veal glaze may be found in specialty food shops, delis or food halls (be prepared to pay premium prices). Glaze may also refer to painting products to be baked with milk, egg whites or egg wash (milk and eggs) to give them a glossy surface.

GLOBE ARTICHOKE Learning how to prepare this ornamental vegetable is much easier with a demonstration, but I'll attempt an explanation. First remove most of the stem (which is still edible), then the very bottom leaves. Then hold the artichoke in one hand with the thumb positioned on the bottom portion of each leaf, and bend back each leaf until it snaps naturally. Tear off the inedible top part where it snapped. As you get closer to the centre of the artichoke, only pale-green and yellow inner parts of the leaf will show and the edible portion of each leaf will be larger. Remove anything that looks tough from the bottom of the artichoke, and taste if you're not sure. Trim away any dark-green parts, particularly from the bottom, with a sharp knife. Rub the artichoke with a cut lemon to prevent discolouration. Halve the artichoke lengthwise and remove the inner cone and choke (the fluffy bit) with a spoon. It is now ready to use. The stem that you removed at the beginning can be peeled and then poached in a lemon and salt solution and cooled and stored in the cooking liquor. This 'pickled' part of the artichoke can be used in soups, salads, risotto and pasta.

GLUCOSE see 'alternatives to sugar' in SUGAR

GLUTEN is a substance found in flour which affects the elasticity and texture of a dough. Some people require a gluten-free diet, most often those who are diagnosed with coeliac disease, also known as gluten sensitive enteropathy. They must avoid wheat, oats, rye and barley, among other products. See FLOUR for more details and a list of flours that indicates whether they are gluten-free.

★ **Alternatives to products containing gluten**
~ **Xanthan gum** (derived from the fermentation of corn sugar with a bacterium) or guar gum (derived from the seeds of the plant originating in India, Cyamoposis tetragonolobus) help gluten-free baked products to bind and hold their shape. For best results, use a combination of the two gums in the proportions of 2 parts Xanthan to 1 part guar. Add a small quantity of water to the recipe to encourage the gums to become sticky. Add ½ –1 teaspoon of the combined gums and water to a single recipe of biscuits, cakes or bread. For larger quantities, you will have to experiment with the quantities of gum and different proportions of flours.

HOME-MADE GLUTEN-FREE BAKING POWDER
Mix together:
¼ cup bicarbonate of soda
½ cup cream of tartar

HOME-MADE GLUTEN-FREE FLOUR
The following combinations replace one cup of plain flour with a
gluten- and wheat-free alternative:
1½ cups of rolled oats (try putting the rolled oats in the food processor
to change their texture)

OR try one of the following:

Option 1.	¼ cup tapioca flour	½ cup brown rice flour	¼ cup soy flour
Option 2.	½ cup soy flour	½ cup cornflour	
Option 3.	½ cup soy flour	¼ rice flour	¼ potato flour
Option 4.	½ cup soy flour	½ cup rice flour	

GLYCAEMIC INDEX (GI) measures how much your blood sugar
increases in the two or three hours after eating carbohydrates. It ranks
foods (between 1 and 100; glucose rates 100) based on the food's
effect on blood sugar levels. The idea is that people should eat less of
those foods with a high glycaemic index and more of those with a low
– along with eating food high in FIBRE and low in saturated and trans
fats (see FAT) and exercising more . . . The index is especially helpful
for people with diabetes, although it can also be useful to athletes and
people who are overweight. Note, however, that a GI value tells you
only how rapidly a particular carbohydrate turns into sugar, not how
much of that carbohydrate is in a serving of a particular food: it is
about the quality of the carbohydrates, not the quantity.

GOBO see BURDOCK ROOT

GOLDENBERRY see CAPE GOOSEBERRY

GOLDEN SYRUP see MOLASSES

GOOBER PEA see PEANUT

GOOSE usually only appears, if ever, at the Christmas table alongside many other meats. Geese are processed at about 20 weeks old and usually only two or three times a year (young geese or gosling are favoured over mature birds as their meat is more tender). The flavour is similar to duck, although wild geese are gamier. See POULTRY for general information and more cooking tips.

HOW TO ROAST GOOSE
The method is similar to cooking DUCK, as geese also store plenty of fat under the skin. Season the goose inside and out with sea salt and pepper. Roast at 210°C for 20 minutes, reduce the heat to 180°C and cook for a further 30 minutes per kilogram or 45 minutes per kilo if stuffed. Drain the fat every 20 minutes. When cooled, you can store the fat in the fridge for future use in roasts or casseroles.

GOOSEBERRIES have a unique flavour that is savoured by the experienced dessert cook. Known as '**goosegogs**' by true aficionados, these small fruit are very sweet if eaten raw, when yellow, golden and translucent, or red. Most however are sold when still green and very tart. At this stage they are ideal for making jam, chutney or pie, with plenty of sugar added. The fruit is best if fully matured before use. Gooseberries are usually stewed and used in pie or mixed with whipped cream and served as a FOOL. The best varieties are those from Europe (such as the Hinnonmakis Yellow, a native of Finland) or the many British varieties (for example, Early Sulphur). Sweet gooseberries are just that, as well as being smaller with a reddish hue about them.

GOURMET once referred to a person who was a connoisseur of food. Now anyone who values food steers well clear of it, as the word continues to lose all meaning when draped over filthy sandwich bars on industrial sites.

GRIDDLE is the US term for a flat grill plate without a rim, usually made of heavy material such as cast iron.

GRILL is to cook with the heat source either beneath or above the food. If the heat source is beneath, food is cooked on a grill plate or GRIDDLE, either flat or ribbed. If the heat source is above the food, the method refers to using an oven grill or oven broiler. Here, the element does not make contact with the food. Grilling is often referred to as BROILING in the US. See also CHAR-GRILL.

GROUNDNUT see PEANUT

GUAR GUM see 'alternatives' in GLUTEN

GUAVA is a tropical fruit with many cultivated varieties. The most common has a green skin and pink flesh with many edible seeds. Others have pink, yellow, red or white flesh. The particular variety used to make juice is a hard fruit, with inedible seeds and a deep-pink, almost red flesh; although high in vitamin C, it does not make for great eating. Guava is usually sold when green.Ripen to a yellowish stage, slice in half, scoop out and discard the seeds (in most cases), and eat the flesh and skin. Guava can also be grilled, sautéed or stir-fried. Eat guava soon after ripening, as like most tropical fruits it will begin to deteriorate and rot quite rapidly. Unripe fruit can be placed in a paper bag with an apple (the slow release of ethylene from the apple will initiate ethylene production from the neighbouring fruit and ripen the guava).

H.

HALF AND HALF see CREAM

HALOUMI (also **halloumi**) is a a white, semi-hard sheep's cheese, originally from Cyprus now made the world over. It is often sold in a brine solution with mint, which gives the cheese a salty, fresh flavour. Haloumi is ideal for grilling as it holds its shape once heated.

HALVA is a sweet confection made from a blend of sesame seeds (TAHINI), spices (cinnamon and cardamom) and honey or sugar syrup, often with other ingredients such as nuts (pistachio or almond) or dried fruit. Originating in the Balkans and the eastern Mediterranean, halva is also sold as '**halawi**' and '**halwa**'.

HARE The hare is distinguished from the rabbit by longer ears, feet and body. When choosing one to buy, check the lip: its more pronounced on older hares than in young animals. Hare is known for one dish in particular –jugged hare (see JUG). See also RABBIT.

HARISSA is a hot, fiery paste from North Africa with a base of chilli, garlic and oil. Recipes have many variations but often include coriander, cumin and caraway seeds and mint. I like to add a teaspoon of harissa to mashed pumpkin for a bit of kick. It can also be used as a dip for breads, in sandwiches, pasta and cous cous. Green harissa is very similar to shug, a hot accompaniment used in Jewish cuisine. It is made from fresh green chilli, olive oil, and coriander, cumin and caraway seeds, as well as coriander leaves, parsley and mint. Covered with a layer of oil, harissa will last 1–2 months refrigerated.

HAZARD ANALYSIS AND CRITICAL CONTROL POINT (HACCP) is the legal system of food safety control used at various stages in the food supply and service industry, from harvest to consumption. A safeguard for all involved in food handling, it lays out the process by which food must be handled, stored, prepared and served so it is safe and edible when it reaches the consumer.

HERBS See individual herbs for further notes about buying and storage and making effective use of dried herbs. And take my encouragement to try growing fresh herbs at home, in the garden or in pots on the windowsill. If you opt for potted herbs I recommend the following four as a starting combination: flat-leaf parsley, rosemary, basil and thyme.

✅ Top tips for herbs

~ Wash herbs only just before using them, as excess water can be absorbed through the leaves, causing black, slimy spots.

~ Store fresh herbs from the market in a plastic bag with the stem end wrapped in wet paper towelling.

~ If the herbs have been purchased with the root still intact, stand them in a small amount of cold water in the fridge covered with a plastic bag.

~ As a general rule, add woodier herbs (rosemary, thyme) early in cooking and soft herbs (basil, mint) at the very end of cooking.

~ Dried herbs certainly have their place in the kitchen, but when they've lost their punch, toss them out and start again: replace any not used within a year of purchase.

~ When substituting dried herbs for fresh, use about half the amount the recipe calls for, as dried herbs contain concentrated oils: 1 tsp fresh herb = 1/2 tsp driedIf you have dried your own recently, it may be wise to use only a third of the dried herb compared to fresh, as the dried herb will still have quite a kick.

🔍 Problem solving

~ **Leftover herbs?** The best option is to avoid leftovers by planning a second recipe to use up the remainder of the bunch when you buy the herb. However, there are many uses for leftovers:Dry your own Not all herbs enjoy being dried. The best are those that contain volatile oils: rosemary, marjoram, savory, bay and thyme. Either hang them over the stove area or place on a tray in a warm, dry area of the house. Once dry, store in airtight jars.

~ **Store in vinegar** - Softer herbs, like parsley, tarragon, basil, dill and mint, lose more in the drying process so a good option is to steep in vinegar, then splash a little on the dish instead of the fresh herb. See also '**herb vinegar**' in VINEGAR.

~ **Store herbs in oil** - Chop finely or crush in a mortar and pestle then mix with a little oil. Store in the fridge for several weeks with the layer of oil sitting on top. Ideal for basil, coriander and dill.

~ **Freeze** - Most herbs can be frozen, left intact on the branch. flat. When you need the herb, just snap off the amount required and cut while still frozen. The less you handle them before freezing, the better chance they have in the freezer. Wash, pat dry carefully (so as not to bruise them and release their oils), then pack in plastic bags, removing as much air as possible before freezing. Remember not to overcrowd the bag and to keep it flat. When you need the herb, just snap off the amount required and cut while still frozen. Defrosting the herb will make it too wet to work with. Another way to freeze herbs is to puree with water then store in ice trays. The ice cubes of herbs can be stored in plastic bags and then used for soups, stews or sauces.

~ **Make herb butter** - Chop and mix with softened butter, roll in aluminium foil and freeze for later use. Try herb bread or take a slice to have with a steak.

See also BOUQUET GARNI; FINES HERBES

HOI SIN SAUCE is a thick, reddish-brown sauce made from brown bean sauce, garlic, mild chilli, salt, spices and additives (check labels). Brands can vary in taste and texture, some being particularly sweet and red, while better brands are more rounded in flavour, less sweet and browner. Hoi sin is used extensively in Chinese cooking, in sauces, sauce mixes, marinades (pork and chicken) and for glazing. Translated, 'hoi sin' means 'sea freshness', although it neither contains nor is used with seafood. Also known also as Chinese barbecue sauce (nothing like the Western version of barbecue sauce), it is found in Asian grocers and in supermarkets.

HOMINY GRITS see CORN

HONEY Only the US and Australia buy the bulk of their honey in liquid form. The rest of the world enjoy **creamed honey**, also known as *spun honey* (US), **whipped honey** and **cream honey**. (New Zealanders are the greatest consumers of creamed honey, per capita, in the world.)

To dispel the myth: creamed honey is pure – nothing is added, no flour, sugar, cream, lard or bees' wax. A starter of crystallised honey is added to the liquid honey, mixed thoroughly then kept cool (not cold) and stirred on occasion. The creamed honey is ready in 1–2 weeks. Liquid honey will granulate naturally, forming coarse, gritty sugar crystals which reduces the commercial value of the product. This naturally crystallising honey is called **set honey** in the UK. See also 'alternatives to sugar' in SUGAR.

HORCHATA is a milk substitute made from chufa (tiger) nuts, the tiny tuberous roots of a Middle Eastern plant or almonds. Mexican horchata, also a dairy substitute, is made from rice and tastes completely different.

HORSERADISH is a root vegetable, which when grated is prized for its heated bite. Most horseradish is sold preserved in jars, but it's worth trying the fresh roots, especially if you like your horseradish hot. Fresh roots may be stored for A good quality root is clean, firm and free from cuts and deep blemishes. The freshly peeled or sliced root is creamy-white, like the paste. Generally, the whiter the root, the fresher it is. You can shave fresh horseradish and serve dressed in lemon juice and sea salt, or make your own. See also WASABI.

HOME-MADE HORSERADISH PASTE
Wash and peel the root as you would a potato and dice it into small cubes. Place the cubes in the blender with a small amount of water. Once pureed add 2–3 tablespoons of vinegar and 1 teaspoon salt for every cup of pureed horseradish.

HOT-SMOKED see FISH, SMOKED

HUSK CHERRY see CAPE GOOSEBERRY

HUSK TOMATO see TOMATILLO

I.

ICACO or **Coco plum** is a coastal plant which bares an edible fruit of white, cottony pulp from the large ribbed seed is relatively flavourless, with a very mild sweetness. Know as **fat pork tree** (Barbados) and **fat poke** (Guyana), the pulp is mixed with sugar to make a jam. The seeds are also edible.

ICE PLANT or **ice vegetable** is an edible succulent also known as *crystal ice plant* and *salty ice plant.* Leaves and stems can be eaten raw or cooked. Although the ice plant leaves have a jelly-like interior they are known to have a slight crunch, are juicy and have a marine-like salinity. When fully ripened, the ice plant becomes sweeter. The Japanese are known to make tempura out of ice plant leaves. Leaves and stems can be pickled or used as a garnish. The flowering buds are also edible and much sought after by chefs.

ILLAWARRA PLUM or **plum pine** is native to the East coast of Australia. Also known as the **brown pine**, The edible 'fruit' has a grape like texture with a sweetish, mild pine flavour. A very versatile native bushfood to cook with and makes delicious sauces and jams. They are particularly high in vitamin C and very high in antioxidants.

INCA BERRIES see PERUVIAN GROUNDCHERRY

INDIAN FIG see PRICKLY PEAR

INDIRECT GRILL A term used mainly to refer to the preparation of ribs. Like PAR-BAKING, it sets the ribs up for their final grill session. The heat comes from around the outside or on one side of the charcoal grill while the middle section or larger portion of
the grill remains off. The meat is placed in the centre of the grill or to the off side, with a bowl of water underneath to catch dripping and to produce steam to help the meat slowly tenderise. The hot coals can be sprinkled with wood chips for a smoky flavour. The meat is covered and cooked until tender. It is then ready for saucing and grilling.

IRISH MOSS see CARRAGEEN

IRRADIATION refers to subjecting food to blasts of radiation to kill harmful bacteria and other bugs. After five decades of research and development, proof of wholesomeness, political debates and public scrutiny, food irradiation is established as a safe and effective method of food processing and preservation. Similar to other food preservation methods, food irradiation still offers advantages and disadvantages relative to the types of food to be treated.

ISINGLASS is a gelatine-like thickener obtained from cleaning and drying the inner lining of the air or swim bladders of a number of fish species, in particular sturgeon and cod. It is used to thicken or clarify especially in the wine industry where it is used as a 'finer'.

> **30 g of isinglass will set 600 ml liquid to a jelly**

For other similar thickeners see also AGAR-AGAR; CARRAGEEN; GELATINE; GELOZONE.

ITALIAN CRESS see LEAFY GREENS

J.

JABOTICABA I came across this fruit in Byron Bay, Australia, in a tropical orchard where small blueberry-like fruit were clinging to the branches of the tree in what appeared to be their hundreds. At this stage the fruit were still quite young – they eventually grow to the size of a muscatel grape. The flesh is a juicy, white, gelatinous pulp that resembles something between a lychee and a sweet fresh muscatel grape in flavour. It is not recommended to eat a lot of this fruit over a long period of time, as they are high in natural tannins. Best eaten from the tree, but can also be made into jam, jellies or even wine and liqueurs. Related to the FEIJOA.

JACKFRUIT, looking like a watermelon dressed in a crocodile suit, is the largest cultivated tree fruit in the world. With an aroma similar to DURIAN when uncut, once opened the yellow-fleshed fruit smells of bananas and pineapple. It is used in fruit salads, poached in coconut milk or cooked like a vegetable, in soup or served with fish. There are two main varieties: one is soft, fibrous, almost sweet, with an oyster-like texture to the flesh; the other is crisp and less sweet. The skin is light-green when immature, turning a yellowy-brown when ripe, and gives slightly when pressed. Before cutting into the fruit, coat the knife, your hands and the cutting board with oil to counter the sticky substance it produces when cut. The seeds of jackfruit can also be eaten: boil for 5 minutes and then roast. The fibrous material in the fruit is called rags; these can be saved and frozen for later use, as they make an excellent agent for setting jam. Jackfruit is readily available throughout Asia and Australia, but difficult to find elsewhere. The tinned variety will suffice as a substitute. See also CHEMPEDAK.

JAMAICA PEPPER see ALLSPICE

JAPANESE PLUM are a native of China, however, for over 1000 years have been a staple of Japan as an ornamental tree, due to the dusky, yellow fruit it produces, as well as the harvested fruit.
Like other plums, the Japanese plum is a smooth-skinned, firm fruit and is naturally very sweet.
See also UMEBOSHI and UMESHU

JAPANESE GREENS see LEAFY GREENS

JAPANESE ISINGLASS see AGAR-AGAR

JAPANESE MOOLI see DAIKON

JAVA APPLE see WAX JAMBU

JELLIED MELON see KIWANO

JELLYFISH is often sold dried and salted. It is favoured for its crunchy texture rather than flavour. Soak for 24 hours, changing the water several times, then drop into boiling water for 15–20 seconds. I suggest shredding finely and using in a salad.

JERKY is meat that has been cut into strips and dried. It originates from a South American Indigenous word (ch'arki) which literally means dried, salted meat. Biltong (Dutch for "meat strip") is air dried as a whole piece and then sliced into bite-sized pieces. Due to the drying and slicing process, most biltong is softer and fluffier in texture whereas beef jerky has more of a steak-like chew.

JERUSALEM ARTICHOKE, as is always written, has nothing to do with either the city Jerusalem (they are native to central North America) or artichokes (the flavour being only faintly similar) – and so it is written again. They are also known as **sunchokes**, a name derived from their relation to the sunflower family; the tuber grows underground like a potato, where it clings to the base of a tall, yellow-flowering plant. Although they are usually considered a starchy vegetable, Jerusalem artichokes in fact contain carbohydrates that don't convert to sugar in the body, so they can be eaten with reckless abandon by the diet-conscious and diabetics. They can be cooked or eaten raw as well as pickled. Other names include **sunroot, wild sunflower, topinambur** or **earth apple.**

 Top tips for Jerusalem artichokes
    ~ when buying, be aware that they are not the most sought-after vegetable so check for freshness: look for firm, plump specimens with no drying or wrinkling, and avoid any with tinges of green, blotches or signs of sprouting.
    ~ Peeling this knobby tuber can be frustrating, and the nutrients are found just below the surface, so I recommend you don't peel, simply scrub with a vegetable brush (it requires some elbow grease).
    ~ Once cut, place in ACIDULATED WATER to avoid discolouring.
    ~ Jerusalem artichokes can be treated the same as potatoes or eaten raw in a salad. Beware of the flatulence caused by the

fructose in these sweet, earthy-flavoured tubers.

JICAMA or **yam bean** is a large tuber that can be eaten raw or cooked. Peeled, shaved or sliced thin, it adds a crunchy texture to salads. Jicama makes for a good alternative to water chestnuts.

JOULES like CALORIES are a direct measurement of energy within food. 1000 joules = 1 kilojoule = 1 Btu (British thermal unit)

JOSTABERRY The fruit can be found growing in European countries. The nearly black berry, which is smaller than a gooseberry and a bit larger than a blackcurrant, is edible both raw and cooked.Best described as having a taste between a gooseberry and a blackcurrant, with the gooseberry flavour more dominant in the unripe fruit, and the blackcurrant notes developing as the fruit ripens.

JUG is an old English cooking technique. Jugged hare involves the hare being placed in a tall jug, set deep in a pan of water, and cooked slowly over a long period. The blood is drained before cooking and reserved and (with its natural clotting abilities) used to the thicken the sauce. Jugged kippers is a favoured method to avoid the house smelling of fish. The kippers' head and tail are removed, then they are placed in a jug head-end first with boiling water poured on top, and covered with a lid or plate and left to stand for 4–5 minutes.

JUJUBE a small fruit also known as the **Chinese date**. The skin turns from a yellowish-green to red when ripe (although it can be eaten before it is fully ripe). Both the skin and flesh are crisp and sweet, and it can be stewed, candied, dried or simply eaten fresh.

JUNIPER BERRY is generally used for cooking in its dried form. Often used in dishes involving furred game (venison, buffalo, hare, rabbit, wild boar), pork and kangaroo, juniper berries are crushed then added to the sauce or marinade. They lend food a strong, bitter-sweet taste, so exercisecaution so they don't overpower the dish. The distilled volatile oil from juniper berries is the flavour behind gin.

JUNKET Remember when Little Miss Muffet sat on her tuffet eating her curds and whey? She was eating junket. Junket is a warm, just-set milk dish, made with junket tablets (actually rennet tablets, used to make cheese). This cheap food is associated with harsh times and lean budgets. The tablets are also available in different flavours.

K.

KALAMANSI also known as **musk lime**, is related to the lime, lemon and cumquat, and closely related to the CALAMONDIN. A small, sour citrus fruit native to the Philippines, kalamansi is too sour to eat as is but is often used as a condiment, as Westerners use lemon. The fruit when ripe is yellow/orange.

KALE is a member of the cabbage family, and is a close relative of COLLARD. Unlike regular cabbage which has a round head, kale and collard form a looser, open head. The flavour is more bitter than regular cabbage so is best eaten with other sweeter ingredients like pears, roasted capsicum or caramelised onions. Kale is available in many varieties, including *Russian kale* and *dinosaur kale*. **Chinese kale** is another name for **Chinese broccoli.**
Cavelo nero is **Italian kale** or **Tuscan kale** and is harvested as long, narrow shards of dark green and firm leaves.

KALONJI see NIGELLA

KANGAROO Recipes for VENISON and kangaroo can be interchanged, due to the similarities in texture, colour and, in some cases, flavour. The primary cuts (fillet, loin and rump) from kangaroo are better-suited to being cooked rare to medium-rare due to the leanness of the meat. At less than 2% fat, kangaroo is marketed as the leanest and healthiest red meat in the world. Kangaroo is sold vacuum-packed to protect this meat from oxidising and dehydrating during storage while still allowing the natural tenderising process of ageing.(Don't open the package until you intend to use the meat as it oxidises quickly.)

KANTEN BAR see AGAR-AGAR

KASHA see BUCKWHEAT

KEBSA is a spice mix from Saudi Arabia and the Gulf. A mix of cardamom, cinnamon, cumin, cloves, nutmeg, coriander seed, loomi, red chilli and black pepper, it is used in soups, as a dipping spice for bread and olive oil and as a rub for meats. A very quick kebsa spice blend can be as simple as cinnamon, cumin and allspice. There is also a meal known as kebsa, a Saudi tradition of hospitality, a feast of goat, lamb, chicken, salads and fruit.

KECAP MANIS see SOY SAUCE

KELP see SEAWEED

KENPO NASHI see RAISIN-TREE FRUIT

KID (baby goat) is rarely cooked outside Italy, the Middle East, Africa and Asia (and their communities in the world's major cities), which is a shame. Asia is the largest consumer of kid meat in the world, followed by Africa. **Capretto** is slightly larger than kid. Kid meat is light pink in colour, fine textured, low in fat and high in protein. It is prepared similarly to lamb. Many recipes for LAMB or even RABBIT can be interchanged with capretto. Also known as **cabrito**.

KILOCALORIE (kcal) is 1000 calories but is equivalent to 1 dietary Calorie. See also CALORIE.

KILOJOULE Naturally there are 1000 joules to a kilojoule, a measure of energy. And there are approximately 4.2 kilojoules to 1 KILOCALORIE. A piece of buttered toast is said to contain 315 kilojoules (315 000 joules) of energy. You could then take that energy and run for six minutes or ride a bike for 10 minutes. See also CALORIE.

KITCHEN HAND A person who helps the chef or cook prepare food in a large kitchen, usually hotels and resorts. In a smaller kitchen, the kitchen hand may do a little food preparation, but the majority of their shift is spent scrubbing dishes. Also known as a pot walloper, a dish pig or, professionally, a steward. See also WASHING UP.

KIWANO is an exotic fruit from the MELON family that is also known as African horned cucumber, jellied melon or hedgehog gourd, names derived from the orange spiked skin on the outside (which is inedible) and the green jelly-like cluster of seeds on the inside. The pulp and seeds should be scooped out before eating, and the remaining flesh may be sprinkled with a little sugar if too bitter for your taste. The pulp can be strained of seeds and used in drinks or sauces. The taste of the kiwano is reminiscent of cucumber. It keeps for 4–6 months in a cool place and should not be refrigerated.

KIWIFRUIT is about the size of an egg and covered with a brown, fuzzy skin. Sliced open, it reveals an emerald green flesh dotted by small, black seeds. The flavour can described as a mix of strawberry, citrus and melon, a sweet, tangy and sometimes tart sensation. Ripe kiwifruit should be soft to the touch, like a ripe peach or avocado.

They can be eaten whole, furry skin and all. If this seems a little too barbaric, slice in half and eat with a teaspoon. Trying to peel them can turn them to mush, especially when they are overripe, but if you do, source a sharp peeler, not a knife, to save wastage. A hybrid variety called Kiwi Gold, is less tart, less hairy and a pale golden-green colour inside. Kiwifruit can also be used as a meat tenderiser. Rub the surface of the meat with a kiwifruit and let it stand for 15 minutes or add kiwifruit to the marinating meat no more than half an hour before the meat is to be cooked. One kiwifruit will go along way, so be careful of quantities (a whole kiwifruit tossed through a marinade for two hours will turn even tough meat to mush).

Kiwifruit are best stored in a plastic bag in the fridge, or if still immature, left in the plastic bag at room temperature for a few days. Also known as **Chinese gooseberry.**

KNIVES - Buying new knives whether for home or as a gift can be a little daunting, and the price can be off-putting. But remember, your new knife should last long after you're dead and gone, so be prepared to spend well and reap the rewards. Pick up and handle several different brands of the same style of knife and see what feels comfortable. Everybody is different, with different wrist strength, hand size and personal taste in design. What feels light and balanced to one person feels heavy and lopsided to another. This is why I recommend buying sharpening equipment as a gift instead of the knives themselves. This will encourage your friends to start sharpening the knives they already have.

Keep knives in a wooden block, on a mounted magnetic strip or in a case, to preserve the blade. Never store good knives in a kitchen draw. The continual knocking and battering can damage the blade and is a safety risk to anyone reaching in without looking, especially children.

Knives were not meant for the dishwasher. Wash in warm soapy water, rinse and dry well before storing.

Sharpening knives is probably the most neglected job in the kitchen. There are several options, the best of which is a live-in Samurai swordsman. Next best, you can try asking your favourite local butcher. (But be warned, to professionals like butchers and chefs, knife sharpening is a chore so expect to pay big money). Finally, learn how to sharpen them yourself. You could ask at a local restaurant or butcher's to be shown the moves. Never, ever, under any circumstances, leave this job to the so-called 'Knife Sharpeners' found lurking in shopping centres or in the Yellow Pages. The method is aggressive, taking large amounts of metal off the knife over a period of time and wearing the knife down quickly on the course edge of the machine. Your expensive German Wüsthofs will be no more in a mere 3 years. Knives are forever, so care for them as you would your young. Sharpen **poultry scissors** by cutting a piece of sandpaper into strips. (Keep the strips of sandpaper for fiddly sanding jobs.)

HOW TO SHARPEN A KNIFE

I recommend the Japanese variety of sharpening stone, a smooth orange block, and a diamond-finished steel to keep the edge on the blade.

1. Submerge the stone in water a soak for 15–20 minutes.

2. the stone from the water and place on a damp cloth or towel to prevent it from moving.

3. Place the knife perpendicular to the stone, with the blade at a 45–60° angle to the surface of the stone. Hold the handle with your strong hand and spread the fingers of the other hand along the blade of the knife for even pressure.

4. Keeping your shoulders, arms and elbows relaxed, start to move the blade of the knife along the length of the stone, starting with the tip and finishing with the neck. Turn the knife over and work the other side.

5. On average, a blunt knife will take about 15 minutes of solid work to refine the edge. If you have different grades of stone, you can now change from a coarse/medium to a medium/fine stone, and continue sharpening for a further 5 minutes. Once finished with the stone, scrub with detergent to remove any grey, metallic build up.

6. The knife's edge will have built up a metal burr which can be removed on the steel. Holding the steel in one hand, with the thumb and forefinger tucked behind the guard, place the knife's edge on the steel at the same angle at which it was sharpened, and run it down the steel. This time, start with the end of the knife that is closest to the handle and run it down towards the tip. I sharpen my knives towards the guard of the steel, but some people prefer to run the knife in the opposite direction, away from the guard and towards the tip of the steel. All it takes to remove the burr is 3–4 strokes either side.

KNOB CELERY see CELERIAC

KOHLRABI is a member of the BRASSICA or cabbage family, rather than the root vegetable family, yet it's the bulb that is of most interest to cooks. Kohlrabi bulb has a nutty, sweet, turnip-like flavour. There are green, white and purple varieties which are all white inside. When buying, look for small bulbs with fresh tops and thin rinds as large bulbs tend to be tough and woody. Avoid bulbs with cracks and blemishes. Dice and use in soups and casseroles, or cook whole with the skin on, then peel and slice or dice for salads.

KOKUM is rarely used outside Southern Indian cuisine. It is the dried rind of a fruit which imparts a pink or purple colour and a slightly sweet, sour taste. If you can find it, the darker the colour, the better the kokum; if you can't, substitute with TAMARIND.

KOMBU is a primary ingredient in DASHI. This seaweed enhances the taste of many dishes as it is an outstanding source of monosodium glutamic acid, the natural version of the chemical flavour-enhancer MONOSODIUM GLUTAMATE. Look for very dark, almost black examples of this dried seaweed, remembering not to wipe off the white residue on the surface which contains much flavour.

KUMARA see 'sweet potato' in POTATO.

KUMQUAT see CUMQUAT

L.

LABNA / LABNEH is a Middle Eastern cream cheese made by straining YOGHURT. It is available from Middle Eastern grocers but would have to be the easiest cheese to make. Labna can be eaten on its own as a cheese, drizzled with extra virgin olive oil (an indentation in the top will help hold the oil), and is delicious served as an appetiser with grilled vegetables, olives and toasted pita bread. It can be mixed with HARISSA as a dip for breads, and it is a great accompaniment to hot and spicy dishes. For desserts, use labna like a slightly tart cream cheese or quark cheese. It can be mixed with honey, orange blossom water or rosewater.

HOME-MADE LABNA

Place a large square of cheesecloth (a new handkerchief will do at a pinch) over a strainer, and place that in turn over a deep bowl or bucket (to catch the whey). Pour yoghurt into the cheesecloth. For savoury dishes, mix 1 kg of yoghurt with 1 tsp salt; for sweet dishes don't add salt. Cover or tie the top of the cloth and stand in the refrigerator for 24 hours. The longer you leave it, the firmer the labna will become. (Make sure the strainer or cheesecloth is suspended above the base of the bucket or bowl so the whey does not touch the labna.)

LAMB

 Top tips for lamb

~ **Milk-fed lamb** has pale, tender meat which lacks the flavour of older lamb; it is slaughtered between three and six weeks of age. Spring lamb has a darker, rosy-coloured meat and is anywhere from three to 12 months old at slaughter.

~ Select your cut of lamb with a cooking method in mind: cheap or secondary cuts are not suitable for grilling, while more expensive cuts like fillet are not suited for braises or stews. Lean cuts (fillet, loin) have less fat, and fat carries flavour. That is why the more expensive lean cuts are not recommended for slow or long cooking; the result can be dry and tasteless.

~ Spice pastes and herb rubs can transform a regular slab of lamb into a multicultural feast. HARISSA, SUMAC, curry and tandoor paste, cajun or herb mixes can all be smeared inside and out before cooking.

See also MUTTON.

LARD commonly refers to RENDERED and clarified pork fat. The best lard is known as leaf lard and comes from around the pig's kidneys. Also known as speck, it will keep refrigerated for about five days or frozen for up to six months.

The technique of larding means to cut a piece of fat (usually pork, sometimes bacon) into 'lardons' (strips) and sew it through a lean piece of meat using a larding needle. This is done to add succulence to a piece of meat that has no marbling (fatty streaks) to speak of. Larding is seldom done these days, as leaner or trim cuts of meat are in higher demand. Larding should not be confused with the similar practice of BARDING. See also FAT.

LAVER see 'nori' in SEAWEED.

LEAFY GREENS refers to lettuces and other edible leaf matter. The most important thing with these vegetables is how you handle and prepare them. Wash leafy greens in water to remove dirt, then lift gently out of the water, leaving behind any dirt and other foreign matter. Do not pull the plug or pour the washed greens in to a colander followed by the soiled water, this defeats the purpose. A lettuce spinner is an essential piece of equipment. The centrifugal method of drying leaves ensures that they are not damaged and that dressings and sauces are not watered down by badly strained greens.

Butter lettuce or **butterhead lettuce** is light-and begin to brown quickly.

Lamb's lettuce, mâche lettuce, lamb's tongue lettuce, corn salad lettuce or **field lettuce** is a loose-leaf lettuce, medium-green and mild in flavour with a semi-firm, small, elongated leaf (about the size, length and look of a lamb's tongue, hence the name). Can be seasonal, and is one of my favourites.

Mesclun, mesclun mix, spring salad mix and **field greens** are all used for a pre-mixed selection of loose-leaf lettuces, usually young and thin-leafed. The mix may include **frisée, mizuna, tasoi, baby chard, oakleaf (red and green), rocket, mustard greens** and **radicchio**. Although these lettuce mixes may look clean, many bare hands have rummaged through the mix before you, and insects and dirt always manage to cling to some leaves; wash and spin dry just before dressing. Assess the age or condition of these mixed lettuces by looking at the cut ends – brown means old – and at the middle or bottom of the box or container it sits in – slimy leaves indicate poor storage and handling or old stock.

Mizuna or **Japanese greens** has a flavour similar to salad rocket, although milder. It is distinguishable by its medium-green, thin yet sharp-cut leaves, as if someone has taken to a fat rocket leaf with a pair of scissors and tried to shape a Christmas tree from it.

Oak leaf lettuce is a loose-leaf style and mild, resembling the coral lettuce in flavour. Its leaves are medium size, with rounded edges and can be red, purple or green.

Radicchio, **red chicory** or **red Italian chicory** is prized for its bitterness. It is the shape of a small iceburg lettuce, with a tight head and leaves that cling close to the heart, although some new varieties can be loose-head. It is cooked almost as often as it's eaten raw: mixed into pasta sauce or cut into quarters and grilled.

Red coral lettuce or **lollo rosso** is a larger, soft, loose-leaf lettuce with ruffled ends with a very mild, pleasant bitterness. A bunch of it can resemble sea coral. Also available is the all-green version *lollo biondo* with medium-green leaves, exactly the same shape and size as the lollo rosso but perhaps a bit sweeter in flavour.

Rocket, **arugula**, **roquette**, **rucola** and **Italian cress** are some of the names of a very popular loose-leaf lettuce which is sold as salad rocket or wild rocket. Salad rocket has a milder flavour and softer, fatter leaf which can bruise easily, and cooks and eats just as well as spinach. **Wild rocket** (by name only) has a thinner, darker leaf and more peppery flavour. It has a better shelf life, and should not be cooked, as the stem becomes stringy and unpalatable. For best flavour, choose the bunch of fat leaf rocket which has a far superior peppery bite than the pre-cut, loose leaf, mass harvested, so-called "wild rocket", looking more like lawn clippings than excellent fresh salad leaf.

LECITHIN is a fatty substance used to preserve, emulsify and moisturise. Its primary source is egg yolks and soy beans. The effectiveness of egg yolks as a binding agent is due to them being high in lecithin. Lecithin is also said to have health benefits: it is essential for the breakdown of fats and cholesterol, it helps prevent arterial congestion, aids in the distribution of body weight, increases immunity to virus infections, cleans the liver and purifies the kidneys. Some people take lecithin as a supplement in tablet or capsule form, and it can also be purchased at health food shops in the form of granules or powder to sprinkle over cereal, or mix into shakes, salad dressings, soups, bread and other baked goods. Quantities vary from 1 tablespoon sprinkled on cereal or yoghurt to 3–4 tablespoons in a bread dough.

LEECHEE see LYCHEE

LEGUMES plant species whose seed pods split along both sides when ripe. They are noted for their flavour, digestibility and high protein content. Common legumes are beans, peas and peanuts. The dried seeds of legumes are called pulses. Common pulses are dried beans, lentils and dried peas. See individual legumes and BEANS, DRIED for more information.

LEMON The three main varieties of lemon are Eureka, Lisbon and Meyer. The Meyer is the most with its thin skin and less tart flavour.

 Top tips for lemons

~ Always wash and dry lemons before grating or using the zest in cooking. This removes dust, mould and dirt which could affect the dish being cooked, and in the case of non-organic lemons, removes the insecticides, colour dye or wax they can be sprayed with (these can all be removed with soapy water).

~ When grating the zest, place a piece of baking or silicon paper over the outside of the grater where it will stick to the rough edges. Grate to your heart's content, peel off the paper and all the zest will come off with it. ~ To get more juice from your lemon, roll it on the bench with pressure from the palm of your hand. This 'bruising' will tenderise the membranes within. Or microwave for 20–30 seconds before juicing.

~ For a dinner party, lemon halves wrapped and tied in muslin make an attractive addition to the table. A half lemon should last each person the entire meal, and the muslin prevents seeds from popping everywhere.

Q Problem solving

~ Excess lemons (or limes)? Squeeze the juice and freeze in an ice tray. The cubes can be transferred to bags when frozen. The zest can also be frozen.

LEMONGRASS is a tall, stemmed, grass-like tropical plant used as a herb and a spice. The most important piece of the stem is the pale lower third – usually sliced then pounded into a paste for a curry – but the remaining portion still has much to offer. Often the whole stem is tied in a knot and simmered in a soup or curry. Bruise the stem with the back of a knife before adding to stocks, soups and sauces, and remove the stem before serving. Wrap any leftover lemongrass well and store in the freezer. Or make a lemongrass tea, infused with some ginger.

LENTILS are an indispensable item in the pantry, low in fat, high in fibre and quick to cook. Unlike many dried beans and pulses, lentils don't need to be soaked before cooking, although some cooks and recipes recommend soaking – in the end it comes down to how you like your lentil and how you plan to use it. Soaking can reduce cooking time and makes the lentils swell which can help them cook quickly when added to dishes without much liquid. Soaking or not, first rinse them under clean water, then pick over them carefully to remove foreign matter (usually stones). If you choose to soak, do so for only 2–3 hours, as leaving them overnight will cause a sour smell and taste or even sprouting.

The French **Le Puy lentil** (sometimes called **French green lentil** or simply **Puy lentil**) is considered one of the finest, ready to eat in 20 minutes (although cook them for longer if you're not used to lentils with a bit of bite – personally I prefer them after 30–40 minutes as I find the flavour is richer when the core of the lentil has been softened). This green lentil holds its shape once cooked, making it perfect for salads or as a base for meats.

To my mind, the lesser known **Castelluccio** lentils from Italy are equally good. Like Le Puy, they are never soaked before cooking. Castelluccio lentils can be green, reddish or grained in colour, they are tender and have a long shelf life.

Brown lentils (also called **German lentils, Egyptian lentils, Indian brown lentils** and **green lentils**), are the most common, and hold their shape when cooked, but they tend to be pasty on the inside. They take 20 minutes to an hour to cook, depending on the job in hand and depending on their size and age (the bigger and older they are, the longer they will take). For salad, I recommend you start checking after 15 minutes then every five minutes after that; for soup, cook them longer; while for something like lentil burgers, give them a full hour to really break down.

Red lentils and **yellow lentils** are split lentils (halved, with the hulls removed), similar to the split peas you'll find in the supermarket or health food store. Without the firm outer skin to hold the shape of the lentil, they have a soft, creamy texture when fully cooked, in 15–20 minutes.

LETTUCE see LEAFY GREENS

LIAISON is a mixture of cream and egg yolks used for thickening white sauces and soups. It must be heated very gently. (As the word derives from the French, meaning 'to bind', it can also be used to refer to other thickening processes).

LIME Most of the tips mentioned under LEMONS can be applied to limes. Lime juice has a much stronger flavour profile than lemon, so if you are substituting one for the other use half as much lime as lemon - as long as the recipe is not compromised.

Kaffir lime is particularly common in Thai recipes, where the juice, zest and the leaves of the tree are all used. The fruit is larger and rougher in shape than the regular lime. When using the zest, be careful not to include any of the very bitter white pith. Kaffir lime leaves have a remarkable aroma and add character to a dish that no other ingredient can replicate. The leaves grow in a distinctive double shape and are finely shredded before being added to a dish. If you can't find or afford kaffir limes, you could substitute regular limes or substitute the kaffir lime leaf for the zest at a ratio of 3 leaves to 1 teaspoon of zest. Can be bought fresh or dried. Also known as **kiefer lime**.

Mexican limes, also known as **key limes**, are smaller and contain many seeds.

Tahitian limes or **Persian limes** are the most common supermarket variety.

LITCHI see LYCHEE

LO BAK / LOH BAAK see DAIKON

LOBSTER see ROCK LOBSTER

LONGAN is a brownish-yellow fruit that resembles a nut and is sold in clusters on a small branch. The word comes from the Chinese and literally means 'dragon eye' (to which it bears an uncanny resemblance when peeled). The longan is closely related to the LYCHEE although it is less perfumed, less acidic and milder in flavour. It is available fresh, frozen (claimed to be as good as fresh), dried and canned (said to taste better than canned lychees). Available from Asian grocers.

LOQUAT These can be eaten raw, in fruit salads or cooked in a sauce to serve with meat. They can also be treated like APPLES, in that the slightly unripe fruit can be used in pies or stewed (tastes great stewed with apple and rhubarb). When ripe, loquats can be stored in the fridge for up to two weeks. Peel the skin before eating.

LOTUS ROOT is not always available fresh but can be bought canned. Drain and rinse canned lotus root before using. Look for lotus root in Asian grocers.

LOVAGE is a herb that resembles flat-leaf parsley yet tastes like wild celery. You can make an alternative by mixing flat-leaf parsley with the pale inner leaves of a bunch of celery in equal parts.

LUFFA is picked, sold and used when unripe. (The overly mature fruit forms sponge-like fibres which when dried are made into those scratchy bath sponges women love and men just don't get.) The many varieties available are found in Asian grocers, some resembling large okra, named **angled luffa** or **Chinese okra,** others called **dishcloth luffa** or **sponge gourd**. In most cases, treat luffa as you would ZUCCHINI.

LYCHEE is too often served from the tin in far too much sweet syrup.

To eat lychees fresh is by far the most enjoyable way. Refrigerated, they keep well for up to 5 weeks but will deteriorate within 3 days when left at room temperature. Lychees will freeze. Also known as **litchi** (US) or **leechee**. The RAMBUTAN and LONGAN are relatives of the lychee. Sun-dried lychee are called **lychee nuts**.

M.

MACE the spice has nothing to do with chemical spray, "Mace", which is a brand name only and often known as "pepper spray" see CHILLI. Mace is the red lacy coating (called the aril) that encases the nutmeg seed. Once dried, the net-like coating becomes a golden-brown spice that is sold ground or as blades (pieces). Mace is similar to NUTMEG and is therefore interchangeable when cooking, but recommended for use in savoury dishes due to it being slightly more pungent.

MAIZE see CORN

MALABAR PLUM see ROSE APPLE

MANDARIN (or **mandarin orange**) is a group of hybrids, similar in taste to oranges, with varying levels of sweetness and sourness. Clementine is a common cultivar sold in supermarkets. Tangerine, murcott, satsuma and temple mandarin are all classed as mandarins although often sold under their own names. Varying levels of sweet and tart, with or without seeds, and loose or tight peel are some of the characteristics that differ between the hybrids. Best eaten fresh.

MANGO is one of the great seasonal fruits (although in fact a member of the cashew and pistachio family). Depending on the cultivar, skin colour can vary from green through yellow and orange to red or even deep purple – so check for ripeness by touch and smell, not colour.The nectar-sweet flesh that clings desperately to a fibrous seed can be served in many ways, but devouring it fresh is without doubt the single best way to eat this fruit. Mangoes do not like refrigeration; they store best at room temperature, stem side down in the tray in which they are bought, then covered with a damp cloth to alleviate wrinkling of the skin.

MANGOSTEEN is a delicious fruit that must be tried at least once in a lifetime. A slightly squashed round shape, 2–7 cm in diameter, it has a thick purple skin. Open the fruit by cutting through the skin only, and then lightly pulling and twisting it apart (beware of the bitter, sticky, milky substance within, as it can stain clothes). Inside, you'll find triangular segments of snow-white, juicy, soft flesh which is mildly acidic. The seeds (if there are any) are edible boiled or roasted. When buying, choose fruit with lots of lobes at their leafy top end; the more lobes, the more fruit segments and the fewer seeds within. Best eaten fresh, mangosteen keeps at room temperature for several days (ideally at 10°C for up to 20 days) or wrapped in paper in the least cold part of the fridge for two weeks. The whole fruit can also be frozen.

MANJA see PALM OIL

MAPLE (crystals or syrup) see 'alternatives to sugar' in SUGAR

MARINARA MIX or **seafood extender** might be convenient but resembles cat food in its quality. This pre-mixed array of poor-quality seafood will never be touched by anyone who values the succulence of fresh seafood. Instead, try making your own as a special occasion treat: simply combine a selection of fresh seafood and fish pieces.

MARJORAM and **oregano** are very similar herbs of the same genus, origanum. Oregano is said to be a hardier plant, liking arid soils, is stronger in flavour and more pungent; it is suited to a Mediterranean style of cooking, with strong flavours. Marjoram is more delicate, appreciates a lighter cooking style (added to sauces or soups towards the end of cooking, or eaten raw in a salad) and is ideal as a pot herb. (Oregano has a root system that does not take to potting.) However, the difference isn't substantial, and their flavour can be just as strongly determined by where the herb is grown: in plenty of sunlight, essential oils within the plant are more prominent and heighten the flavour. Both herbs like to be dried. Use fresh in salads, especially where tomatoes and onions feature.

Problem solving
~ Leftover marjoram or oregano? Mix with oil (see HERBS for method) and spread on the base of pizzas or crusty breads or use to baste roasts or steaks. **MARRON** see CRAYFISH

MASCARPONE is a smooth, soft, white cheese with a mildly acidic taste and a high fat content (47–50%). It is made by a similar method to ricotta, except with cream rather than milk: the cream has tartaric acid added, is heated, the curd and whey are separated and the resulting cheese is lightly salted and whipped. If necessary, replace with whipped RICOTTA or COTTAGE CHEESE or mix 250 g cream cheese with teo tablespoons of sour cream or whipping cream (see CREAM).

MATZO see FLOUR

MEASUREMENTS What a luxury it would be if metric were to become the universal measurement, which seems rational in these modern times. See weight and liquid conversion tables (page 253 and 258) for equivalents for **US Customary, British Imperial** and **metric** measurements.

✅ Top tips for measurements
~ Cookbooks assume you will use proper cup and teaspoon measuring utensils. Household cups and teaspoons are not useful. Keep this in mind when working from these books, especially when baking delicate goods.
~ Australian cookbooks tend to use a mix of metric and British Imperial.
~ US cookbook measurements refer to volumerather than weight for dry ingredients.
~ Take particular care with cup measurements, as all three are different:
1 US cup = 237 ml
1 British cup = 284 ml

1 Australian cup = 250 ml

~ When measuring with a cup or spoon, always use level quantity (scant) unless the recipe states 'heaped'.

~ **Scant**, as in scant 1/2 cup, scant pinch of salt, is also known as a struck measure. It means only just the measurement specified. See also conversions and equivalents on pages ...

MEAT Hints and information are included under listings for individual meats. But only the more common ones, so if you're looking for tips on baking buffalo, broiling bison, casseroling camel or grilling giraffe, try another source. Another way of thinking about different types of meat – rather than the usual divide between white and red – is whether the animal is ruminant or non-ruminant. Ruminant refers to any cud-chewing or cloven-hoofed animal with four legs. Keep in mind that recipes for one animal could lend themselves to another. Horse meat, although not eaten in many countries, is popular in many European countries, especially Belgium, France and Sweden, where it outsells lamb and mutton combined. The best mince meat is the type you make yourself. If you don't have a mincing machine, try cutting larger pieces of meat (usually scraps, off-cuts or cheaper cuts like skirt or flank) into 1–2 cm pieces and putting in the food processor on pulse so you can control how finely it is chopped. Hand-cutting meat for a good meat sauce is better left to a chef.

Cuts of meat and common terms

Chuck steak is known as **round steak** in the US, and can be called **stewing beef** or **casserole beef**.

Corned beef is known as **cured beef** or **corned silverside** in the UK and can be called **salt beef**.

Canned corned beef is known as **bully beef** in the UK.

A **cutlet** is the lean loin with the bone on.

A **chop** is a cut, bone in, from the shoulder and neck, and also the middle loin.

Eye fillet steak or **fillet steak** is known as **tenderloin steak** in the US and is also called *filet mignon*.

Flat iron steak (US) is my favourite cut. The most flavour filled slice of beef. Known as **butler's steak** (UK) and wrongly described as

Oyster blade steak in Australia. Misnamed for the simple reason is that true flat iron steak is a flat cut from only one side of the oyster blades signature line of sinew that separates two different grains of meat. As opposed to a simple cross section cut of the whole slab of oyster blade. Flat iron steak fetches a greater price per kilogram (or pound) due to the labour involved in separating these to muscle.

Hanger steak (US) is a flat steak but not to be confused at all with flat iron steak. Known also as **butcher's steak** due to it being a favourite cut of meat often kept by the butcher as they break down the carcass. known as **skirt steak** (UK) which is different in the US.

Mince is referred to as **ground meat** in the US.

Offal is known as **variety meats** or **organ meat** in the US.

Rump steak is called sirloin steak (or bottom sirloin) in the US, while sirloin in Australia or the UK refers to what Americans call porterhouse.

Sirloin or Strip (US) refers specifically to the large strip of meat from the sub-primal posterior of the beast. The whole strip is then cut into steaks with various names including sirloin, strip-loin, porterhouse and entrecôte.

Skirt steak is called **flank steak** in the US and can be called **stewing steak.**

T-bone is a cross section cut of the bone-in, sub primal posterior section of the beast. Made up of two specific muscle or steaks and separated by the signature "T" bone. On one side of the bone the sirloin or porterhouse steak, on the other side of the bone is the small, yet more tender eye fillet or tenderloin steak.

A **joint of meat** is a large cut of meat with the bone in.

HOW TO COOK MEAT

Bring meat to room temperature before cooking. Meat to be roasted, pan-grilled or barbecued should be left out of the fridge for a period of time (30 minutes to 11/2 hours) to reach room temperature. This reduces the core temperature and the overall cooking time of the meat.

Rest grilled or roasted meat after cooking. When raw meat hits the pan or oven it begins to contract, and as it cooks and contracts, the juices (blood) are forced to the centre of the meat. If you cut into it immediately it is cooked, the juices will still be concentrated in the centre. Allowing the meat to rest and cool a little, relaxes the meat fibres and lets the juices redistribute evenly throughout the meat. The more juices, the more flavour and tenderness. The larger the cut of meat the longer the resting time required. Rest the average steak in a warm place for 5–10 minutes, and a large roast for up to 1 hour covered in foil. (Braised or stewed meats do not need to be rested.)

FRYING OR GRILLING

Remember hot when exposing meat to a pan or grill top; a continual sizzling sound should always be present. Brown the meat on both sides in a hot pan then adjust the heat to finish, but be careful not to drop the heat so much that the meat starts to stew. It is sometimes recommended that thick-cut steaks be finished in a hot oven. This practice helps those who are in the habit of turning their meat fifty times to stop it from burning before it is cooked, but is really only suitable for those who enjoy cremating their food.

Sealing meat to lock in the juices New research shows that it is in fact a fallacy that moisture is retained by sealing meat (see also BRAISE). However, browning the meat before finishing the cooking does enhance its flavour and texture: it adds a delicious crust that contrasts satisfyingly with a rare centre.

To salt or not to salt? When anything with a water content, whether meat, fruit or vegetables, comes into contact with salt, the salt will begin to draw out the water. The amount of salt and the time the food is exposed to it will determine the extraction rate of moisture. So a steak that is salted and left to sit while the pan heats up will lose valuable juices, while a steak that is salted after it is cooked misses the point, as the meat has already been sealed. The best option is to season the meat with salt just before it hits the pan, ready to be sealed. This way the salt cooks onto the meat, enhancing the flavour of the cut, without drawing out valuable juices. Watch as crystal salt flakes caramelise on the surface of the meat when exposed to a hot pan. Season the joint with salt and pepper, spice rubs or pastes or chopped herbs. Sealing a joint before moving it to the oven will form a crust and cook on the seasonings, and allows the oven to be kept on a lower temperature (160°C).

CRUMBING OR BREADING

Never add salt to meat before crumbing. It will draw out the moisture and make the crumbs turn soggy. Instead, season the egg mixture and the flour with salt and pepper. To add flavour to the meat, you can stuff it or marinate it (remember to pat it dry in paper towelling before crumbing). To add flavour to breadcrumbs, rub in fresh crushed garlic (2 teaspoons of crushed garlic for every 500 grams of breadcrumbs will get you started) or add fresh cracked black pepper and torn or roughly shredded flat-leaf parsley. Your home-made parmigiana will never taste the same.

BRAISING

For most braised dishes the cut of meat is first dredged through flour then pan-fried. The flour acts as a thickening agent as well as adding colour to the sauce. The purpose of this is not to lock in the Juices, as braising meat may take several hours in which time any juices that were 'locked in' have well and truly escaped into the braising liquor. Never assume that the longer meat braises the better off it will be. Meat can over braise to the point where it falls off the bone or turns into mush. Depending on the type, size and cut of meat, stick to the requested time limit, check for done-ness, then give or take time after checking.

POT ROASTING

Resist adding too much liquid or it will become a stew. Basically, pot roasting is meat that is cooked very slowly with a small amount of liquid in a covered pot.

Problem solving

~ **Steak curls as it cooks?** Some cuts of meat have a tough membrane attached to the meat that when exposed to heat causes the cut of meat to curl or twist, making the opposite side near impossible to brown evenly. Simply place small incisions at intervals in the membrane making sure the cut goes through to the meat.

~ **Is the steak done?** When pressed with a finger, a cooked steak will feel different (softer, firmer, springier) depending on how well it is done. The professional cook learns by experience to tell a rare from a medium-rare steak, but for domestic cooks who don't cook hundreds of steaks a year, telling the difference can be difficult. A good way to learn is to make a small incision in one side of the steak and look to see how done it is. (Remember to serve with the cut side down.) Of course the sealed surface area has now been cut, allowing valuable juices to escape. So once the incision has been made, also press the meat with a finger and remember what that pressure feels like. Soon you will be able to tell what a rare steak feels like without having to cut into it.

~ **Undercooked one person's steak?** Slice it in two (lengthways) and place back in the pan for another minute or so; now you have two steaks.

~ **Undercooked roast?** As you usually don't discover it's undercooked until you've started carving, placing it back in the oven is not an option.The best thing to do is slice the meat a bit thicker and finish cooking each piece as a steak.

~ **Burnt a casserole, stew or soup?** Don't stir it! Plonk the pot immediately into a sink of cold water to stop the cooking. This is an important step. Then lift out the ingredients without disturbing the bottom of the pot, and place in a fresh pot or dish. Taste the food to assess whether the burnt flavour has permeated the liquid and if so, how much. If it's really bad, the bin is the only option. If it tastes only slightly burnt, try masking the flavour with a sauce such as Worcestershire sauce, barbecue sauce or tomato paste, or with other strong flavours such as garlic, chilli or onion (sautéed first in a separate pan) or spices (dry-roasted first).

✪ Alternatives to meat

~ Ardent meat lovers would argue that there are none, but that does not help the vegetarians, vegans or anyone changing the way they eat.

~ **Meat alternatives** are growing in popularity. As consumers are question the ethical consumption of meat and the effects that our diets have on animals, the environment, and our health. Many techniques and accompaniments that work with meat can successfully be applied to non-meat products.

~ **Mushrooms** have long been considered meat for vegetarians. Cut into large chunks or kept whole, mushrooms bulk out a curry, stir-fry or casserole perfectly, adding a meaty texture that other vegetables fail to deliver.

~ **Pureed nuts** and seeds are a good source of protein in place of meat.

~ **Seitan** is made from wheat gluten, is high in protein and has a meat-like texture when cooked. Seitan absorbs flavours well and can be sliced and diced, then used in stir-fries, casseroles or cooked in a sauce.

~ **Synthetic meats** are a form of cellular agriculture, along with synthetic milk and hen free egg whites. Lab-grown meat comes in many other names; *cultured meat, in vitro meat and synthetic meat,* and is made by growing muscle cells in a nutrient serum and encouraging them into muscle-like fibres.

~ **Tempeh** is a fermented soy bean product that makes for an excellent high-protein meat substitute. Tempeh is one of the most versatile alternatives to meat and it takes to marinating, stir-frying, grilling, braising, sautéing and baking.

~ **Tofu**, another soy product, can be purchased ready-made (burgers, steaks, hot dogs) as well as in blocks.

~ **TVP** (Textured Vegetable Protein) is dried, minced soy protein used as a substitute for minced meat. TVP has no discernible flavour of its own so relies on added flavour profiles for a boost. Any recipe made from minced beef can be recreated using TVP.

MELON There are three types of melon: winter melon, musk melon and rock melon. (WATERMELON is a different fruit.) Melons are highly perishable so growers pick them early, making it difficult to choose a melon packed with sweet, nectar-like flavour. Melons do not ripen after picking and only keep for about two weeks after that, at which point they only grow softer. Choose a melon that is heavy for its size and free of bruises. Look at the navel, where the stem was attached, to detect mould or excessive softness. A melon's ripeness can sometimes be detected by a delicate aroma, or by tapping it lightly for a hollow sound. Hard melons can be good if left to soften at room temperature for a couple of days. Store ripe melons in the refrigerator and, if cut, be sure they are tightly covered.

Musk melon has a rough, netted skin (that is, the skin looks as if it is draped in a net), and is also known as netted melon, nutmeg melon, American cantaloupe, false cantaloupe or Persian melon.

Rock melon is also known as **cantaloupe** (a name derived from the Italian area where they were first cultivated). Rock melons have a smoother and paler skin than musk melons. The **Charentais** is an excellent quality rock melon. Note that in the US 'cantaloupe' refers to a type of musk melon; the true rock melon isn't commercially grown there.

Winter melon or **American melon** refers to a group of smooth-to rough-skinned melons with less perfume than the rock and musk melon varieties. Some well-known winter melons include **honeydew melon** (cream skin, pale-green flesh), **galaisa melon** (a rockmelon–honeydew cross with yellow-green skin and green flesh), **casaba melon** (yellow skin, creamy-white flesh), **orange flesh melon** (cream skin, orange flesh) and the **Crenshaw melon** (creamy yellow skin, golden-pink flesh).

MERINGUE

French meringue is made by beating egg whites to a soft peak before adding sugar in small amounts then beating for a further 10 minutes to produce a smooth, shiny mix. Sifted icing sugar is then gently folded into the mix, taking great care not to overwork this mixture. These meringues are now ready to bake in an oven preheated to 120°C, reduced to 100°C when the meringues go in, where they will stay for 13/4 hours. They are ready when both the top and bottom are dry. Keep for up to 2 weeks in an airtight container.

Italian meringue is made by adding a hot sugar syrup (121°C) to whisked egg whites. The trick is to add the syrup at just the right moment when the egg whites have been whisked firm. The mixer is then turned to the lowest speed and the syrup is gently poured in a thin stream, not allowing it to get on the whisk, as this will form strands of sugar in the meringue. The meringue continues to be whisked at a low speed until completely cooled. Italian meringue is used to make excellent 'buttercream', used as a topping for lemon meringue pie.

Swiss meringues are made from egg whites and sugar mixed together in a bowl then whisked with the base of the bowl sitting in a double-boiler set over a direct heat. (A more experienced cook would chance doing this over a naked flame, but risks burning and discolouring the mix.) When the mix heats to approximately 40°C it is removed from the heat source and beaten until completely cold. This mix is now ready to bake like a French meringue, either spooned or piped onto baking sheets or parchment paper.

Snow eggs are a classic, soft poached or baked meringue. Made with egg whites and sugar then served on CRÈME ANGLAISE, these meringues are made by beating egg whites to a soft peak, adding the sugar then poaching spoonfuls (quenelles) in slightly sweetened milk for 6 minutes, turning once. They can also be piped into small tins or ramekins and baked at 140°C for 10 minutes.

Vacherins are French meringues piped into cup or vol au vent shapes before cooking, then filled with fruits, ice-cream, creams or custards.

 Top tips for meringues

~ Success with meringues and pavlova relies on persistence and correct oven TEMPERATURES.

~ Meringues made on a rainy or humid day will struggle to dry properly.

~ If beads form on the surface of the meringue or liquid seeps from the base, the oven temperature is too low –try increasing by 10°C.

~ Allow meringues to finish cooling in the oven after the temperature has been turned off. Cracks form when the meringue has cooled too quickly, because it has been removed from the oven while still warm.

~ **Overcooked meringues?** Once they have cooled, they can be crushed and used in, on or around cakes, or mixed into or sprinkled over ice-cream. (And, let's face it, overdone or underdone, to a child, any meringue is good).

MESCLUN see LEAFY GREENS

MICROWAVE The first microwave oven was built in 1947. It was nearly 6 feet tall, weighed over 750 pounds and cost US$5000 to buy. Now these compact metal boxes are standard-issue equipment in most households in developed countries. Microwaves are a form of electromagnetic radiation that is very similar to sunlight and radio waves. Microwave energy occurs when an electric current flows through a conductor. Thanks to Dr Percy LeBaron Spencer whose chocolate bar melted in his pocket while he was toying with a new experiment which had nothing to do with food, we now have the microwave oven. There are many and varied books on cooking in a microwave, but many avid cooks like me see it simply as the best tool for reheating or melting food rather than a way to cook dishes from scratch. No doubt microwave cooks would beg to differ.

MILK

Alcoholic fermented milk On your cornflakes? Think again. **Koumiss** is one such milk, an age-old fermented drink, once made from mare's milk. Basically, alcoholic fermented milks are made by lactic ferments and yeast cell extracts, instead of 'live' cells. They are mostly consumed in Europe, North Africa and the Middle East.

Buttermilk, also known as cultured buttermilk, is made from skim or low-fat cow's milk that has been soured with Streptococcus lactis bacteria (traditionally it was the liquid left after butter was churned). It should be kept chilled, as it may separate when warmed. Buttermilk is ideal for baking goods such as pancakes, cornbread and scones. It is very stable and lasts well, and adds a delicious tang to baked goods, salad dressing, soups and sauces. Buttermilk can be substituted with YOGHURT or sour cream (see CREAM) with only slight variations in the result.

HOME-MADE BUTTERMILK
to make one cup of buttermilk, combine:
¼ cup milk
¾ cup yoghurt

Buttermilk powder is an excellent product to use in bread machines where a dough needs to sit for long periods before being turned on to bake. It is sold in tins or packets in health food shops and supermarkets. Once the packet has been opened, store in the fridge for up to one year.

> *1 cup fresh buttermilk = 1/4 cup powdered buttermilk and 1 cup water*

Cultured milk products include YOGHURT, yoghurt drinks, buttermilk, crème fraîche (see CREAM) and sour cream (see CREAM).

Evaporated milk or **unsweetened condensed milk** is whole or skimmed milk reduced by 60%. It generally has a high fat content (8%), and can be reconstituted by adding its volume again in water. Sold in cans (once opened, store in a clean container for 3–5 days).

Goat's milk contains lactose (as does the milk of all mammals) but some people find it more digestible than cow's milk, so it is sometimes recommended as an alternative to cow's milk.

Homogenised milk has undergone a treatment (homogenisation) that prevents the cream component rising to the top.

Lactose-reduced milk is exactly that. Lactose has been reduced by 40–100%. People with lactose intolerance can look into these brands, but for those allergic to milk proteins, move on.
Pasteurised milk has undergone a heat process to destroy potentially harmful bacteria.

Powdered milk is easily reconstituted by adding water. Favoured for baking and by those on a budget.

Raw milk is a bitter sweet experience for me as a 10-year-old. It was my job to get up at six a.m. and hand-milk our two cows before school. This raw milk would sit in the fridge all day, then my mother would skim the cream from the top... then whipped and served with hot scones and home-made preserves – which all but made up for the early starts. The milk itself was watery, a little like skim milk now sold in supermarkets. Raw milk is not sold commercially because of the risk of bacteria (listeria and salmonella).

Sheep's milk or **ewe's milk** contains more than twice the fat of cow's milk (81/2% for ewe's milk and 4% for cow's milk). This is one of the reasons that it makes excellent cheese.

Sweetened condensed milk has been evaporated by a third, with 20% sugar added before reduction, the sugar acting as a preservative. Sold in cans.

UHT (ultra-high temperature) milk or *long-life milk* can be stored without refrigeration for about six months. It is packed in sterilised, aseptically sealed cartons, and like canned milk requires refrigeration after opening.

Fat content in milk Milk is sold by different names in different countries. As a general guide, extra cream milk (4.8 % fat) is known as breakfast milk or Channel Island milk (5.2% fat) in the UK. Regular milk (4% fat) is known as whole milk (3.5–5% fat) in the UK and US. Reduced fat milk (2% fat) is known as semi-skimmed milk in the US (1.5– 1.8% fat). Low-fat milk (1% fat) is also called light milk. Skim milk, skimmed milk or non-fat milk has a varying fat content (0.15–0.5% fat).

⭐ Alternatives to milk

~ **Almond milk** is a great option that can be easily made at home. It tastes great, has no cholesterol and can be substituted for dairy milk measure for measure when baking.

~ **Fruit milks** are usually made from very ripe bananas, cantaloupe or honeydew melon. For banana milk, simply blend one very ripe banana with one cup of water. For the cantaloupe and honeydew, scoop the flesh straight into the blender and puree to form a creamy, milky texture.

~ **Horchata** and Mexican horchata are both used as milk substitutes.

~ **Non-dairy creamers** and whiteners are common in the US but rare elsewhere. These dairy alternatives, usually reserved for beverages, contain corn syrup solids and palm oil, and are free of lactose, cholesterol, allergens and milk protein. Some contain coconut oil, canola oil or other such ingredients.

~ **Oat milk** is a very good replacement for drinking and in cooking, with excellent health benefits.

~ **Rice milk** can be used on cereal, for drinking, in baking and as a thickening agent.

~ **Soy milk** is an alternative although some people are allergic to it.

~ See also '**goat's milk**' and '**lactose-reduced milk**' in the list above.

MINT The three main types are **spearmint, peppermint and pennyroyal**. Spearmint (garden mint) is the one most often used in the kitchen. See also HERBS.

✪ **Problem solving**

~ **Leftover mint?** The best use is mixed in salads, especially Asian-style salads. Tear up mint, basil and coriander, and mix with small lettuce leaves such as cress and snow pea sprouts. Add a non-creamy dressing and sprinkle with fried shallots.

MIOGA GINGER is the bud from a member of the ginger family, used in pickles and in salads, as a garnish for soups such as laksa, and the Japanese dishes tempura and sashimi.

MIRIN is a sweet alcohol used in Japanese cuisine. Generally used only for cooking, it is made from 'mochigome' and 'komekoji' (yeast). There are two types of mirin: 'hon' and 'shin'. Shin mirin has less than 1%alcohol. It enhances flavour and adds alustre to cooked food. Although hon mirin tastes the same, it is 14% alcohol so is less popular for cooking.

MIRITON see CHOKO

MIXED SPICE is used in biscuits, cakes and puddings in Western cuisine. It is a mix of allspice, cinnamon, cloves, ginger, nutmeg and a small amount of black pepper. Making your own mixed spice can be an exercise in individuality; play with the quantities or add other sweet spices such as ground coriander, cardamom or anise.

MIZUNA see LEAFY GREENS

MOLASSES is the by-product of sugar cane and sugar beet refining, once the primary sweetener used in America for breads, cakes, biscuits and making rum. Only the molasses from sugar cane is edible; the molasses from sugar beet is not for human consumption. This black sticky substance goes through several refining stages. The first creates blackstrap molasses, a thick, black, bitter-tasting molasses, also known as **dark treacle** (Australia) and **black treacle** (UK). Next comes **treacle**, a refined dark molasses, still strong, but edible and often used in puddings, baked goods and tarts. A further step produces the light **golden syrup,** used as a spread as well as in cooking. See also POMEGRANATE MOLASSES.

MOLE SAUCE, a Mexican sauce to accompany meat, was invented by a nun, based on an ancient festival dish eaten by the Aztecs. It is made with Mexican chocolate (not the same as chocolate used to make sweets and desserts – see CHOCOLATE), often as little as 30 g for a recipe to serve with a whole chicken. Other ingredients in this thick sauce include plenty of red chilli, onion, garlic, herbs (oregano, thyme, parsley), tomatoes, sesame seeds, allspice, cloves and cinnamon. Mole served with chicken and turkey tastes better than it sounds.

MONOSODIUM GLUTAMATE (MSG) is two things: a naturally occurring glutamic acid, which is found in the human body and in unprocessed, unadulterated food like tomatoes, and a synthetic glutamic acid which is a crystallised, salt-like product used as a flavour enhancer in processed foodstuffs and some restaurant food. The former is good for you, while the latter, touted as being bad, is made through a fermentation process involving genetically modified bacteria. As with all additives, consumption of MSG should be treated cautiously, particularly if you know you are sensitive to additives. Naturally occurring MSG, like that found in seaweed, combined with natural salts is a better way to enhance the flavour of food. See also CHINESE RESTAURANT SYNDROME.

MOYA see CUSTARD APPLE

MURCOTT see MANDARIN

MUSHROOM Although we think of mushrooms as vegetables, their DNA suggests they are closer to the *animal kingdom* than they are to the plant world. The fruiting bodies of higher fungi is the sexual stage in the life cycle of the fungus. There are over 1.5million species in the fungi kingdom, of that, only about 20, 000 species produce mushrooms. Wild foraging for mushrooms in season is a growing industry that should be led by experienced experts to avoid picking and consuming deadly varieties. Farmed mushrooms are the most common, safe and accessible for the majority of consumers.

✅ Top tips for mushrooms

~ When buying mushrooms look for smooth, firm caps, free from major blemishes. The mushroom's surface should be dry, but not dried-out looking.

~ Once home, refrigerate mushrooms immediately. Store them in paper bags or, if packaged, remove their plastic wrap and cover the package loosely with paper towel. They will keep five days or longer. Avoid airtight plastic bags – this causes moisture condensation which speeds degradation.

~ Most mushrooms can be frozen successfully: the texture will change, but the flavour won't. (Add to the dish while still frozen.) Delicate mushrooms such as oyster or enokitaki should not be frozen.
~ Before using fresh mushrooms, brush off any dirt or foreign matter with a damp cloth or paper towelling. Alternatively, use a pastry brush to remove other debris clinging to the underneath or stem of the fungi.

~ Despite previous opinions on washing mushrooms (allegedly absorbing too much water) - they can in fact be briefly washed in water to remove excessive dirt - often limited to cultivated button mushrooms.

~ The white flesh of mushrooms will brown after being sliced. This does not affect the taste but you can avoid it by brushing with lemon juice.

~ Remember that not all mushrooms should be prepared in the same manner; some shine with moist cooking methods, in soups, stews, ragouts, sauces and stir-fry, while others love oil and butter. European mushrooms do well sautéed or used in cream sauces, while Asian varieties excel in soups and stir-fries.

Fresh cultivated mushrooms, the standard button and field mushrooms, are mass-produced in controlled conditions and are fine to eat raw as well as cooked. Exotic mushrooms (often sold pre-packed) are also great fresh, although a dried mushroom can offer better or more concentrated flavour than its fresh counterpart (for example, in the case of *shitake* and straw mushrooms). The delicate oyster (abalone) and enokitaki (enoki) mushrooms are ideal raw in salads, and if cooked should be added towards the very end of cooking so they wilt rather than disintegrate.

Dried mushrooms are interchangeable with fresh. Simply rehydrate by soaking or simmering in enough water to cover. Keep the water, as this can be used as a stock for soups, sauces and risotto (although strain before use to avoid sand, small stones and other heavy foreign matter). Not all types of mushrooms dry well; some that do are *shitake,* wood ear, cloud ear and straw mushrooms. Dried *shitake* are often used over fresh as their flavour is more intense. Drop the *shitake* into simmering water, remove from the heat, then leave to steep for 10 minutes, or soak in hot water for 30 minutes, then drain and squeeze out excess water, slice and use. *Forestière* is a mix of broken pieces of other mushroom varieties. Treat these like *shitake* but rinse well and discard the lower portion of soaking liquid as this mix is very sandy. Morels, chanterelles (girole), black chanterelles (black trumpet) and cepes (cep, porcini, bolete) can all be rehydrated by soaking in hot water for 15–30 minutes.

Powdered mushrooms can add another dimension to mashed vegetables, dips, rubs for meat, soups, risottos and pasta. They're also good mixed with oil for dipping bread. Any dried mushroom can be ground in a food processor into a powder. Porcini powder is commercially available albeit expensive.

Canned mushrooms are in most cases the last resort, as their texture tends to be rubbery. Tinned straw mushrooms are one of the exceptions and often used in Asian stir-fries and soups.

Medicinal mushrooms are often a dried extract from species of mushrooms that proving to aid or support human function, like immune systems, nerve repair, enhance brain function etc. Although the traditional use of mushrooms as medicine has been around for over two thousand years, modern medicines have vastly overshadowed the potential mushrooms possess. New studies are now starting to show results and gaining momentum in popularity. Very few of the medicinal mushrooms can be eaten raw, however, a favourite of mine is **Lion's mane.** The dried extract thought to enhance brain function, mood and boost focus. But it's the raw version that is worth cooking, with a taste and texture to lobster or crab meat.

MUSK LIME see KALAMANSI

MUSSELS, like all shellfish, are at their best when still alive and in their shell. Before buying, check whether they're alive by tapping the shell, which will then tightly close. Any with gaping shells are dead, and should not be purchased. The 'beard' of a mussel is actually the byssal threads, produced by glands near the foot area. which allow the mussel to cling to rocks or hard surfaces in the water.

HOW TO DE-BEARD A MUSSEL

To remove the beard, yank it firmly towards the hinge of the mussel rather than the opening end.(Pulling towards the opening will kill the mussel and can rip out some of the inner flesh.)

MUTTON was often considered tough and stringy, but due to modern breeding and farming methods the meat produced now is both tender and flavourful. Mutton has a more robust flavour than LAMB, an off-white fat that springs back to the touch (lamb has a firm, creamy-white fat), and it turns cherry-red when cut, then darkens with age (lamb stays a pinkish-red colour). Darker mutton may still be good, strong in aroma, and should be cooked and eaten immediately. As mutton is a tougher piece of meat, marinating or tenderising with a meat mallet will soften the connective tissues. Mutton is not easily available, but can be purchased at butchers.

N.

NAM PLA see FISH SAUCE

NASTURTIUM is one of my favourites. The flower, leaf and seed are all edible, with the young leaf being the choice ingredient. The peppery bite these leaves offer make for a great salad. The flowers are less tasty but can be an attractive addition to salads; the seeds can be pickled.

NEEPS is another name for SWEDE.

NIGELLA, also known as **kalonji** or **charnushka** (US), are the teardrop-shaped, black and pungent seeds from a bush found throughout India. This aromatic, slightly bitter spice is used to give a nutty edge to curries and breads, and in Middle Eastern and Turkish cuisine. Kalonji should not be confused with black sesame seeds (kalonji have a more angular shape to the seeds), black onion seeds which is a misnomer, or black cumin (although, to confuse matters, 'black cumin' is the literal translation of the Hindi word for kalonji).

NOODLES are like pasta in many ways. There are many styles available and, as with pasta, there can be confusion about what is the right noodle to use in soups, salads or in stir-fry. Some noodles are merely soaked before being cooked, others need washing before being blanched and then finally cooked. There are egg noodles which are favoured in soups. There are Japanese noodles like soba (buckwheat), somen and udon which require a specific cooking process before being used in thefinal dish. Then there are the many forms of rice noodles, from the very thick to fine, hair-like cellophane noodles. Considering entire books are devoted to both noodles and pasta, all that is needed here are some quick guidelines that should encourage you to look into and further develop the use of these ingredients. **For those with allergies**, look for noodles made with potato starch (harusame), agar agar, bean curd skin, arrowroot, mung beans, buckwheat, seaweed, sweet potato, yams (shirataki), tapioca and soybeans.

　　Bean thread vermicelli are very fine noodles made from mung bean starch and tapioca. They are often used in soups and salads more for texture and appearance than flavour. They can also be deep-fried straight from the packet and used as a garnish. Soak in cold water for 20–30 minutes (hot water softens them too much) before cooking – the noodles are ready when they become transparent. They have more names than just about all other noodles combined, including **cellophane noodles, jelly noodles, glass noodles, invisible noodles, mung bean noodles, shiny noodles** and **slippery noodles,** as well as a dozen names from different Asian countries.

Chinese noodles are commonly divided into two groups: those made with wheat (mian), favoured in the cooler north, and those made from rice (fen). A third type, egg noodles are a Cantonese specialty (see **egg noodles** and **rice noodles** below). A rule of thumb that applies to most noodles is that flat noodles are used for stir-fry dishes and round noodles are used in soups.

Egg noodles come fresh or dried and in a number of varieties: chow mein noodles are formed into patties or pancakes once cooked then fried on both sides, **hokkein noodles**, common in the cuisines of Malaysia and Singapore, resemble thick yellow spaghetti, **Hong Kong noodles** are used in the classic dish chow mein, while **Cantonese noodles (lo mein)** come in various sizes, flat and round. Fresh egg noodles should be blanched in boiling water for 20 seconds before being added to soups or stir-fries.

Dried egg noodles should be cooked in boiling water until al dente (or longer if you prefer a soft noodle), then cooled ready for further use in soups or fried.

Japanese noodles are most commonly made from wheat or buckwheat. **Soba** is the classic buckwheat noodle, with green tea

HOW TO COOK DRIED JAPANESE NOODLES

Although most packets carry clear cooking methods, the following is a method that works for most dried noodles. Add noodles to plenty of unsalted boiling water. (Take care not to add in a clump as these dry, starchy noodles have a tendency to stick together.) Once sprinkled in, stir to ensure the noodles stay separated. When the water returns to the boil, add a cup of cold water and continue stirring, then repeat this method 2–3 times more. The added cold water and stirring ensures the noodles release excess starches. Drain and rinse in cold water. The noodles can be reheated before adding to soups or stir-fries.

sometimes added to make the soft-green chasoba. **Somen**, made from fine wheat flour and oil, and hiyamugi are quite thin and fragile and are usually eaten cold with dipping sauces. The thick and chewy **udon** can be made from wheat or buckwheat, while ramen are long curly noodles formed into blocks. **Konyyaku** or **devil's tongue noodles** are made from yam flour and come in thick or thin sheets or balls. They should be boiled before use to remove any harsh flavours. **Harusame** are made from mung beans.

Rice noodles come fresh and dried. Fresh noodles need only be reheated in boiling water for 15–20 seconds before use in soups or stir-fries. Fresh vermicelli noodles are delicate and are best steamed to heat through. They can also be eaten (on the day of purchase) at room temperature in salads. Fresh rice noodles toughen as they age or if refrigerated. Dried rice noodles like vermicelli and rice sticks can be rehydrated in warm water for 15 minutes, drained and then used. Alternatively, soak them in cold water for 1–2 hours to allow them to keep their crunch. They will remain quite firm, just no longer brittle, but will wilt and soften when combined with other hot ingredients ready to serve.

Soy noodles come in two varieties. **Tofu noodles** (also known as **tofu shreds, soy bean** and **bean curd noodles)** are made from compressed tofu and resemble a pack of rubber bands. Available dried, fresh or frozen, these nutritious noodles are used in salads, stir-fries and soups. Soak dried noodles in warm water until soft. **Bean curd skin noodles** are made from YUBA and are chewier than tofu noodles but used in the same way.

Wheat flour noodles are made with wheat flour, salt and water, available fresh or dried. Sometimes eggs and flavourings are added. Depending on thickness, boil fresh noodles for 3–4 minutes before use and dried noodles for 5–10 minutes.

NORI see SEAWEED

NUNGU FRUIT, the flesh of which is a translucent, sweet jelly and also known as **ice apple**. Nungu palm grows in the dry, tropical regions of mid and southern India., where it is known as **doub palm, palmyra palm, tala** or **tal palm, toddy palm** or **wine palm**. The tender fruit pulp is eaten raw during summer because it gives a cooling effect to the body. The ripened fibrous outer layer of the fruit can be eaten raw, boiled, or roasted.

152

NUT MEAL see 'nut flour' in FLOUR

NUTMEG can be bought whole or powdered. The whole kernels can be grated directly onto or into food, but be careful not to add too much. In its natural state, the nutmeg kernel has a lacy, scarlet covering, known as MACE, which, when removed and dried, turns an orange/yellow colour and has the flavour of nutmeg. The general rule is, nutmeg to be used for sweet dishes, mace for savoury.

O.

OCTOPUS The best tip for cooking octopus is to tenderise the flesh before cooking. Ideally this is done by beating over a rock in the Greek Islands. Alternatively, precook very briefly by blanching in vinegar water. Or rub with grated DAIKON for its tenderising properties. Italians swear by cooking the octopus with wine AND the cork from the wine bottle, without being able to explain the chemistry behind why that works..."Capiche!" Larger, raw tentacles benefit from being frozen as the freezing and thawing begins the tenderizering process. Typically, as any food defrosts, (the moisture within has formed expanded ice crystals), the ice crystals defrost and that moisture naturally leaves the food. It's the excess water content within the octopus that contributes to the rubbery texture when cooked, by removing as much of this moisture before cooking it will help produce a more tender product."Rubbery" and "chewy" are two words often associated with cooked octopus, which is a shame really because it can be very tender yet still "AL DENTE". The simplest way to cook octopus is to simmer it in liquid. Fill a saucepan with salted water and bring to the boil. Add the octopus, reduce the heat immediately and simmer gently for 45–60 minutes. It's important that the water is turned down to a gentle simmer once the octopus is in the pan. Cooking it too quickly will result in a rubbery texture.

Buy tentacles (frozen) or a whole baby octopus fresh, and if you don't fancy cleaning the whole octopus at home, buy them pre-cleaned. They should be firm to touch and sweet to smell, with no slimy residue or wafts of ammonia.

Known as **polpo** in Italy, **pulpo** in Spain and **oktapodi** in Greece.

OIL

 Top tips for oil

~ Always check the use-by date on oil before buying. Oils should also carry a 'packaged on' date and the closer to the packaged date you can buy an oil, the fresher it is. Be wary of oils that are reduced in price, as they could well be old.

~ Buy oil in smaller quantities if you keep it near the stove.

~ Keeping oil in the fridge is not necessary but is an option. Oils higher in fat content, such as olive oils, to solidify and turn white in the fridge. Simply bring to room temperature before use. If preparing fresh chopped garlic or chillies to store in the fridge, it would be best to use a vegetable oil to avoid having it solidify in cold storage.

~ Keep oil out of direct sunlight. Store in a place that is cool, dry and dark, such as a pantry or cupboard. Buying oil in a tin is advantageous, as light cannot penetrate the container.

~ All fats and oils eventually break down and become rancid with prolonged exposure to air, light and heat. The only way to tell if an oil is old or rancid is to open it and smell. Rancid oils have a stale, soapy smell and lose the strong characteristics of that particular oil as well as forming free radicals (which change cell membranes, suppress the immune system and promote the development of cancer and arteriosclerosis). If an oil is rancid, take it back to the shop if it is newly purchased or throw it out, there is nothing that can be done. Once you are used to detecting the rancid odour, you may well be surprised at how often you encounter the smell in other fat- or oil-based products.

~ Oils made from nuts are the most unstable of all oils (although macadamia is the best of them), so buy in smaller quantities and try to use well before the use-by date.

~ If you deep-fry at home, you can strain the used oil through paper towelling and store in the fridge to reuse later. The oil can be used for day--to-day cooking as well as further deep-frying. Polyunsaturated oils can only be used once, while olive oil, rice bran oil and d unrefined peanut oil last longer and can be strained and reused two or three times.

~ Never get in the habit of pouring oil down the sink. Pour cold oil into an empty plastic or metal container with a lid (old milk or cream containers, jam jars and the like) before putting in the rubbish. Some countries have depots where used cooking oil can be dropped off. If you feel you go through enough oil to justify a trip to the depot, then I suggest giving your local council a call to find out if this service is available to you.

The following fats and oils are low in essential fatty acids (see FAT), therefore produce the lowest amount of toxic molecules when heated, so although most of them are saturated fats, they are considered the better option for cooking: butter, lard, tropical fats (coconut and palm oil), high oleic sunflower (not ordinary sunflower) oil, high oleic safflower (not ordinary safflower) oil, peanut oil, sesame oil, canola oil and olive oil, in that order of preference.

THE BEST OIL FOR THE JOB

For salads and other cold dishes where the oil will be tasted clearly, try the stronger oils like walnut, hazelnut, macadamia and extra virgin olive oil. Flavoured oils like citrus, chilli, coffee, herb, garlic and others are intended to give flavour and lift to an otherwise drab dish or salad. **Sesame oil** is misunderstood and often abused: use it in small quantities as a seasoning, as you would salt and pepper, in stir-fries or Asian-style dressings.

For cooking, use unrefined oils (see below). A good roasted peanut oil is good for cooking as well as salads but unrefined peanut oil is better for frying. There is a school of thought that believes any oil becomes toxic once heated and so oil should never be used for cooking — here is not the place to analyse that theory. Certainly, the hotter the oil gets, the faster it will oxidise and break down. Shortly before smoking point, oils begin decomposition, thus forming free radicals and acrolein, a toxic smoke. Oil at smoking point is generally considered not fit for human consumption, as it cannot be properly digested by the liver.

Refined oils are unbalanced oils. They have had vital elements removed to extend shelf-life and profitability. Often removed are LETHICIN (which makes digesting oil easier), anti-oxidants (like vitamin E and carotene), phytosterols (which provide protection for the immune and cardiovascular system) and chlorophyll (an essential source of magnesium, which is required for muscle, heart, and nerve functions). In addition, these elements are removed with corrosive bases, window-washing acids and bleaching clays. The oils are then heated to frying temperatures before being packed into bottles or tins. Choose unrefined oil where possible. Sunflower, safflower, canola, soybean, corn and vegetable oils are just some of those on the supermarket shelf that are worth thinking twice about.

OKRA also known in many English speaking countries as **ladies' fingers** or **ochro.** A member of the *Mallow* family of plants which include DURIAN, COCAO and cotton. Okra is prized for its edible green seed pods and favoured in Southern United States, West Africa, India and southern Asia. When cooked, the characteristic slime or gooey texture is valued for its ability to assist in thickening wet dishes like sauces, soup (Gumbo) and stews. Dried okra can also thicken sauces. The viscous mucilage can be reduced by adding acidic foods like tomatoes.   Young okra leaves may be cooked in a similar way to the greens of beets or dandelions, or in salads. Okra seeds may be roasted and ground to form a caffeine-free substitute for coffee.

OLIVES come in many styles, from the buttery Ligurian to the salty, meaty Kalamata – right down to those horrid, rubbery black things you sometimes find on cheap pizza. The olive fruit has a bitter component (oleuropein), a low sugar content (2.6–6%) and a high oil content (12–30%), depending on the time of year or variety. These characteristics are what make the olive a fruit inmost cases cannot be consumed directly from the tree. Olives are cured or pickled before consumption, using various methods including oil-cured, water-cured, brine-cured, lye-cured (green olives) and dry-cured. The best-known French olives are the green picholine and the renowned niçoise. Greek olives are divided into three classes: round (black and green), long (black and green) and the kalamata olive. Kalamata olives are highly prized, with a low oleuropein content. An incision is made in the fruit to facilitate washing with water or brine, the olives are immersed in wine vinegar for one or two days, then packed in fresh brine, usually with pieces of lemon. Olive oil is often added to form a surface film. The best known Italian olives are the Ligurian, lugano, gaeta and the ponentine. Moroccan olives are reasonably small with a soft meat. The very tasty manzanilla or the larger gordal (which can be as heavy as 20 g) are the best Spanish olives.

Green olives are harvested earlier in the ripening cycle, when they have reached normal size but their colour hasn't changed. Most green olives are cured with lye, sweetened and pickled and are ready for consumption about 45 days after harvesting. They are often sold pitted and stuffed. They will last up to several weeks after opening. The excellent green olives found especially in Spain are treated differently, with hydrolysis, leaching and fermentation, resulting in a softer, juicier olive.**Dried olives** have a bolder flavour than brined olives and can be bitter. These salt-cured, wrinkled black olives are added towards the end of cooking or marinated in herbs, chilli and oil.

 Top tips for olives

~ An opened jar of olives should be refrigerated in their own liquid in a non-metal container.

~ If you're having trouble removing the stone, trying squashing the olive gently with the bottom of a glass before sliding the seed out.

OMEGA 3 and **OMEGA 6** see **'essential fatty acids'** in FAT.

ONION

Problem solving

~ **How to prevent tears while working with onion?**There's no perfect answer, short of engineering a genetically modified onion void of all sulphur compounds, but the following can help: keep onions in the fridge, as the cold subdues the substance known as allicin, produced when an onion is cut; peel onions under water, but this washes away the natural 'bite' onions produce; leave the root end intact when peeling, as this contains the largest amount of sulphuric compounds. Onions grown in soil that contains a higher level of sulphur compounds produce strong, tear-inducing onions.

Brown onion (yellow onion in the US) is the most common cooking onion. Usually too strong to be eaten raw.

Green onion is a general term used to describe both the **salad onion** and the **spring onion** (see below) and any harvested bulb with green shoots in tact.

Pickling onions are small and good for cooking as well as pickling. **Pearl onions, boiling onions** (*small brown onions)* and **cippolini onions** are all pickling onions.

Red onions are sweeter than brown and are often eaten raw but cook just as well. There are several varieties of red onion, some a little more elongated with a bit of a green sprout at the top (**Burmuda onions**). Red onions are sometimes mistakenly called **Spanish onions**.

Salad onion A slightly more developed spring onion, harvested from 4 months on, giving it a more rounded bulb. Salad onions have the advantage that they are sold separately, not in a bunch, so if ever a recipe calls for a small amount of spring onions, you can buy a salad onion or two instead, and use the inner green leaves only. The bulbous part can be used in salads or in cooking. Known as **spring onion** in the US and **green onion** in the UK.

Shallot grows as a small group or cluster of onion bulbs. Popular in French and Asian cuisines, shallots have a brown/golden skin or a pink/purple skin. Shallots are favoured in sauces for their mild flavour. 'Shallot' is a name used for the spring onion in some parts of the world where the word **'éschalot'** refers to the true shallot.

Spanish onions are similar to brown onions only larger and sweeter and they are seasonal (spring to summer).

Spring onions are **green onions**, harvested from 8 weeks after seed to prevent a bulbous end forming (so they are an even width from top to bottom). Buying a whole bunch can mean wastage so, to lengthen storage time, divide into three smaller bunches, wrap each in cling film and keep in the fridge. In many parts of the world the misnomer 'scallion' or 'shallot' is used to describe spring onion.

White onions are sharper and spicier than brown onions but lack their big, rounded flavour. Their tang makes them a popular choice in Hispanic cooking.

158

ORANGE As there are many cultivated varieties of orange available and much seasonal variation, it is better to buy from a grocer rather than the supermarket, as the grocer can tell you what state the oranges are in and when others are coming into season. As a guide, small-to medium-sized oranges are sweeter than large ones, while the thin-skinned varieties contain more juice than the thick-skinned.

Jaffa oranges are similar to the **Valenciaoranges** only sweeter, Valencias being the choice orange for juicing. Valencias have a slightly green skin even when ripe.

Navel oranges are the all-round good guys, easy to peel and segment, with good juice content, no seeds and a sweet flavour.

For cooking, turn to the very sour **Seville orange** (great in marmalade).

Blood oranges are named for their deep-pink or red-streaked flesh, and their skins too may have a red blush. They are smaller than an average orange with slightly rougher skin. The flavour is sweet and mildly acidic, some say 'an orange kissed by a raspberry'. Blood oranges keep for about two weeks either refrigerated or at room temperature.

Before zesting an orange be sure the orange isn't coated in wax (if it has been waxed, wash with soapy water). Take care not to grate in the bitter white pith.

---

1 medium-sized orange will yield about 3–4 teaspoons of grated zest
2–4 medium-sized oranges will yield about 1 cup orange juice

ORANGE MINT see BERGAMOT

OREGANO see MARJORAM

OVENS Accurate oven temperatures are important, especially for baking. Unfortunately the thermostat is often the first thing that breaks on an oven. Ten degrees out and that delicate baked custard could resemble omelette when the timer goes off. The best solution is to get to know your oven, or invest in an oven thermometer. The more expensive solution is to call in a specialist, to check and/or replace your thermostat.

Conventional ovens have a gas burner or an electric element(s) heating from the bottom. As the heat rises, it creates different temperature areas or zones within the oven. The hottest area is at the top, the centre is moderate while the coolest part is at the bottom of the oven. This can limit the amount of food that can be cooked at the one time or cause problems with baked goods if the oven is overloaded.

Gas ovens can cook at a lower temperature than electric, while electric ovens can produce a higher, more consistent heat. The following types of oven, less common in the domestic market, are sometimes referred to as zoned ovens.

Fan-assisted ovens (available in gas and electric) operate like conventional ovens but with the addition of a fan at the rear. As the heat rises from the bottom it's circulated by the fan to create a more even temperature. The fan can be turned on or off so, for example, a pie can be baked using the fan-assisted function, and then its top browned using the oven conventionally.

Fan-forced or convection ovens have an in-built fan that circulates heated air around the oven. This results in an even temperature throughout the entire oven, allowing all shelves to be used simultaneously. Fan-forced ovens heat more quickly, can cook food at lower temperatures, and use up to 35% less energy than conventional ovens. Available in electric only.

Combination cookers combine convection and microwave cooking in the same oven. The advantage of these ovens is that food can be browned or crisped on the outside using convection cooking, while the microwave energy reduces the actual cooking time. See also the table of temperature conversions on page 257.

OYSTER All shellfish should be bought when still alive and in their shell, but this is particularly important with oysters. They are far better when opened (shucked) at home, so they retain their precious liquid or nectar. If you buy oysters that have already been shucked, they should be plump, with a natural creamy colour and a clear liquid.

OYSTER PLANT see SALSIFY

OYSTER SAUCE is a staple in Chinese cuisine. On its own or combined with other sauces and pastes, oyster sauce lends itself well to seafood, beef, chicken and pork as well as soups. Are there oysters in oyster sauce? Most oyster and 'oyster-flavoured sauce' sold commercially and especially in supermarkets, is made from water, sugar, thickeners, monosodium glutamate, caramel colouring and an ingredient called 'oyster extractive', a flavour that is extracted from oysters but, due to refining, contains none of the oysters' proteins. However, quality oyster sauce is made with fresh (giant Asian Pacific) oysters that have been boiled in water with soy sauce, salt and spices, and preserved then processed in a way that retains the oysters' proteins. Cheap brands tend to be salty and contain wheat flour, while quality brands are thickened with starch, and are milder in salt content. Once opened, always store in the fridge where it will keep for many months.

P.

PAK CHI FARANG see CORIANDER

PALM BUTTER is a thick red paste made from palm nuts which have been boiled, pounded to a pulp and strained. It is used as a base for soups and sauces, and excellent with seafood. Canned palm butter can be purchased in most African food stores.

PALM OIL can be white or red. Red palm oil is extracted from the fibrous flesh around the nut of the fruit of the oil palm, while the white oil comes from the palm kernel itself. It is used liberally in soups and sauces, yet without making them greasy or oily. Both palm oils are high in saturated fats, although the red (50%) has far less than the white (80%). Also known as **manja** or **zomi.**

PANADA is a paste made from bread, flour or rice combined with a liquid (stock, milk, water, butter), used to thicken soups and sauces and bind stuffings and meatballs. The mixture is heated until the paste leaves the side of the pan, then cooled, before being added to the dish. A bread panada is made from butter, milk, fresh breadcrumbs and salt. A flour panada is made from butter, water, flour and salt. It resembles choux pastry when cooked, and can be smeared with a knob of butter to prevent a skin from forming as it cools. A frangipane panada contains flour, milk and egg yolks.

PAN BROIL To cook in a non-stick or ribbed pan on the stove top with little or preferably no oil and no lid. Any fats that may build up during cooking are drained as the food cooks. The idea is for the meat or vegetable to cook quickly over a high heat, so food to be pan broiled is cut thinner or smaller than usual to help it cook fast.

PANCH PHORA see BENGALI FIVE SPICE

PANDANUS LEAF is a long, dark-green, tough, blade-like leaf important as a flavouring and colouring in Thai and Malaysian cuisine. It is used in both savoury and sweet dishes. A piece of pandan leaf added to rice after the heat source has been turned off imparts a very subtle, jasmine-like aroma, and two or three leaves can be simmered in a curry. The leaves can be pounded or blended with a little water to release the colour and flavour. They are then used in cakes and desserts, and added to impart their mild scent to poaching water and desserts that are cooked or warmed and then cooled. Like vanilla pods, the flavour is extracted when heated, then the leaf is removed before serving. Available fresh, frozen and dried in Asian grocers, in bunches or packs of 6–8 leaves. If the fresh is unavailable, head to the freezer. I find the frozen product as good as the fresh for many recipes. Dried pandan leaves lack colour and flavour and are not recommended. Also known as **pandan leaf, screw-pine leaf** and **daun pandan**.

PAN FRY also known as sauté. To cook in oil or fat in a pan on the stove top with no lid.

PAN SEAR Refers to searing or browning meat (often steak, meat or fish) in a pan before finishing it in the oven.

PAPAYA comes in two main varieties: the Hawaiian solo papaya and the Mexican papaya. The smaller, sweeter, pink-fleshed Hawaiian papaya is used in salads or for dessert. The Mexican papaya is large, round and less sweet, often reserved for savoury dishes. Try sprinkling a few of the peppery, edible black seeds into a salad or as a garnish. The juice of the green (unripe) papaya can be rubbed into meat or octopus as a tenderiser, and its flesh is often shredded or sliced wafer thin and used in Asian salads or cooked as a vegetable. Although the name is sometimes interchanged with PAWPAW, the two are actually different fruit.

PAPRIKA generally refers to the ground spice, although some countries use this term to describe capsicum and chilli. Paprika is the dried and ground outer flesh (mesocarp) of different types of chilli plant. The various types of paprika are determined by when the plant is harvested. Mild, sweet paprika is made from a very mild chilli, with few of the veins, seeds and placenta of the chilli included. These parts of the chilli, left over from sweet paprika, are used to make hot paprika, which in some cases can be as hot as cayenne pepper and used in a similar fashion.

The flavour of smoked paprika, also known as hot smoked paprika and available sweet, bitter or hot, derives from being exposed to woodsmoke as it is being dried. Paprika powder is high in sugar and can therefore burn or caramelise very quickly; be aware of this when frying in oil. Paprika is an and an exceptional spice for sauces, meats and seafood. The very best paprika comes form the Balkan countries.

PAR-BAKE refers to breads and occasionally biscuits that have been PROVEN, then partly baked (to hold the shape) then frozen so the home cook can finish the baking. Different levels of par-baked bread are available. Some are frozen immediately after the proving stage, allowing the home or commercial cook to do all the baking. Others are 90% baked and sold at room temperature so that they only require 5 minutes of final baking time at home. Par-baking is also used in reference to spare ribs that are partly cooked before being finished on the grill.

PARBOIL see BLANCH

PARISIAN ESSENCE or BURNT CARAMEL is an almost flavourless, rich-brown concentrate used mostly as a gravy browning agent. It can also be used to enhance the rich appearance of a Christmas cake or in microwave cooking where the sugars won't brown. Known as **blackjack** on the professional circuit.

PARSLEY The two main varieties of this herb are prepared quite differently.

Curly parsley can be chopped ferociously, this way and that, and still present well. (The old method of wrapping the finely chopped parsley in a towel, washing it and then squeezing out whatever flavour and chlorophyll was left in it, ready to sprinkle over every dish on the menu, must surely be vanquished.)

Flat-leaf parsley (also *Italian parsley* or **continental parsley**) should be torn by hand or run through with the blade of a knife once or twice only – a chiffonade of leaf, if you will. Any attacks on this type of parsley would bruise and damage the leaf. Flat-leaf parsley has more flavour and less bitterness than curly parsley.

A third common variety is **celery-leaf parsley**: this is often tagged Italian parsley but is in fact a different breed altogether, and has a much tougher texture and stronger flavour.

PARSLEY ROOT, also known as **turnip-rooted parsley and Hamburg parsley** (although the Germans call it **Dutch parsley** – seems nobody wants to own up to its origin), is a subspecies grown for its beige root, which tastes like a parsley–CELERIAC cross. It's used in parts of Europe in soups, stews and simply as a vegetable. Choose firm roots with feathery, bright-green leaves. Store refrigerated in a plastic bag for up to a week.

PASSIONFRUIT has three common varieties: the small purple **granadilla**; the larger, elongated **Panama passionfruit** (also purple) and the **banana passionfruit**. The granadilla is ripe when its skin begins to wrinkle (a smooth-skinned granadilla will be quite acidic so allow to sit at room temperature for a few days to mature), while the Panama is smooth-skinned when ripe. The banana passionfruit is not readily available as it is not seen as a commercially viable crop. It lacks the rich flavour of ordinary passionfruit, but can be used in the same manner. Buy passionfruit that are heavy for their size. The best tool for cutting them is a knife with a serrated edge. If you're fortunate enough to have an abundance of fruit, you can freeze it for up to 6 months – either scoop the pulp from the shells or simply freeze the fruit whole.

PASTA is often made with durum wheat (semolina) flour (see FLOUR) because of its high protein content (15%, too high for successful bread-making). The protein forms strong gluten strands which help the dough retain elasticity when it is extruded through the pasta machines. Pasta made with soft wheat flour is usually mixed with eggs to reinforce the dough, which is not necessary with the strong durum flour. However, eggs can be added to any flour for a richer pasta (pasta all'uovo). Experiment with hen's or duck's eggs. Starting with 1 egg for every 200g flour.
Some brands of dried pasta (pasta asciutta) can be just as good as fresh pasta (pasta fresca). Dried pasta has a shelf life of up to two years. Fresh pasta is best used immediately or stored in an airtight

500g (1 lb) of dried pasta will give the same cooked volume as 750 g (1½ lb) fresh.
The size of a single serve varies, of course, but a good starting point is 75g-100 g of dried or 150 g of fresh per person.

container in the fridge for up to five days. It may also be stored in a cupboard for up to a month but obviously will dry in that time.

 Top tips for cooking pasta
~ The most important thing is plenty of boiling, salted water: 1 litre plus a very generous pinch of salt for every serve (100 g) of pasta. Salt is important, as it brings out the flavour of the pasta. (Obviously you'll make your own judgement if you are trying to reduce your salt intake.)
~ Fresh pasta should be ready in 2–3 minutes, gnocchi are ready when they rise to the top, and dried pasta is ready in 5–12

minutes, depending on the type (follow the instructions on the packet). I suggest to undercook the pasta slightly and then finish cooking it in the sauce.

~ Adding oil to pasta water is absolutely not necessary. With the exception of fresh lasagne sheets, pasta does not benefit from the addition of oil. The real secret to stopping it sticking together is to stir the pasta for the first two minutes after adding it to the pot. Move the pasta around the pot with a wooden spoon, as this allows the water to cook the outer part of the pasta, making it slippery, not a starchy glue.

~ Once it is cooked, drain the pasta, setting some of the cooking water aside as this can be used to thin pasta sauces if stock is not available.

~ Never rinse it in water after draining as this washes away the natural sticky starches that help the sauce stick.

~ If you are keeping the pasta for later use, toss it in olive or vegetable oil after draining, then spread thinly on trays, allowing the pasta to cool quickly. To reheat, either drop it in boiling water for 10–15 seconds or microwave, covered for 30 seconds.

Problem solving

~ **Pasta stuck together?** Cooked pasta that is really stuck together is best kept for a baked pasta dish. Cool the stuck pasta, then mix with sauce, vegetables or tinned tuna and cheese, and place in a hot oven for 30 minutes.

PASTEURISE A heat treatment used in some countries to kill off harmful bacteria in dairy products and some alcoholic drinks (beer, wine, cider). It extends the life of milk, purportedly without affecting its taste and nutrient value. Purists and admirers of raw milk cheese argue that, although this process may kill bad bacteria, it also kills good bacteria and changes the molecular make-up and therefore the taste of the milk and what is made from it. (I should know, I lived on a farm, and on winter mornings would squirt warm cows milk directly into my mouth. As for bacteria, it's hard to say if any of us became sick after I defrosted my hands in the bucket of very warm milk before I brought the pail back to the house.)

PASTRY Store bought pastry, although handy, will never match the quality of fresh home-made pastry: mass-produced commercial pastry is made in bulk using a rolling machine and inferior fats, and pastry made at home with butter and in small batches will always be tastier, not to mention an incredible sense of achievement.

✅ Top tips for pastry

~ Always chill raw pastry for 30 minutes before rolling it, then for another 20–30 minutes before putting it in the oven. This allows the gluten in the flour to relax, preventing unnecessary shrinkage while baking.

~ Pastry rolled out on marble is significantly better than other surfaces due to the marble's capacity to absorb heat. This keeps the butter or fats within the pastry cool and workable. ~ Brush a little water around the top edge of the pie base before covering with the pastry lid. This helps strengthen the seal when the two are crimped together.

~ Once the dough or pastry has been moulded into the tin or dish, allow it to rest in the fridge for at least 20 minutes before baking.

~ For a glossy pie crust, brush with egg white before baking. Puff pastry, whether bought or home-made, should be glazed carefully before baking for the best presentation.

~ Splashing milk or egg wash over the outer cut edges of the pastry will act as a glue and retard the rising of the pastry when baked.

~ Get into the habit of placing a tray or large baking dish in the oven under the pie to catch spillage.

~ Transferring pastry from the bench to the tart or pie ring can be the cause of much frustration. Work quickly and confidently. The longer you work it, the warmer it gets, becoming soft and unmanageable. This is especially true of short or sweet pastries.

Here are two methods:

1. Roll out the dough between layers of plastic wrap. Ensure the plastic wrap is wide enough that the pastry won't spill out the sides.Work quickly. Then remove the top layer of plastic, pick up the bottom piece with the pastry stuck to it and transfer to the pie dish.

2. Roll out the dough on a bench, dust lightly with flour, fold into quarters, transfer to the dish with the point of the fold in the centre of the dish, then simply unfold.

Blind baking pastry is the technique of partially cooking the pastry case before the filling is put in it. This ensures that the pastry is cooked through and that it is crisp so it doesn't get soggy when the filling is added.

(It is particularly useful for wet fillings.) To prevent steam building under the pastry, causing it to bubble upwards, the uncooked pastry is weighed down in the dish or pricked all over before baking. To blind bake, cover the pastry with a sheet of greaseproof paper, then scatter rice, dried beans or pie weights on top. Cook for 10–12 minutes. Alternatively, you could freeze the prepared flan for 15–20 minutes before baking. If any bubbles appear while the pastry is baking, pop them with the tip of the knife.

Docking pastry means placing small holes around the dough with a pastry docker or a fork. This helps prevent the dough from bulging while it is baking. The downside is that it leaves these small holes in the cooked pastry.

A **pie funnel** is a hollow funnel, usually about 3 inches tall, that is placed in the centre of the pie before cooking. It aids heat distribution, supports the top pastry crust and allows liquids to reduce, thus enhancing flavour and helping avoid soggy pastry. It is also known as a pie bird, as many are made to resemble blackbirds, and other shapes like elephants, chefs and songbirds are common. I've also seen 'tweety bird' and 'naked women' pie birds.

to avoid soggy pastry in a tart case, remove it from the oven after blind baking, take out the paper lining filled with beans or rice, then, while still hot, brush with a beaten egg and return to the oven for the prescribed time, usually another 10 minutes. The egg will cook, forming a glaze or impervious layer, ready for the filling. Alternatively, you could brush a thin layer of melted chocolate inside the case when it is cold. Allow the chocolate to set before filling.

~ **Soggy lid?** Use a pie funnel. If you don't have one, try putting a piece of dried pasta such as rigatoni or large macaroni into the centre of the pie. This will act as a chimney, allowing excess heat and steam to escape.

~ **Shrunk pastry?** Pastry shrinks during baking because of high water content in the dough. As the water evaporates, the dough loses volume. So try using less water next time. If the dough was made without water yet still shrinks, chances are the pastry was stretched and forced into the dish, or that you didn't rest it in the fridge before baking.

PAWPAW is not in fact related to PAPAYA, although it is used as an alternative name for papaya in Australia and Africa. It is a fruit of the CHERIMOYA family, which includes CUSTARD APPLES. Surrounded by a smooth yellow skin, the meat of this elongated, curved fruit is sweet, creamy, soft, yellow and fragrant, reminiscent of bananas and pears, hence the nickname **poor man's banana.**
It is often eaten fresh, but can also be used in desserts.

PEANUT Not really a nut but a LEGUME, peanuts are also known as **groundnuts** because of their unusual pod development. After the flowers are fertilised, they wither to the ground and bury themselves where the pods mature subterraneously. They are usually harvested by uprooting the whole plant to dry the nuts. Another common name for peanuts in parts of the US is **goober pea**, which comes straight from the African name 'nguba'.

PEARS although there are over 3000 varieties of pears worldwide, they can be divided into two groups:
    European pears, also known as **Winter pears** often need more time to ripen. They are very good for cooking and as wll as eating out of hand for their crunchy, tart texture and taste even when fully mature. The European pears are one of the few fruits that are best when ripened off the tree and at room temperature (preferably next to some apples).
    Asian pears, native to Japan and China, are ready-to-eat, straight from harvest. They are crunchy pears that require no ripening time and are best eaten as they are or in salads, although they can be cooked. There are three groups of Asian pears, including **20th century, Nashi** and **Ya Li**.

Q Problem solving
~ Parts of the pastry colouring too quickly? Remove from the oven and cover the 'burning' pastry with a strip of foil.

PECTIN is found in the skins of fruit, and forms a jelly when combined with sugar and acid, so acts as a setting agent in fruit jams and jellies.

BEST USE FOR DIFFERENT VARIETIES OF PEAR
The following varieties of winter pear are divided into those that are best fresh and those that are best used for cooking.
Fresh: Bartlett (also known as Williams'), d'Anjou, Comice, Seckel, Packham, Corella, Conference
Cooking: St Germain, Kieffer, Catillac, Conference, Winter Nelis
Bosc pears (also known as Beurre Bosc or Kaiser Alexander) can be good either fresh or cooked

---

Fruit high in pectin include citrus, apples, grapes, plums and quinces, although pectin levels can also depend on how fresh and/or ripe the particular fruit is. If fruit is low in pectin, additional pectin, available as a powder and a liquid, can be added. Powdered pectin should be discarded if it's caked together or browned. Liquid pectin, if stored in the fridge, should be left out for 1 hour before use. If the liquid is too runny, or is set and won't syrup down, then it should be discarded. Powdered and liquid pectin cannot be interchanged in recipes.

PEPINELLA see CHOKO

PEPINO, also known as tree melon, is an oblong fruit with a purple-striped yellow/golden skin and a melon-like flavour. Flesh and skin vary in colour
depending on the variety. If the fruit has a soapy aftertaste, it is of a poor cultivar. When ripe, pepino should give slightly to pressure.

PEPITAS see PUMPKIN SEEDS

PEPPER, no matter what its colour, begins life as the unripe, green peppercorn.
　　Black pepper is the most aromatic pepper, produced by picking the clusters of berries when not quite ripe, then leaving them in piles to ferment. After a few days, the individual berries are spread out and left to dry in the sun for two or three more days or until they

are shrivelled and nearly black. Black pepper from India is regarded as the best, especially the Malabar and Tellicherry varieties. One of the hottest black peppers is from Lampong province in Sumatra and it too is highly regarded.

White pepper is the most pungent of the peppers, but the least aromatic. It is produced from the fully ripened berries that are just about to turn red. After harvest, the clusters are packed in bags and soaked in water for more than a week. This softens the outer coating, or pericarp, so that it may be removed to reveal the grey centres. The peppercorns are then spread out to dry in the sun where they naturally bleach to white.

Green peppercorns are harvested while still immature and cured in brine. They can be used in curry pastes (soak in cold water for 30 minutes then pound into the paste), or added whole (first rinse in cold water) to cream sauces or stews, and to pâtés, terrines and dressings, for a musky, peppery bite with far less pungency than black or white.

Tasmanian pepper, also known as **mountain pepper** and **native pepper**, is native to Australia and hard to source from outside the country. It resembles black pepper in size and appearance, but there is no substitute for this flavour. Tasmanian pepper has gained popularity through the 'indigenous food' movement in Australia. See also PINK PEPPERCORNS.

PERILLA see SHISO

PERSIAN FAIRY FLOSS is a spun sugar made from sesame oil and sugar. Eating it is like eating melting fibreglass, and it is much coarser than the fairy floss sold at school fairs. Flavours include pistachio, chocolate, vanilla and saffron. This is my favourite end to a meal: it looks amazing and tastes great. Persian fairy floss needs to be kept in an airtight container to avoid moisture breaking down the sugar. Available at some, not all, Middle Eastern grocers. Also available in some large chain supermarkets.

PERSIMMON has two common varieties. The paler, orange, tomato-shaped **Fuyu** can be eaten while still a little bit firm, while the oblong, red-orange **Hachiya** should be completely soft, almost squishy, before consumption (if it's not, be prepared to pucker up). Once at the squishy stage and bold orange in colour, the Hachiya is beautifully sweet and can be scooped straight out of the skin. The Fuyu is better suited to slicing into segments or dicing and using in chutney or in salads. Except for the seeds and the calyx (stem leaves), the rest of the fruit is edible.

PICKLING SPICE is a mixture of herbs and spices used to season pickles, onions or other vegetables. It often includes dill weed and/or seed, coriander seed, cinnamon stick, peppercorns and bay leaves.

PIE see PASTRY

PIMENTO is sometimes used to refer to ALLSPICE (from the Spanish word for peppercorn, which allspice resembles), but probably more often refers to a particular variety of red CAPSICUM.

PINEAPPLE For the sweetest pineapples, ask for hybrid varieties by the name of Bethonga Gold (Australia), Golden Supreme (US), Kona Sugarloaf (US), prickly leafed roughie pineapple (Australia), or the small Queen Victoria pineapple of South Africa. These varieties have as much as four times more vitamin C than the common Cayenne variety. They also have a very short season, so ask your local fruit supplier when they are due in. When buying a pineapple, check for ripeness by removing a leaf from the very centre of the dislodges with little resistance the pineapple is ready, but if after a bit of effort the leaf remains intact, the pineapple is still quite green. The juice tends to accumulate at the base of a pineapple, so the night before you want to eat it, cut the top off then turn it upside-down onto a plate and place in the refrigerator. When you turn it over the sweet juice will have distributed throughout the entire pineapple. Like kiwifruit, pineapple makes an excellent meat tenderiser as it contains the enzyme bromelin.

PINEAPPLE GUAVA see FEIJOA

PINK PEPPERCORNS are not actually peppercorns but berries. They are sweet and aromatic and make a good (although less fragrant) alternative to JUNIPER BERRIES. Sold either dried or in brine, they are used in sauces, with fish or poultry, or ground to use as a final dusting for garnish. Freeze-dried pink peppercorns are often sold mixed with black and white peppercorns for people to use in clear grinders – the purpose is more display than flavour. They should be used in moderation, as large quantities have been said to cause respiratory ailments or irritation of mucous membranes.

PITAYA / PITAHAYA see DRAGONFRUIT

PLANTAIN see BANANA

POACH The delicate process of cooking food in a liquid set below simmering point (approx 75–80°C). The liquid (water, stock, sugar syrup, alcohol) should never come to the boil. The idea is to preserve the natural shape of the food and retain a delicate flavour. The foods most commonly poached are eggs, fish, meat, poultry and fruit.

POÊLÉ A method of slow-cooking meat or vegetables in butter in a covered pan in the oven at a temperature hot enough to braise the food, yet not so hot as to colour the butter solids. Sometimes wrongly referred to as 'butter roasting', POT ROASTING or **white braising** (see BRAISING).

POLENTA see CORN

POMEGRANATE Also known as **Chinese apple**.
is a labour-intensive fruit that needs love and understanding. The hard, leathery skin encases stunning, ruby-red, pulp-coated seeds, which are held in place by a bitter, cream-coloured membrane – here's where the work begins. To choose ripe fruit, tap it gently and listen for a somewhat metallic sound. Cut the pomegranate in half then pry out the pulp-encased seeds, removing any of the bitter membrane still attached. The seeds can be eaten then and there, added to fruit salad, sprinkled over salads or used in other savoury dishes. To make juice, take half a pomegranate and press it into a bowl, squashing out the juices, or warm it slightly, roll and press gently on the bench top (as you would a lemon), then cut a hole in the stem

and place over a glass, squeezing now and then to extract more juice. Pomegranate is also made into the syrup known as grenadine and into a POMEGRANATE MOLASSES. Pomegranates store well in the fridge for some time, getting better with age.

POMEGRANATE MOLASSES, also known as **pomegranate syrup**, is a Middle Eastern bottled condiment made from yellow, sour pomegranates cooked with sugar. It is used to give a fruity tang to savoury dishes and sauces. Pomegranate molasses is as thick as sugar molasses, but with a reddish-brown hue. The best brands are dark-brown, tart and fruity, while lesser quality brands tend to be quite sweet, purple in colour and resemble a thick grenadine syrup.

POMELO was once described to me as the doofus big brother of the grapefruit. It has an extremely thick layer of pith, but after spending a year or two fighting your way through that, you will find a pulp that resembles grapefruit except that it is less acidic and sweeter, so worth the battle. Also known as **Chinese grapefruit**.

POOR MAN'S BANANA see PAWPAW

POPPY SEEDS have a very short shelf life - we are talking weeks before degradation sets in and the pungency that once was is no more. Buy in small quantities and always check the date on the packaging. Poppy seeds can be black, brown, beige or white. The best are from Holland and they have a blueish tinge. **White poppy seeds** are used in chutney as well as lightly crushed and used to thicken sauces and curries. Roasting them also brings out the nuttiness from the oils. Being harvested from the flower of the opium poppy, poppy seeds can produce a positive result in a drug test. It has been reported that people with a love of bagels or cakes with poppy seeds have lost their jobs because of a positive reading to a morphine test, only to be reinstated some time later . . . this is not urban myth.

PORK is often associated in Western countries with a roast and the crackling that accompanies it. Yet there is so much more on offer, from the lean fillets to the very tasty neck. Pork is the most important meat in Chinese cuisine, and in fact is the most consumed meat in the world (it makes up 44% of the world's consumption compared to 28% beef and 24% chicken).

Roast pork is ready when the juices run clear after being speared with a skewer. Overcooked pork meat is, in general, dry and tough and needs a bucket of moist apple sauce to compensate. People tend to overcook it for fear of the disease trichinosis which is caused by a parasite. However, trichinosis is in fact associated with raw pork products and wild game, and has never been reported in Australia. It's important to follow correct food handling and storage methods, but there's no need to cook pork until it becomes a leather substitute.

HOW TO MAKE PORK CRACKLING

Prepare the skin (off the joint) with olive oil and salt, place directly on the oven's wire rack (with a catchment tray underneath) at 210°C for 20 minutes, then turn the temperature down to 180°C and cook until crisp. At the point when you turn down the temperature, place the pork roast in the oven in the catchment tray, underneath the crackling, so the crackling bastes the meat below. If the crackling is ready ahead of the meat, set it aside on paper towelling until needed – it will not lose any crunchiness. In fact, it is better if the crackling is ready beforehand so the oven can be turned down even further (160–70°C) allowing the pork to cook at a gentle rate, resulting in tender, juicy meat.

Crackling or pork rind: there never seems to be enough of the stuff. I admit to once standing over a spit roast with a large joint of pork rotating in front of me, and with one other's help successfully eating the entire provision of crisp, bubbled rind in a very short period of time. Funny thing, karma – I broke a tooth, such were my gluttonous ways. I suggest you ask for an extra slab of pork rind, fat intact, when you buy your roasting joint.(The fat that runs along the back of the pig, just under the skin is also called fatback or speck and, when rendered, becomes LARD.) You can remove the skin from the joint to maximise the yield of crackling, remembering that roasting the crackling (rind/skin) off the meat can mean major shrinkage because the skin will no longer protect the tender white meat from drying out too much. So here's what you do:If you're desperate for crackling and can't manage the above, try buying a packet of pork scratchings.

POTATO New and old, waxy or floury: so many styles and varieties, cooking with potatoes can be a laboratory full of experiments. Selecting the best potatoes for boiling, frying, mashing, roasting, salads, gratins, baking, steaming, sautés or even for gnocchi can be a trial-and-error journey. In general, waxy are good for salads, steaming and boiling and do not take well to mashing, roasting and baking. Floury potatoes are better suited to dry baking, roasting, mash and chips. They can be used like waxy if they are not overcooked, as they will dry and crumble.

BEST USE FOR DIFFERENT VARIETIES OF POTATO

Baking (dry): King Edward (the best), Bintje, Pontiac, Crystal, Sebago, Delaware, Kennebec, Wilwash
Frying: Idaho (Russet Burbank, the best), Kennebec, Maris Piper, Cystal, Sputna, Delaware
Gnocchi: Desiree (the best), Toolangi Delight, Purple Congo (although the colour may be too much for some)
Mashing: Sebago (the best), Pontiac, Toolangi Delight, Desiree, Spunta, Bison, Kennebec
Roasting: Desiree (the best), Spunta, Crystal, Delaware, Idaho (Russet Burbank), Kennebec, Pontiac, Bison
Salad: Choose the waxy variety, whose starches settle and hold firm after cooking (take care not to overcook them and allow to cool thoroughly before use) Kipfler (the best), Ratte, Pink fir, Pink eye, (Southern Gold), Bintje, Wilwash, Wilja, Coliban, Pontiac, Nicola, Patrone

For fluffy mashed potato, heat the milk or cream before adding it with a touch of butter to the mashed potatoes. Potatoes can also be mashed with a good extra virgin olive oil or a non-dairy dip instead of milk, cream or butter.

Sweet potato comes in differing shapes, colours and sizes. Due to the texture of all sweet potatoes, they are best roasted or baked whole in their skins or wrapped in foil with butter/oil and seasonings, or sliced and grilled. They shouldn't be boiled as, like pumpkin, they lose too much texture, volume and, more importantly, flavour. Sweet potato can be white- or orange-fleshed with orange, white, brown or purple skins. The orange-fleshed, brown-skinned sweet potato is known as a yam in the US, where sweet potato refers only to the white-fleshed variety. (The true yam is called a tropical yam in the US.) Boniato is a type of sweet potato favoured for its fluffier texture once cooked, but lacking the sweetness and flavour of regular sweet potato. **Kumara** is a cultivar of sweet potato popular in New Zealand and the Pacific region.

POT ROAST is a similar method to BRAISE, only it is used for larger joints or cuts of meat. The meat (e.g. beef topside, oyster blade or fresh silverside in a 1.5–2 kg piece) is cooked in a deep, covered pot with very little or no liquid. The meat is first seared or browned in a little butter or oil, then placed on a bed of browned root vegetables, or bones and vegetables. The pot is tightly covered and the meat cooked gently. A pot roast may be cooked in a pot, a pressure cooker or in the oven. The small amount of liquid and the vegetables together produce sufficient steam to make this moist heat method ideal for the medium-tender roasting cuts.

POULTRY refers to domesticated or game birds, but most often chicken. (See entries for DUCK, GAME, GOOSE and TURKEY for specific information on those birds but note that much of the information here is relevant to them too.) If there is one thing that passionate cooks despise, it is the declining quality of most chicken meat available to the general public. Meat from poorly reared birds lacks flavour and texture and can be more susceptible to harmful bacteria. Of course, mass-produced chicken is cheaper so it's up to the individual to balance the pros and cons of cost, differences in flavour and texture, and the risk of bacteria, such as E. coli, salmonella and Campylobacter. All poultry is highly susceptible to the growth of harmful (and not so harmful) bacteria, from the moment it is killed to the time you ingest it. There is not much you can do about the first phases of meat production, but once at home you can reduce contamination through proper storage and cooking.   All poultry should be kept refrigerated at 0–4°C and used within two days. If frozen, whole or in pieces, the meat must be kept cold while defrosting. When freezing pieces of chicken, separate each piece with plastic wrap or baking paper. This way if only one piece is needed it can be removed easily without having to defrost a whole lump of chicken. Also, freeze as flat as possible, (not pushed into a ball at the back of the freezer) before piling into one bag. This will ensure that the meat freezes quickly, halting bacteria growth, but also that it defrosts evenly. Never defrost poultry by leaving it out at roomtemperature. Leave it in the fridge for a day or two until it is completely thawed before cooking.

HOW TO COOK POULTRY

Poultry meat can be broken into three categories: **red meat**, **white meat** and **giblet**s, each of which is treated differently when cooked.

The **'red' meat** is the working muscles of the bird, the legs and wings, which produce a tough, fibrous, dark meat better suited to long, slow cooking (although nothing like the cooking times required for tough red meat from beef or lamb). Having said that, leg meat with sinew and gristle removed is tender enough to stir-fry, sauté, barbecue or bake to shred for sandwiches. The red meat is considered to have more flavour than the white meat – the source of many arguments over the drumstick of a roasted bird.

The **'white' meat** is the breast of the bird. In chicken and turkey it is white and delicate; it must be cooked through, but overcooking will render it dry and tough. The 'white' meat of game bird isn't really considered white meat at all and can be treated like a beef steak, in that it is best served rare to medium rare. (Asking for the breast of game to be cooked well done in a restaurant is frowned upon as much as a well-done steak.)

Giblets are the heart, liver and gizzards of poultry. Often sautéed, grilled, fried or used to make gravy, they can also be steamed or simmered and then ground into a stuffing.

When chicken and turkey – whole or as pieces – are cooked perfectly, the juices will run clear rather than cloudy-white or pink.As chicken and turkey are soft proteins, they prefer gentle rather than fierce cooking methods. This allows the proteins to set rather than having them contract too fast and force out valuable juices.

Skin off versus skin on? The skin tends to be the fattiest part of poultry so does little for the waistline, which is why it is often recommended to buy chicken breast skin-off. On the other hand, the skin is poultry's built-in baste mechanism. So, although it takes a little more self-control, I recommend that you buy chicken breast and cook it with the skin on, letting the fat from the skin render, basting the lean white meat beneath, then remove the skin before eating the succulent meat. (This method doesn't work with poaching and steaming.)

COOKING A WHOLE BIRD

Preparation: Remove any bits and fat left inside the carcass. Rinse in cold running water and then pat dry, inside and out, with a lint-free towel (paper towels, especially cheap ones, can leave paper fibres on the meat). If stuffing the cavity, remember not to pack it in too tight because the mixture will expand as it cooks.

Cooking times: When roasting whole birds, the breast will cook faster than the legs. (If you want to avoid this, try packing a stuffing between the breast skin and breast or cutting 2–3 lines into the leg muscles to allow heat to penetrate.) And a stuffed bird will take a little longer than one without stuffing because it takes longer for the heat to penetrate to the centre. Allow two minutes resting time per kilogram before you carve the beast, and remove the wishbone for easy carving. (Hang the wishbone out to dry for the kids to fight over – the smart child will have figured out that whoever keeps their little finger above their opponent's will always win.)

Battery hen is a term for a practice that will one day end. This barbaric method of supplying eggs to meet high demand is appalling, and you need only witness the conditions under which these eggs have been produced to change the way you eat. Once these chickens are deemed useless as productive layers (their lifespan is no more than 18 months), they are transported, bruised and broken-boned, to a slaughterhouse, where their calcium-deficient, toxin-infused, pathetic excuse for a carcass is transformed into food such as pies, loaves, soups, pet food and other chicken by-products that conceal the true state of the battery chicken's flesh and miserable lives. That's why you should buy only certified free-range eggs – and here endeth the lesson.

Boiler hen (or **stewing hen** in the US) is a tough-fleshed hen reserved for stocks, pies, broth and – if desperate – picked over for chicken salad or sandwiches. Not for roasting. The hen needs to be cooked or boiled for several hours. The flavour of boiler chicken is strong and the flesh firm, making for an ideal stock.

Broiler hen is a US term for a meat-producing hen (as opposed to an egg-producing one). A broiler's genetic make-up means it is inappropriate as an egg layer. The broiler is slaughtered at about 6–7 weeks. Also marketed as fryers.

Capon is a surgically neutered rooster, slaughtered at 10–12 weeks. It has a heavier carcass than ordinary chicken, yielding lighter, generous amounts of white flesh and is sold particularly for roasting.

Cockscomb is the often red, fleshy excrescence found on the head of roosters and other poultry. Traditionally served in France as a garnish or a small entree. Not likely to make a comeback because of their scarcity apart from anything else – you'll have more fun with a bag of parson's nose.

Corn-fed chicken is a label that is occasionally abused. In many cases it has been shown that no more than 50% of the hens' feed has included corn or maize during the fattening stage. The best corn-fed chickens are also free-range, fed on a diet of corn and corn gluten meal (70%) and soybean meal (15–20%) with the remainder made up of salts, vitamins and minerals. The resulting chicken is plump, meaty and has a yellow tinge, not just on the skin, but also to the flesh. This yellow pigmentation is derived from the natural yellow colouring in corn called xanthophyll.

Free-range chicken is a marketing term that should be broken into two groups for the consumer. For a chicken to be free-range, at least half its life must be spent outside. 'Traditional free-range' requires greater access to outside living, fewer chickens in the space and a higher minimum age at slaughter. Then there is 'free-range total freedom': similar to traditional but with no restrictions to daytime open-air living. Be rightfully suspicious of labels such as 'farm fresh' and 'country fresh'; these do not guarantee free-range conditions.

Grain-fed chicken is fed on a blend of wheat, corn and sometimes barley, which makes up about 70% of its feed. The other

30% is made up of mainly protein such as soybean or occasionally canola or fish meal, as well as vitamins and minerals.

Male chickens refers to the thousands of millions of those cute, fluffy new chickens that were unfortunate enough to be hatched at a commercial egg farm. No sentiment is wasted on these 'useless' animals which are either ground up while still alive for fertiliser, gassed or suffocated in bags or containers. This information may have little to do with your cooking, but it will give
you something to mull over next time you order sunny-side-up.

Poussin is a chicken that is slaughtered at 21–28 days old. These young chickens are usually reserved for grilling or roasting and can be served as an individual portion.

Spatchcock is another word for poussin that can also describe a method in which it is cooked – butterflied and grilled – which is both quick and easy.old.(After that she becomes known as a hen.)

Young roaster a US term for a broiler-style chicken, generally older and heavier than a broiler, slaughtered at around 10 weeks.

POUSSIN see POULTRY

PRAWN is usually known as **shrimp** in the US (although sometimes 'prawn' there can be used to denote large, extra-large and jumbo prawns), but elsewhere 'shrimp' refers to very small peeled prawns, as in the classic retro dish, shrimp cocktail – usually frozen or in brine or those labelled for the US export market. Sometimes called jumbo shrimp or shrimp scampi in the US. (See SCAMPI for more cryptic crustaceans.) The many species of prawns available worldwide ensure varied flavours, but wherever you are, the methods for buying and handling prawns is the same.

Uncooked prawns are green-grey and can be purchased with the shell on or as cutlets (shell off). I advise you to buy whole green prawns and boil them at home, but if you do buy precooked, they should be plump and bright orange, with no signs of having been defrosted. (Frozen cooked prawns can be watery, rubbery or flavourless when defrosted).

Preparing and de-veining prawns: Most recipes suggest de-veining prawns (removing their digestive sac, also known as sand vein) either before or after cooking, as it is too unsightly or gritty for many people. However, it is edible, and others don't mind it. Occasionally a batch of prawns can have a very clean vein, and usually the veins of small prawns or shrimp are too small to be removed and contain little if any digestive matter. Sometimes a mass of green, beige or orange goop covers the digestive sac from head to tail, mostly at the head end. This is the prawn ovary, the different colours representing the different stages of the ovary, which turns orange or cream once cooked. (But now you know what it is, will you ever eat it again?) While prawns can be peeled and de-veined either before or after cooking, the former is probably better if they are to be served whole, the latter if they are to be presented in a salad.

HOW TO DE-VEIN WHOLE GREEN PRAWNS

Use a skewer or even a toothpick to pierce the meat at the top of the head end, just below where the vein runs. Gently lift and jiggle the skewer, and as you lift the vein should begin to release itself from the body of meat.

OR

Run a small knife blade along the back of the prawn, enough to pierce the flesh and scrape out the vein. This method is great if the prawns are to be butterflied for quick cooking and presentation.

HOW TO COOK WHOLE RAW PRAWNS

Bring seawater or salted water (1 litre water to 1/2 cup rock salt) to a vigorous boil, then add the prawns and cook until they curl and turn a bright orange. (Another sign they are cooked is when they float on the surface.) Lift out the prawns and drop into ice water. Do not reheat or recook precooked prawns.

325 g cooked prawns in the shell will yield 1 cup of prawn meat

PRICKLY PEAR is the flower or red fruit berry that grows on the cactus pad. The colour of the fruit may vary from white to yellowish-green to purplish-red. Prickly pear with a purple inside is the sweetest. The fruit is sold after having its nasty spikes removed, but be careful when buying as some spikes may be left. Hold it in a towel while peeling to avoid needle punctures. A ripe prickly pear fruit gives slightly when pressed and when fully ripe should be stored in the fridge for up to a week. It is customary in Italy to present the fruit in a bowl of cold water. Used in jams, sweets, syrups, baking and ices. Indian fig is sometimes used as an alternative name; in fact it is a close relative but not the same fruit. Cochineal are cultivated on the prickly pear family.

PULLET see POULTRY

PULSE see LEGUME

PUMPKIN in the US and UK refers to a type of sweet pumpkin reserved for making pumpkin pie or jack-o'-lanterns (these have a large seed cavity and pale orange flesh). Pumpkin in Australia and New Zealand refers to all hard-skinned SQUASH including the likes of butternut, Japola, golden nugget and Queensland blue. These and several other cultivars are all known as **winter squash** in the US or **squash** in the UK.

 Top tips for pumpkin

~ Pumpkin and squash can leave sticky residue on your hands while peeling and cutting, which once dried is hard to remove. Try wearing a latex glove on the hand not holding the knife.

~ When cutting pumpkin, always cut into it with a cut flat surface facing down. Trying to cut on the rounded edge is asking for a knife wound.

PUMPKIN SEEDS of all varieties of pumpkins and squash may be consumed raw, roasted and salted, toasted, baked, with or without their shell (shelled pumpkin seed kernels are called **pepitas** or **pumpkin seed meats**). Like all nuts and seeds, pumpkin seeds can turn rancid quickly and should be kept in an airtight container in the refrigerator or freezer where they will last for several months. For nutritional value, pumpkin seeds are best eaten raw, added to salads or chopped or ground then added to baked goods, soups, stews and dressings. Roasting them heightens the flavour but breaks down their essential fatty acids (see FAT). Pepitas make for a great snack, added to cereal and muesli, sprinkled over or in baked goods and used in soups, stews and dressings. desserts.

PURSLANE is an edible weed, classed as a succulent. Its leaves are thick and tender, with a faintly sour and peppery flavour. The stems are tinged with pink, so the plant is as decorative as it is piquant. Purslane is best eaten raw, or sautéed before use in soups and stews, as it can be slimy, with a texture like okra, when cooked. Alternatives to purslane are hard to find; some say it is similar to watercress or spinach, which is interesting because watercress and spinach don't taste like each other, so I'd suggest you disregard them. As a fresh leaf, the best you can hope for is lamb's tongue lettuce (see LEAFY GREENS), a very distant relative.

QUAHOG or **hard clam, hard shell clam, round clam** or **chowder clam** is a native to the east coast of America. If a recipe call for quahog, simply replace it with the local clam available to you.
QUAIL a small to medium sized bird bred for meat, eggs and hunting. Although nutritious and tasty, any young chef from any high end restaurant will recall the many hundreds of small birds they had to de-bone - whole - from the inside out.

QAIMAAQ see CREAM

QUARK or **quarg** is classified as a *set acid cheese*. Quark is traditional in the cuisines of Baltic, Germanic and Slavic-speaking countries. Commonly mistaken as a curd cheese, (like cottage cheese), the difference being quark is made from soured milk which has been fermented with a mesophile bacteria, and traditionally without rennet - although dairies in the modern era do use rennet. Quark eats like labna (strained yoghurt), although not quite as sour.

Used fresh or in baked dishes, sweet or savoury.

QUATRE ÉPICES (literally 'four spices') is a favourite spice in France, North Africa and the Middle East, made up of white pepper, ground nutmeg, ground ginger and ground cloves. It is used in French charcuterie, and Middle Eastern meat dishes.

QUINCE is best eaten cooked, as the astringent and sour flesh can be unpleasant when raw, should be a golden-yellow when ripe, with a patchy coating of brown down on the surface (wash this off before cooking). The perfume emanating from fresh picked quince resembles that of a jar of mixed boiled candies.

Quince undergoes an amazing metamorphosis once cooked. From a hard, sour fruit comes a deep-pink, sweet, soft one. Although depending on the cultivar, some will turn only barely pink, even a shade of yellow. Once peeled, cored and sliced or diced, quince can be placed in water to avoid browning of the flesh. Whole, the fruit can be kept refrigerated in a plastic bag for up to two months.

Quince is often prepared as jams, jellies, preserves and paste due to its high pectin content, but can also be made into chutney, quince butter, quince honey, vodka, even hand cream or simply baked. The pectin content is highest in early season quinces and slightly under-ripe fruit (starting to turn yellow with blotches of green still evident on the skin), and most of it is in the skin and pips (which is why many recipes tell you to cook the skin and pips in a muslin bag alongside the flesh).

QUINOA pronounced "keen-wa", is a seed harvested from a species of flowering plant in the "amaranth' family. Originating from the Andean region of South America, Quinoa is now harvested in over 70 countries worldwide. Marketed as a super food due to the fact it contains more dietary minerals than most other grains. Rich in protein, vitamin B and fibre. Quinoa is often simply boiled according to instructions on the pack. Which is fine. However, I suggest cooking it more like a pilaf, giving a perfect, fluffy result - according to the following quantities and method:

QUINOA PILAF

1 cup quinoa
1 ¾ cups water or stock

Pre-heat oven to 200C. Place the quinoa in a baking dish, place in the oven and cook (uncovered) for 8 minutes. Remove from oven, turn oven temperature down to 180C. Add one and three quarter cups (1 ¾ cups) water or stock to the quinoa. Cover with foil, place back in the oven for 20minutes. Remove from oven, uncover and stir with a fork. Set aside to cool completely.

The ratio is always the same. 1 part quinoa to 1 and ¾ parts liquid.

R.

RABBIT There is no greater deceit than lying about what you're feeding people, and discovering as a as a kid that the chicken I thought I was eating was in fact rabbit - was just not cool. Although I licked the plate clean, I admit I would not have touched it had I first been told what it was. Some 20 years later I marvel at the comeback and chic appeal of rabbit and hare on restaurant menus. European cooks never lost touch with rabbit and HARE, and have developed countless ways of preparing them.

Marinades are often used, with hare in particular, to improve the flavour, and braising and casserole cooking have long been favoured to retain juiciness. However, a saddle of young hare or rabbit, quickly roasted until well browned but still quite pink in the centre, can be one of the juiciest and most tender cuts of meat. Rabbit and hare are readily available at butcher's and specialty game and poultry shops. Rabbit are low in cholesterol, and they're still an economical meat. Rabbits usually weigh 800 g–1 kg. Farmed white rabbits, known as **New Zealand white rabbits**, are less widely available, as there are very few licensed farms.

Farmed rabbits weigh about 1.5–2 kg and the meat is whiter, more tender and slightly fattier. Due to disease and the release of a killer virus in 1997, wild rabbits are no longer available on the retail market in New Zealand. Incidentally, possum meat is similar in size and taste similar to rabbit and therefore rabbit recipes can be easily adapted.

RACREME see CREAM

RADICCHIO see LEAFY GREENS

RADISH is an edible root vegetable, often consumed raw in salads. Originating in Asia, there are four main types, based on seasons - Summer, Autumn (fall), winter and spring. Ranging in size, shape and colour. Grown not just for the bulbous root but also for seeds, sprouts, flowers and even oil, in the case of daikon.

RAISIN is simply a dried grape. The confusion lays in which country you are from. Commonwealth countries like Australia, New Zealand, Ireland and the UK etc applies the word raisin to a large dried grape and the word **sultana** to a smaller, differing varietal of grape.

In the US, raisin is a what pretty much the rest of the world call a sultana, While the smaller sultana in the US is referred to as a **golden raisin** or **raisin sultana**. These smaller grapes are usually treated with the preservative, sulphur dioxide, after drying.

Golden raisin in many other countries refers to a larger fruit, that is generally dried in dehydrators with controlled temperature and humidity, which allows them to retain a lighter colour and more moisture. They are often treated with sulphur dioxide after drying.

Currants are also a dried grape, smaller again and not at all related to the berry family *Ribes* which include blackcurrants and redcurrants.

RAISIN-TREE FRUIT is not really a fruit but a mature flower stalk. (The fruit – a brown pod – surrounds the stalk but is not edible.) The stem within the pod or the 'raisin' is edible, can be eaten fresh or used in any recipe that calls for dried raisins. You will rarely find raisin tree fruit on sale, so the only way to ensure a supply is to grow your own, in which case, tell your local nursery you want a Hovenia dulcis of the Rhamnaceae family. Also known as *Japanese raisin tree* and *kenpo nashi*.

RAMBUTAN This punk-looking, red or yellow, soft-spiked fruit is related to the LYCHEE, but less sweet and perfumed. Like the lychee, it has a translucent, jelly-like fruit or aril which clings to a smooth brown seed, a bit larger than an almond. To serve, slice around the skin, twist and separate. Best eaten fresh, out of hand.

RAPE is a green vegetable related to mustard and an ancient member of the BRASSICA family. The seedlings can be used in salads, and as it grows older, treat it as you would KALE or COLLARD. Rape has been genetically modified to create canola oil, but this is very different from rapeseed oil itself, made from a subspecies of rape. Rapeseed oil is poisonous and is used as a machinery lubricant, a fuel, in soap and as a synthetic rubber base as well as an illuminant for slick colour pages in magazines.

RAS EL HANOUT is a superbly fragrant and complex Moroccan spice blend. It roughly translates as 'top of the shelf' or 'head of the shop', which for a spice merchant represents the best blend of spices on offer. Although consisting of up to 15 different ingredients, it is subtle, and the addition of rose petals and lavender can impart a fantastic aroma, colour and underlying flavour. Like many of the spice blends, ras el hanout can be made with varied spice combinations and quantities, although often the spices are mixed in equal portions. A basic blend might include black pepper (Tellicherry), cardamom, ginger, cinnamon, mace, turmeric, allspice, nutmeg, saffron, galangal, cayenne, coriander, cassia, cloves and nigella. Ras el hanout can be added to cous cous and rice as they cook, and is also used in meat and potato tagines (casseroles), meatballs and lamb dishes. It is best to roast the ground spice mix before using.

RAY and **skate** are similar fish in appearance, although ray have long wire-like tails, while skate are larger and have a shorter, stumpier tail.

None of this stops the names being used interchangeably. The wings of both are the only edible part. They are sold with or without skin (as it can be hard to remove I suggest you buy skinless). Beware of ray and skate wings being passed off as scallops in cheap restaurants after being cut into disks of the same shape – the taste isn't dissimilar but the texture can be stringy.

REDCLAW see CRAYFISH

RED COOKING is associated with Chinese cooking, a method whereby meat (often pork, but also beef and chicken) is braised in a soy sauce-based liquid which tenderises the meat and colours it a dark reddish-brown. Other ingredients include ginger, onion, sweet rice wine, Chinese five spice and sugar. A cheap form of red cooking might simply mean rubbing the meat with sugar, salt and red food colouring, then slow roasting to produce a piece of meat that looks very red on the outside but normal on the inside.

REDUCE To cook a liquid down to a fraction of its original volume in order to enhance and concentrate its flavour or to thicken it. Don't add salt before reducing as the salty flavour will be concentrated too. Creams are thickened by reduction; a stock can be reduced by many times its volume to produce a glaze.

REFRESH Although this is not exactly a cooking method, it is often used after BLANCHING or parboiling. Food is removed from the water, then placed in iced water to halt the cooking process and lock in the colour. Also known as shock.

RENDER To reduce the fat content of meat. This can be done in a pan, in the oven, in water or on the grill, as long as heat is used to remove the fat. Rendering is best achieved at a lower temperature.

RHUBARB refers to the edible stalks from the flowering plant family whose members include buckwheat and sorrel. Although rhubarb is a vegetable, it is more commonly associated with fruit based dessert recipes. Rhubarb stems can be eaten raw, however, the tart nature of the vegetable lends itself to be complemented by cooking with sugar. The leaves of rhubarb contain high levels of oxalic acid and anthrone glycosides, rendering them inedible.

RICE is a member of the grass family and lives a short life of 3–7 months. The three main categories of rice are short grain, medium grain and long grain. Different varieties have different levels of the two starches found in rice and this affects how they cook: the starch '*amylose*' makes the rice separate and fluffy, while '*amylopectin*' gives it a sticky consistency. There are thousands of subspecies of rice worldwide, each country offering their own version based on national dishes.

All rice should be stored in a dry place below, 18°C. Red, brown and black rice (see below) should be consumed within 6 months of purchase. White rice has a longer storage time.

HOW TO COOK RICE

The various types of rice behave differently when cooked, mainly because of variations in their ratio of the starches amylose and amylopectin. There are many methods to cooking rice and, depending on the type, the times can vary by up to 10 minutes. Very generally speaking, rice takes about 20minutes to cook.

Some recommend that white rice be washed in a small amount of cold water, then rinsed and swirled (but not stirred with a hand or implement as this can break the grains) until the water runs clear. This removes excess rice starch, ensuring the rice is not overly starchy or sticky. Others say that washing is unnecessary.

Opinion is similarly divided about soaking rice: some people swear by it, others abhor the practice. In general, glutinous (short and medium grain) rice does benefit from soaking; long-grain rice does not (it will reduce the cooking time slightly but gives it the potential to become soggy).

There is no exact measure of what proportion of water to rice is best, as rice will absorb water at different rates depending on its type and age (young rice still has a moisture content so needs less water). One method is the 'index finger' gauge, where you add waterto cover the rice to the height of the first knuckle of your index finger with the fingertip touching the rice. My advice is to cook rice often until you find a method and a measure that is foolproof for you.

Adding a small amount of GHEE to the rice before cooking can help keep the grains separate: a method used by some Indian cooks that also adds a bit of flavour.

Whether you salt rice or not is optional. Some say it is best left unseasoned so the focus is cast onto the food it is served with. minutes after cooking. It should be stirred occasionally while standing.

Rice cookers are a brilliant way to cook rice, but need to be cared for. Never use metal implements when removing the rice, and always make sure the base of the bowl is dry before placing it on the element.

For the **stove-top** method, rinse the rice in water to remove excess starch. For every cup of rice, add 11/2 cups cold water. Bring the rice to a boil, covered, on a high heat. As soon as it is boiling, turn the heat down to the lowest setting. Keep the lid on the pot and cook gently gently for another 20 minutes. Let stand for 10 minutes. Fluff up rice before serving.

Steamed rice is a method employed by few outside the Thai community. It takes time and patience, which Western cooks often lack. The rice should be soaked for 3 hours (long-grain jasmine) or overnight (short-grain) then rinsed and drained.

For long-grain rice, add boiling water to only just cover the grains of rice. Place in a steamer basket, covered, over a medium heat, and cook for 30–60 minutes depending on quantity.

For short-grain sticky rice, place directly in a mound in the steamer (only a few grains will drop through so there's no need to use a plate) then cover and cook for approximately 25 minutes. Check the centre of this mound to ensure the rice grains are cooked through, then cover with a cloth to prevent it drying out.

Arborio rice is a commonly available medium-grain rice used for making risotto. This grain has a higher than normal amount of soluble starch and it needs to be cooked slowly and stirred continuously to expose the starch that gives risotto its tell-tale creaminess. Cooking time: 18–20 minutes. See also 'risotto rice', below.

Baldo rice is Italian-grown and used in risotto, desserts, soups and salads. Considered to be the 'daughter' of arborio rice, baldo rice is also popular in other Mediterranean dishes, used in stuffings, salads and desserts. If unavailable, replace with arborio.

Basmati rice is a quality rice with an excellent flavour grown in India. It has long grains which stay separate, fluffy and somewhat dry once cooked. When cooked it will not only swell but also lengthen to 2–3 times its raw size. White basmati rice takes less water and less time to cook than ordinary long-grain rice: try using equal quantities of rice to water. Un-hulled or brown basmati has even more flavour and takes longer to cook.

Bhutanese red rice hails from the small Himalayan kingdom of Bhutan. This is a short-grain red rice that cooks in 20 minutes and finishes with a nutty, earthy flavour and a red russet colour. If unavailable from delis or Asian grocers, substitute with *Christmas rice* (or as a last resort, another short-grain rice).

Black glutinous rice is also known as **black sticky rice** or **black forbidden rice.** It has a much richer flavour than white sticky rice and can be either medium- or long-grain. Once cooked, black rice is a deep, dark-purple with a nutty flavour and a wholegrain texture. Because of its striking appearance, it is often used for festive desserts, steamed in banana leaves or in salads. Before cooking (particularly if you plan to steam the rice), soak in water overnight; this allows the rice to absorb water, swell and then cook in less time.

Black japonica rice is a hybrid of a red medium-grain and a black short-grain japonica type of rice. It is often sold un-hulled and therefore cooks like a brown rice (about 45 minutes).

Broken rice is the damaged white rice which is separated from the intact grain at the production stage, and used in other areas such as animal feed, beer brewing or flour processing.

Brown rice The difference between brown and white rice is that brown has had only the hull or husk removed, leaving the bran intact. This long-grain rice takes longer to cook than white rice (about 40–45 minutes). It has a chewier texture and nuttier flavour, and is a natural source of bran, high in FIBRE and vitamin B.

Calrose rice is also known as sushi rice. It is quite round and short and belongs to the *japonica* sub species of rice.

Carolina rice is a long-grain rice originally grown in that part of America at the end of the 17th century. It is now grown throughout the US.

Christmas rice is a short-grain red rice. When cooked, it has a sticky, dense character and a musky aroma.

Converted rice is also known as parboiled rice. In fact, it hasn't been parboiled but rather soaked, steamed and dried before being husked or hulled. It has retained more nutrients than white rice and, due to reduced surface starch, stays well separated after being cooked. It cooks perfectly in approximately 20 minutes.

Dirty rice is a recipe rather than a type of rice. It is white rice cooked with minced chicken livers, gizzards, onions and seasonings, giving it its 'dirty' appearance. This Cajun specialty is far more tasty than it sounds.

Fermented rice is used in Asian desserts and in savoury dishes where its sweetness can counterbalance a salty or sour dish. This sweet rice has a small alcohol content and is available in most Asian grocers.

Flattened rice (or **rice flakes**) is used in desserts or batters. It sometimes has a slight green colouring, produced by the introduction of PANDANUS.

Glutinous rice - Despite its name, glutinous rice contains no gluten. Rather, the name describes the sticky nature of the rice once cooked. This short-grain rice is used in sushi and Asian desserts. It may also be referred to as **sticky rice, sweet rice or Chinese sweet rice** (again, this is about the way it is used rather than its content: there is no sugar in the grain), as well as **botan rice, Japanese rice, mochi rice, pearl rice, sushi rice** and **waxy rice.**

Himalayan red rice is a long-grain rice which can be substituted for brown rice – the only difference is the colour of the husk.

Instant rice or **precooked rice** as it is sometimes called, is not always readily available, is more expensive and, with its mushy texture and insipid flavour, is less appealing than ordinary rice. It has been precooked and dehydrated and is available white or brown, taking 5 and 10 minutes respectively to cook. Instant rice might help if you're in a hurry but considering normal rice takes only 15–20 minutes to cook, why bother with an inferior product? If a recipe calls for precooked rice, be clear whether this means instant rice or rice that has been boiled or steamed by you earlier.

Jasmine rice has a perfume more like pandanus than jasmine flowers; the name in fact refers to the pearl-like sheen of the grain. This long-grain aromatic rice is favoured in Thailand and has become popular worldwide. Jasmine takes less water and less time to cook than normal long-grain rice: try using equal quantities of rice to water. Leftover cold jasmine rice makes excellent fried rice. Also known as **hom mali rice** or simply **fragrant rice**.

Kalijira rice (also known as **baby basmati rice**) is a fast-cooking, short-grain rice favoured in desserts. Kalijira rice is produced in Bangladesh.

Patna rice is a long-grain rice originally from the region Bihar (the capital of which is Patna) in India. The name now describes a generic, long-grain white rice that is grown the world over.

Pearl rice is another name for short-grain rice (and is different from 'pearled rice' which simply refers to white rice in general).

Pecan rice or **wild pecan rice** is a new hybrid similar to popcorn rice and basmati. It has a long grain with a chewy texture and nutty flavour and aroma.

Popcorn rice is a new hybrid similar to but cheaper than basmati. When cooked, it has the aroma of –what else? – popcorn. Available in white and brown, it is also known as **American basmati, della rice** and **gourmet rice**.

Popped rice is also known as **poona rice**, available in Indian produce stores and is used in festive desserts and sweetmeats.

Risotto rice is, as the name suggests, used specifically for making risotto. It is a medium-grain rice with a characteristic white dot in the centre of the grain. There are several varieties, each claiming to produce the best risotto, including *Carnaroli, Vialone Nano* (or simply *Nano*), **arborio**, *baldo, Padano* and *Roma*. Washing risotto rice is a big no-no. The more starches left with the grain, the creamier the risotto. Some brands claim that no stirring is required, thus freeing you from the stove for 15–20 minutes, but old-school risotto lovers will tell you that the best risotto is one that has been worked constantly with a wooden spoon, so as to have the rice grains trounce one another, rendering maximum starch which in turn produces the creamy texture. Sometimes called **Piedmont rice**.

Rough rice or **paddy rice** is the un-hulled kernel, which is inedible until it is processed for cooking or packaging.

Spanish rice can be medium- or long-grain. Valencia produces a medium- to short-grain style that is favoured for paella (long-grain rice is never used for paella), and another paella rice is **granza rice**. Andalucia produces a long-grain rice perfect for pilaff. For rice dishes of Spain the rice is never washed, the starch too valuable to run down the sink. Other well known rice used for Paella are **Bomba rice, Calasparra** and **Senia.**

White rice is also known as **polished rice, pearled rice** (pearled as in polished) or **fully milled rice**, due to it being stripped of its husk and bran layers.

Wild rice. You've heard it before, now hear it again: wild rice is not a rice at all but a true grass seed (a trifle confusing, as essentially rice is a grass seed too). Also known as **Indian rice**, it takes longer to cook than white rice, has more nutrients and a nutty flavour and chewy texture that suits poultry, game meats and vegetable dishes. Rinse then cook 40–50 minutes, after which time most of the grains will have split open or 'blossomed' but still retain a bite.

Q **Problem solving**

~ **Burnt rice?** Burning can leave a scorched smell through the cooked rice. Take a crust of bread and place it on top of the rice. Depending on the extent of the burning, this can absorb most, if not all, of the aroma.

RICOTTA CHEESE is a by-product of Parmesan and Romano cheese (in its genuine form anyway). Translated literally as 'recooked', it is made from the whey, a cloudy, watery substance that weeps out as the curd is cut and allowed to sit. The firmness of ricotta is simply down to how long the cheese is drained for. **Ricotta salata** is ricotta that is pressed and salted, repeatedly over many days, then dried for several months. Grated over baked eggs or salads.

Firm ricottas are great crumbled into salads or marinated in oil and herbs then lightly grilled and served with a salad. The softer style of ricotta, sold in tubs, is good for cooking in baked cheesecake. Ricotta can be replaced in some instances only, with COTTAGE CHEESE. A simple method for soft ricotta or whipped ricotta is to use firm ricotta from the deli and blend in a food processor for 30 seconds to one minute - do not add anything.

RICOTTA

600ml cold water
1.8litres full cream milk
200ml pure cream (35%)
80ml lemon juice
½ teaspoon salt

Method:

In a heavy based pot add the cold water to cover the bottom. This will help stop the milk from scalding on the base of pot.

Sprinkle the salt in the pot with the water. Pour the milk and cream mix over the water. Then pour the lemon juice evenly over the milk mix. Place over a very low heat and gently bring to 90°C.   DO NOT STIR. DO NOT BRING TO THE BOIL.

The heating process will take at least 30mins-45mins. Keep an eye on the temperature.

Once temperature is reached, gently remove pan from the heat and sit to cool for 30minutes before gently removing the curds into a ricotta basket or a strainer lined with cheese cloth.

Strain and pour the remaining whey into a container and keep for cooking.

Refrigerate the ricotta. Will last 5-7days.

⭐ *Left over whey from the ricotta can be used for baking in bread recipes where it asks for water. It can also be used in muffin recipes or for braising meats.*

ROAST To cook meat or vegetables in the dry heat of the oven. See also BAKE.

ROCKET see LEAFY GREENS

ROCK LOBSTER and **crayfish** are names that are continually interchanged, and shouldn't be. The rock lobsters of Australia (in Europe called **spiny lobster, lobster** or **European lobster**) do not have front claws; while the American lobster is prized for its large front claws; and the Norwegian lobster, while smaller, is also adorned with front claws. Flat lobsters are also known as **shovel-nosed lobsters**, **butterfly crays** and **slipper lobsters**. Two common Australian species are the **Balmain bug** and the **Moreton Bay bug**.

ROSE APPLE also known as the **malabar plum**, is not related to the apple family. It is a smallish (2–5 cm), ovoid fruit which may be green or a dull yellow with pink flushes when ripe. The aroma once cut resembles rosewater, and the mild flavour of its firm, juicy and whitish flesh also shows hints of rosewater. Distilled fruit is said to produce a rosewater of quality to match the best made from rose petals. Rose apples can bruise easily and lose their crispness. Although able to be eaten fresh, they are ideal for preserves and jams, as their pulp is high in PECTIN (best mixed with other fruits for flavour). The flowers can also be eaten, often dried or candied, and the seeds are an intoxicant.

ROSEMARY is a tough herb that can be added at the beginning of cooking. Remove the leaves and grind in a mortar and pestle with sea salt to make a rub for lamb, chicken, beef or veal cuts. Rosemary keeps well in the fridge, but not in water: keep it dry in an airtight bag. You can also tie a string around the end of the bunch and hang it in the kitchen to dry. Rosemary flowers are also edible, if slightly bitter.

ROUX is a mixture used to thicken sauces and soups, made from equal parts flour and fat (oil, butter, bacon fat, duck fat, peanut oil and lard are some examples). The mix is cooked to varying degrees depending on the liquid to be thickened, but it is important that it is long enough to cook the flour. A **brown roux** is cooked with oil rather than butter (5 parts flour to 4 parts oil or lard) until it is light-brown, and is reserved for dark sauces and stews. **Blond roux** and **white roux** are usually always butter-based (equal parts flour and butter). A white roux is primarily used for béchamel sauce, while a blond roux is cooked a little longer (until fawn-coloured) for velouté or lighter-coloured sauces. See also BEURRE MANIÉ.

RUBBER HUSBAND is not a marital aid, but a hollow rubber tube used to peel garlic quickly. A clove of garlic is placed in the tube and rolled backwards and forwards several times, and the skin just comes off. Handy to keep in the drawer and available at good kitchenware shops.

RUTABAGA see SWEDE

S.

SAFFRON or **saffron crocus** and **saffron threads** as they are also known, are the stigma from the *Crocus sativus* flower. This expensive spice attracts its high price tag from the labour intensive cultivation and harvesting methods. Fetching as much as $11,000/kg (and as little as $4000/kg for lesser grades), it takes about 150 flowers to produce 1g of dried saffron threads. To maximise the flavour before use -
The best way to extract flavour from saffron is to soak the threads in very hot (not boiling) liquid for 10 to 20 minutes. Or use a bit of the hot stock from the dish being prepared. Use a blender of stick blender to maximise the extraction before adding to the recipe.

SAGE has a powerful flavour so tends to be used one or two leaves at a time. Drying the remainder is an excellent option, as dried sage holds well in cooking for long periods. One way to use a bunch of fresh sage quickly is to make a chicken or veal ragout, a long slow-cooking process well matched to this herb. Sage butter and sage oil are delicious (see HERBS for method) and, need I say it, sage stuffing. Store in the same way as rosemary, dry and airtight in the fridge.

SAGO, known also as **sago palm**, is a starch produced from a several species of palm, sold as a starch (flour), as flakes or pearls. Pearl sago has been heat-treated to form small balls of starch which then need to be cooked in water to soften. Like **pearl tapioca** (which can be substituted successfully), it is used to thicken soups and in desserts. Cooking time for sago depends on the size of the pearl; small pearls take about 15 minutes and large 25–30 minutes. The pearls have a tendency to sit at the bottom of the pot and stick – and believe me, trying to clean them is a nightmare – so when you add them to the water or other liquid, stir until the pearls begin to surface. Sago pudding has a Western and Eastern version. In the West it was used in hard times as a cheap dessert, and now is favoured as a gluten-free offering. Made with milk, sugar, citrus zest, eggs and butter, this pudding is a stark contrast to gula melaka, a Malay pudding made with sago cooked in water flavoured with PANDANUS LEAF then served with coconut cream and a sugar syrup made with palm sugar.

SALAMANDER A commercial oven grill used in restaurants. It is designed to finish off a dish by giving it a crust, or to flash the food with a quick heat source before serving.

SALSIFY is a thin, long (approx. 15 cm) root vegetable that resembles teenage parsnip (unkempt). The flavour is hard to describe; references to flavour talk of 'delicate', 'faint' and 'mild' all of which are great adjectives, but where's the noun? Even so this is a popular vegetable in France and Spain (Spanish salsify is a different cultivar). The size of the root makes salsify just as annoying to peel as baby carrots, so bake or boil it whole before peeling or, even better, scraping. If you do peel it before cooking, it will begin to darken, so have handy a bowl of acidulated water. (Also available in tins, but what's the point?) The leaves and stem can also be eaten, cooked like spinach or raw in salads. The innermost pale leaves are tender and best eaten raw. The flowers are also edible, as are the seeds - often sprouted.
    Black salsify is more highly regarded than the more common white and can be used to replace BURDOCK ROOT if necessary. Known as **oyster plant** or **vegetable oyster**, because of its texture once cooked. Also known as **Jerusalem star, Jack go to bed, goatsbeard** and **purple salsify.**

SALT is essential to our diets. As our bodies cannot produce salts for themselves, they rely on us to find it. Then it becomes an issue of what type and how much we should feed our bodies.
Some home cooks, made paranoid by the propaganda of "too much salt causes high blood pressure and heart attacks" began to omit salt from all cooking, presenting the family with bland meals. Meals in restaurants often taste significantly better than those cooked at home. Other than the fact that food cooked by anyone other than yourself

seems to taste better anyway, the reason for this could be as simple as the professional cook's respect for salt's place in food. Basically, good quality salt enhances the natural flavour of food. You should add salt not once but several times in small amounts, tasting and testing in between each addition.

As well as standard table and cooking salts, many new salts are now on the market. These can be better for you but unfortunately often carry heavy price tags, so rarely grace the home kitchen.

✓ Top tips for using salt

~ Add small amounts of salt several times, stirring and tasting between each addition

~ Before reaching for the salt shaker on the table - whether at home or in a restaurant - taste the food first! Chances are, the cook has added just the right amount. High on the list of what chefs hate is the customer who dowses the meal in salt and pepper before trying even one mouthful. (*Equally annoying to the customer is the waiter with the baseball-bat-sized pepper grinder offering you pepper before you've tasted your meal –next time ask them to leave the grinder with you until you've tried your* meal).

⌕ Problem solving

~ **Added to much salt?** Act immediately! Remove everything you dropped in, even if it means scooping out some of the other ingredients (they can always be replaced). Stir the mixture well. Or add a peeled potato or two and cook gently until the potatoes have absorbed most of the salt. Gently remove and discard the potato.

~ **Still too salty and you can't bring yourself to throw it out?** Cool down completely then freeze in smaller portions. Use one of these frozen salt blocks the next time you prepare the same dish by adding it (defrosted overnight) to the new batch.

~ **Need to eat less salt?** First, note that salt is important to our natural diet and it's not recommended to omit it completely. If you need to reduce your salt intake for medical reasons:

– use a salt that is low in sodium
– replace salt with seaweed granules
– use salt-reduced products

– check product labels for key words: sodium, salt, soy sauce, brine, corned, pickled, cured and smoked. These can indicate excess salt.

– make your own stocks instead of using packaged cubes or tetra packs

Black salt is a true misnomer if ever there was one, as this is a pink/grey salt, mined from the Indian food stores. Its characteristic smoky flavour means you cannot make a true Indian chaat (a type of salad) without it.

Celtic sea salt is a hand-farmed salt from the marshlands of Brittany. (Like any farmed product, a good crop depends on the weather.) Natural Celtic sea salt is sold as fine white crystals or larger grey crystals. The unwashed, almost dirty, appearance of this salt ensures that it retains all its natural minerals - highly recommended for your health.

Cooking salt is slightly coarser than TABLE SALT, and often made up of several salts. It is used in bulk in commercial kitchens. This is the best salt to season the water for cooking pasta rather than wasting your good sea salt or salt flake.

Fleur de sel translates as 'flower of salt'. It is hand-harvested like CELTIC SEA SALT, and used as a finishing salt, in small quantities. Fleur de sel is produced from the salt crust on top of the salt pond, so it is the least salty and purest part of the saline. It is taken from a single day's harvest. Also full of essential minerals. See also SEL GRIS.

Hawaiian black lava salt is a sea salt that is evaporated with purified black lava rock, then mixed with activated charcoal for its colour and apparent detoxifying effects. Although hard to find, it can be ordered over the internet.

Hawaiian red clay salt or **red alae salt** is a sea salt harvested in ponds, with baked Hawaiian clay added after it is dried. Can be ordered over the internet.

Iodised salt has a small amount of potassium iodide added to help prevent goitre, a thyroid condition. As little as 40 mg of potassium iodide is added per kilogram of near pure sodium chloride.

Korean bamboo salt or **red bamboo salt** (biosalt) is made from sun-dried salt stuffed into bamboo hollows and sealed with yellow clay. It is then baked 9 times, for 8 hours each time. After each baking period the bamboo stub is replaced. The resultant salt is red in colour, sweet-flavoured, and very salty, and its odour may not be appealing. High in minerals, bamboo salt is favoured in medicine, cosmetics and cleaning, and as a finishing salt in cooking.

Kosher salt, because it is. Kosher salt can be an overly refined salt with little nutrient value, sourced, like table salt from land deposits, or Kosher sea salt, a crystal salt with no additives, ideal for pickling meats because of its larger crystal that absorbs moisture. Kosher sea salt is best in a salt grinder if it is to be used as a table salt.

Malian red clay salt or **Saharan salt** is valued in Africa. Sourced from salt mines just south of the Sahara in Mali, Africa.

Pink Peruvian lake salt is a form of sea salt harvested from wells lined with rose quartz. The pink colouring comes from the tiny pieces of rose quartz present in the salts. The Incas and Mayans have used this salt for its powerful spiritual and healing properties. You can eat it at a top New York restaurant, then contemplate the spiritual healing the salt has brought you as you pay for the meal. If money isn't an issue, buy a quarter of a pound of the stuff and bathe in it.

Rock salt is procured from halite, a mineral that was once a sea salt but is now buried underground, sometimes in very large deposits. The rock salt is mined and ground into coarse chunks. Further refining to different sized grains produces cooking salt or table salt. The coarse rock crystals can be used in a salt mill or dropped straight into water for cooking pasta. They are also used when curing some meats or preserving lemons and in baking where large cuts of meat or whole fish are coated in a thick slurry of salt mixed with a little water or egg white.

Saltpetre or **potassium nitrate** is classed as a salt and preserving agent. A pinch of saltpetre added to a duck liver parfait mixture before it is cooked keeps it pink on the inside long after it has cooled.

Salt spray is a pure form of seawater used as a seasoning and sold in pump spray bottles. On the rare occasion I've used salt spray, I have found its simplicity appealing, although it is similar to fish sauce, in that it requires delicate handling to avoid over salting. Use a ratio of two sprays = 1 pinch of regular salt.

Sea salt and rock salt are the preferred salts for everyday cooking. Sea salt has a high mineral content and a clean salty flavour, and is sold as coarse crystals, flakes or granules. In a bygone era, it was referred to as **bay salt**. *Maldon sea salt* is a globally recognised salt-flake brand, which has spawned the trend for other countries to cash in on this abundant mineral.

Sel gris is from the same farmers who bring you CELTIC SEA SALT and FLEUR DE SEL. However, sel gris is harvested throughout an entire season (for every 150 kg of sel gris produced, only about 10 kg of fleur de sel is harvested). These salts by far are the healthiest in terms of mineral offerings for the human body and mind.

Smoked salt can lend a little of its smoky character to a casserole or steak. Styles available include hickory-smoked sea salt, Mediterranean oak-smoked sea salt and the elusive and extremely expensive smoked Danish salt.

Table salt is the most refined product of rock salt. It contains ANTI-CAKING AGENTS such as calcium silicate added (at less than 0.5%) to ensure that it flows freely in any weather condition, especially in the tropics where humidity plays havoc with dry food. Table salt is a very fine-grained, harsh-tasting salt.

SALTPETRE see SALT

SANSHO PEPPER see SICHUAN PEPPER

SAPODILLA see SAPOTE

SAPOTE, also known as **chocolate fruit, chocolate pudding fruit,** or more appropriately **black persimmon**, should only be eaten in season; trying to ripen this fruit out of season is futile. The fruit ranges in shape from elongated to spherical, and may weigh up to 3 kg, but common varieties are about the size of a tennis ball to a softball. The dull-red skin is hard, rough and brittle. The flesh is red, orange or greyish in colour; it is aromatic, sweet and soft when ripe with a soft, chocolatey flavour. It can be eaten as is or used in mousses, trifle, cakes, fruit shakes, ice-cream or sorbet. Usually, the fruit has some fibres in the flesh and contains one or more seeds.

To open a sapote, slice the skin around its 'equator' then twist the two halves open (as you would a mangosteen). If the fruit is too ripe, the skin may squish in the hands, so be careful. Once ripe, refrigerate and use within a few days. Sapote do not freeze well.

White sapote, sapodilla, Mamey sapote and **yellow sapote** are species with differing characteristics in flavour and colour. Some may be slightly more bitter than others, and flavours might resemble pears, bananas, peaches or brown sugar.

SATSUMA see MANDARIN

SAUCES Ah, sauces! That magical liquid that can cover a cook's feeble mistakes or, at best, lift the main ingredient to new heights. For some, a meat without sauce is like the moon without darkness, while for others, making a sauce is an arduous task. Think of Bolognese or any stew or casserole for that matter.

Butter sauces vary from the rich **beurre blanc** to a simple herb or flavoured butter which becomes a sauce as it melts over the meat or dish. Add butter to pan juices with wine or stock, to help thicken the sauce. The trick is to remove the pan from the heat, then add small cubes of butter, whisking or stirring until it has melted. Do not re-boil or heat once the butter has been incorporated as it will split. Flavoured butters can be rolled first in plastic wrap, then in foil to hold their shape, then refrigerated until solid. When hard, cut into rounds and freeze in a plastic bag for later use.

The most common **egg-based sauces** are **emulsion sauces,** made up of eggs (or more often just egg yolks) combined slowly with a fat, either oil or butter; **mayonnaise** (cold) and **hollandaise** (warm) - with its ten or so derivatives - are probably the best known. **Sabayon** can be either sweet or savoury and consists of eggs or egg yolks combined with a liquid (stock, juice or alcohol), then whisked until light or ribbon stage. It is cooked over a double boiler, and great care must be taken not to overcook or *"scramble"* the egg. Sabayon can be the beginning of a hollandaise sauce or can be used as a sauce on its own, as in **zabaglione**, a sweetened sabayon served with sponge biscuits. Another common egg-based sauce is **crème anglaise** or **English custard**, a sweetened egg yolk mix cooked with cream then gently heated to thicken (again with great care as boiling the sauce can lead to separation or curdling). Cold, hard egg sauces such as sauce **Gribiche, sauce Vincent, Cambridge sauce** and **sauce Sardalaise** are often served with fish, shellfish, tongue or, if you're in the mood, (and who isn't?) calf's head terrine.

Purees, whether from fruit, nuts or vegetables, make a good alternative to other more time-consuming sauces. Cook the ingredients then thicken with a béchamel (white) sauce, cream, butter, flour (or other starch) or by reducing to enhance the quality of this style of sauce.

HOW TO THICKEN A SAUCE

DEGLAZE the pan but don't let the liquid evaporate entirely. Now thicken the sauce by REDUCING it, (continue to cook the sauce over a high heat until much of it evaporates and the remaining liquid is intensified in flavour) or by adding another ingredient, such as butter, cream, blue cheese, cornflour, arrowroot or potato or rice flour (mixed first with a little cold water) and cooking gently to combine. A BEURRE MANIÉ (2 parts soft butter mixed with 1 part flour) is another thickening option but I don't favour it as the flour particles need time to cook out and the method doesn't provide this extra time. (The method is to add a beurre manié to the boiling liquid, bring it back to the boil, then turn off the heat source. This leaves the sauce with a grainy texture.)

Q **Problem solving**

~ **Burnt sauce?** Try to disguise it by adding a strong flavour profile, such as Vegemite, peanut butter, fruit juice, vinegar, Worcestershire sauce or chilli sauce. Or throw the sauce away and serve the meal with a wedge of lemon instead.

~ **Lumpy sauce or gravy?** Strain the sauce through a sieve. To avoid lumpy sauce in future, use a sauce whisk (metal or plastic) as you begin to bring the sauce together, then use a wooden spoon while the sauce simmers.

~ **Added too much salt?** The only answer is to sacrifice the few to save the many: ladle out the drop zone, including sauce, then bulk out the remaining sauce with stock, cream or wine. Or, if you've mixed in the salt already, pour off two-thirds of it (freeze this in an ice tray and use later as instant salt cubes to add flavour to future sauces), then bulk out the remaining sauce with stock, cream or wine.

~ **Curdled or split/separated dressing or sauce?**Remember Rule No. 1: follow the recipe. If a method states 'add slowly', then snail' pace is fast enough. There is no rushing the first stage of making a mayonnaise or hollandaise (or any derivative of these emulsion-type sauces). Get it right the first time and spare yourself the agony of repairing it. If an emulsion sauce is looking a bit thin, start adding small amounts of very hot water – this will aid in 'cooking' the egg within the sauce, helping to bring it back. Then, slowly add the oil again. If the sauce has separated, start again, using one fresh egg yolk. This time add the separated sauce to the egg yolk instead of oil.

For **prepared sauces**, see individual names, e.g. hoi sin sauce, oyster sauce, soy sauce.

SAUTÉ see PAN FRY

SAVORY is a herb with a strong, peppery flavour, and is used in Mediterranean countries to flavour beans, mushrooms, vegetables, and meats. Of the two varieties – winter savory and the milder summer savory – winter savory is best suited to slowly cooked dishes like stews, while summer savory is best suited to sautés, salads and soups. An alternative is thyme mixed with sage or mint in the proportions 3 parts thyme to 1 part sage.

SCALD To heat a liquid (often milk) to a point just before boiling. If you boil milk, you will burn the proteins and the result will be scorched milk. Milk (raw) was once to be scalded to kill bacteria, but we now have pasteurisation to do that job. These days, a recipe may suggest scalding milk to make working with other ingredients easier (for instance, to help added ingredients to dissolve or melt in the hot liquid).

SCALLION is the US term for SPRING ONION. **Bunching onion** and **green onion** are also used.

SCALLOP are rarely sold live, as they must be gutted as well as shucked, leaving only the white adductor muscle and the roe (the orange, pink or light tan-coloured flesh attached to the meat). Shucked scallops should be plump, with no sign of damage to the roe. (Scallops are hermaphrodites – i.e. a single scallop has both male and female organs – and the roe or gonad takes on an orange, pink or purple colour (female ovary) or white to pale tan colour (male testis) at different times.)

Scallops should be served medium-rare, in other words barely cooked on the inside, for the best flavour and to retain succulence. Cook them quickly on a high heat: 30 seconds to 1 minute is all it takes in most cases. Frozen scallops, although of a good standard, do retain water. After defrosting, cook them separately from the sauce so they don't water it down, then add to the sauce just before serving. Some recipes ask for the roe (the pinky-orange bit) to be removed from the eye or abductor muscle (the round, white bit). This is because some people don't like the stronger flavour of the roe (or the fact that it is the reproductive gland) – so it's really a matter of personal preference.

In the US the *eye of the scallop* is preferred and is sold without the roe; in Europe the roe is often kept on. The best scallops are, of course, bought fresh, in the shell, to be shucked yourself.

Dried scallops are used sparingly (they're expensive) to sweeten or add flavour to soups, stews and stocks, especially high-quality stock. They should be soaked in water for 30 minutes before use.

SCAMPI are also known as **Dublin Bay prawns, Norway lobsters, deep sea lobsters, lobsterettes** (US) or **langoustines** (France). Scampi resemble giant prawns (hence the confusion) although the species is classified as a lobster. True scampi, like those caught in deep-sea fishing off New Zealand or Australia, are a narrow pincer-clawed species with slender bodies and a more delicate flavour than rock lobster. Be wary of restaurants in the US that serve 'shrimp scampi', believing diners will think of it as a special Italian dish because it's cooked with garlic and olive oil or butter.

SCONE Known in the US as a **biscuit**. See also BAKING.

SCREW-PINE LEAF see PANDANUS LEAF

SEAFOOD see CRAYFISH; FISH; MUSSELS; OYSTER; PRAWN; ROCK LOBSTER; SCALLOP; SCAMPI; SQUID

 Alternatives to seafood
~ For those allergic to seafood, there is no substitute. Allergic reactions to seafood (which includes fish and shellfish, the most common being prawns or shrimp) are the third most common food allergy after eggs and milk. The allergy is usually life-long, and if anything, the reactions can become more aggressive after each exposure to seafood. In severe cases, even the vapours from cooked seafood can trigger a reaction.

SEAFOOD EXTENDER see MARINARA MIX

SEA GREENS see SEAWEED

SEA LEGS see CRAB STICKS

SEAR To seal the surface of meat or fish with a high heat in a pan or on a grill, with or without oil, either as a style of cooking (for example for fresh tuna) or as a first step before further cooking. The idea is that it locks in the juices, although the validity of this theory is now being tested and questioned.

SEAWEED also known as **sea greens** or **sea vegetables**, can be very tasty. Some sea greens, such as dulse, contain 10 times more calcium than cow's milk, more vitamin C than oranges and are very high in iron.
  Bladderwrack is said to aid an under-active thyroid gland (and consequently help weight loss) and goitre, among other ailments.
  Chlorella is a seaweed thought of as a super food for its very high levels of chlorophyll, vitamins, minerals and proteins.
  Dulse has the highest iron content of any food, and so is excellent for those with anaemia. It prevents seasickness, inhibits the herpes virus and is a good salt substitute. Dulse is found in many health food stores or fish markets. Fresh, this red seaweed can be

eaten straight off the rocks, sun-dried it can be used in salads, sandwiches, toasted, roasted, fried or boiled.

Kelp is also known as brown seaweed. To clean, rinse with fresh water and remove the olive-coloured membrane. Boil in water for 20–30 minutes. Serve hot as a soup with added seasonings, or cooled as a jelly. Unlike the Japanese KOMBU, kelp cooks relatively quickly and should only be added to a soup or stews in the last 20 minutes of cooking (do not boil first).

Nori is made from porphyra which is farmed in Japan and is the most widely consumed seaweed in the world. Also known as **laver** and **sloke**, nori can be eaten roasted, used in sushi, salads, soups or crumbled. Rehydrate before using in salads or a side dish: rinse under cold water then drop into boiling water for 15 minutes. The flat dried sheets are known as **sushi nori** (US), **nori sheets** or **seaweed sheets**.

Spirulina is a blue green algae, sold as a powder or sometimes as a spirulina drink. It is classed as a 'superfood' as it contains over 60% vegetable protein, the highest of any food. In powder form it can be purchased as green spirulina or blue spirulina - which is a bright blue that is at odds with natural food colours.

Wakame is a cultivated seaweed, that can be mistaken for its close relative **alaria**. Alaria is collected wild whereas wakame is a cultivated vegetable. Alaria has a more delicate flavour thanwakame, and both are very high in calcium and vitamin A, and high in all vitamin Bs. Alaria and wakame should be soaked for about 20 minutes prior to cooking. The water in which they have been cooked will be high in nutrients and should be strained and used as a stock. For eating raw in salads, first soak or marinate in lemon juice or rice vinegar. Used as a flavour component in miso soup.

SEITAN see 'alternatives' in MEAT

SEL GRIS see SALT

SESAME SEED comes in different colours: white/yellow, red, brown and black. Black sesame seeds are said to be the most flavoursome. All sesame seeds are high in oil, so should be used within 3 months to avoid staleness or rancidity. Toast sesame seeds to enhance their nutty flavour. There are two main varieties of sesame seed butter: the

Asian variety, which is called sesame butter, and the Middle Eastern variety, which is called TAHINI. The butter is usually made with raw sesame seeds and is thicker than tahini, which is made with roasted seeds. Once opened, keep sesame seed butter/tahini refrigerated for up to three months. Kept in the pantry it will go rancid.

SEVEN-FLAVOUR SPICE see TOGARASHI

SHALLOT see ONION

SHALLOW FRY Similar to PANFRYING, only using a little more fat. The excess fat is then poured from the pan after the cooking.

SHARK A dozen or so edible species of shark are caught for their meat, although as many as half of the 350 species are deemed useless to the fishing industry (only 7% are classed as highly important). Shark is similar in appearance to dogfish, and the several species of dogfish as well as the elephant fish can be referred to as shark. All shark is marketed as flake in its filleted form. Flake is popular in fish and chip shops for its price and the fact that it is boneless.

SHEA NUT is the walnut-sized seed of the shea tree, a west African tree of the sapodilla family. **Sheanut oil** or **shea butter** (also called **galam butter**) is the solid green, yellow or white fat from these seeds. In African countries, shea butter is used in the making of margarine and chocolate.

SHISO is a very popular herb in Japan, where the green leaves are used in salads, to wrap food, and in tempura, sushi and sashimi as a garnish. Also known as **perilla, Chinese basil** and **wild sesame. Red shiso** is named **beefsteak leaf** because of its colour. It is used extensively as a colouring and mild flavouring agent in pickled plums.

SHOCK see REFRESH

SHORTENING is a solid fat made from vegetable oils. It is chemically transformed and solidified through hydrogenation, a process that creates trans fatty acids (see FAT) and converts the mixture into a saturated fat, thereby destroying any polyunsaturated benefits. Vegetable shortening is virtually flavourless and may be replaced with other fats in baking and cooking. It can be stored at room temperature for up to a year. It is available in all supermarkets and is sold as normal- or 'butter'-flavoured. Some companies make a solid vegetable fat that is marketed as vegetable SUET.

SHOYU see SOY SAUCE

SHRIMP For fresh or frozen shrimps see PRAWN. **Dried shrimps** are used in many Asian countries as a seasoning in stocks and sauces. They are an integral ingredient in master stock. Dried shrimps are usually soaked in warm water for 15 minutes or rice wine to soften before adding to soups and stir-fry.

SICHUAN PEPPER is also known as **anise pepper, Chinese pepper** and **spice pepper**. It has an aromatic, woody/lemony flavour with a slight anaesthetic feel on the tongue. The aroma comes from the pod and not the seeds. Sichuan pepper is the most common but you can also buy **Indonesian sichuan, North Indian sichuan** and **Nepalese sichuan.** The Japanese version is called **sansho** and is used in TOGARASHI. The seeds will have already been removed from store-bought pepper, as they have an unnecessary bitterness about them. You should also remove any fragments of stem that you find as they are tough and also pointy, which could be harmful on swallowing. Sichuan can be used as a condiment: first mix with salt, dry-toast in a wok until it begins to smoke, then cool and grind coarsely. Chinese Sichuan pepper is the most common but you can also buy Indonesian Sichuan, North Indian Sichuan and Nepalese Sichuan. The Japanese version is called sansho and is used in TOGARASHI.

SILVERBEET or **Swiss chard**, like CHARD, is a close relative of rhubarb. It is tougher and more strongly flavoured than BABY CHARD which is why children have issues eating it. When cooking silverbeet, cut the dark, crinkly leaves from the hard, white stalks and cook separately. The leaves will only need wilting, which may only take 30 seconds to 1 minute, depending on quantity, while the stems, either sliced or cut into batons will take 3–7 minutes to break down, depending on how thickly they are cut and how well cooked you like them. Silverbeet is

sometimes called **sea-kale beet** (UK), **green chard** (US), **spinach beet,**
leaf beet, and **white beet.**

SIMMER is to cook in a liquid just below boiling point, at a
temperature of 85°C, when small rolling bubbles start to break the
surface. The great recipe tautology is the instruction to 'gently simmer'
because 'simmering hard' would mean to boil.

SKATE see RAY

SLOKE see 'nori' in SEAWEED

SMOKE What many professional cooks do as a coping mechanism
faced with the pressure of service. The smoke drawn from a tobacco
stick penetrates the lungs with its aromatic blend of nicotine and
tobacco. Sometimes other herbs and spices are thrown into the mix.
Smoking can also mean the flavouring of meats and vegetables via
the hot or cold smoking method. For a more detailed explanation, see
FISH, SMOKED.

SMOTHER To add a small amount of liquid to a food that has been
sautéed. The pan is then covered with a lid, the temperature r
educed and the food cooked slowly until done.

SNOW EGGS see MERINGUE

SNOW PEAS are sometimes called **mange-tout** (because you eat
every part of them) or **Chinese peas, Chinese snow peas** and **sugar**
peas.

SODA also **SODIUM BICARBONATE** see BICARBONATE OF SODA

SOFT ICING MIXTURE see SUGAR

SOURSOP is a fruit of the moya family, related to the CUSTARD APPLE.
This green fruit with soft spikes is tropical in flavour and very slightly
acidic. Its seeds and peel are inedible. The two best eating varieties
are 'sweet' and 'seedless', their names giving a clue to their

characters. The seedless soursop is said to be insipid and fibrous, but has the advantage of not containing the 30–200 black seeds of other soursops. Depending on the cultivar, soursop can be quite fibrous on the inside, and these are best used for the juice, drinks, ice-cream and sorbet. The immature fruits are often cooked and eaten as a vegetable, steamed, boiled or braised. Check Asian grocers for availability.

SOY SAUCE is made from soya beans fermented in brine and (usually) wheat.

Chinese soy sauce comes as either light or dark (and as salt-reduced or 'lite' soy sauce which contains one-third less sodium). **Light soy sauce** is also marketed as **superior soy sauce** and is the most common of all cooking soy sauce in China (and globally for that matter). It is light in colour, full-flavoured and –surprisingly – saltier than dark soy sauce. **Dark soy sauce** is brewed for longer giving it a very dark, almost black appearance. It is stronger in flavour (not saltiness), thicker and reserved for braising or stewing. It can also be labelled soy superior sauce or **black soy sauce**.

Vietnamese soy sauce is almost identical to Chinese light soy, made with ground soy beans, water, rice flour and salt.

Mushroom soy sauce is dark soy sauce with the infusion of dried straw mushrooms. It is used in much the same way as dark soy sauce.

Japanese soy sauce is fermented and aged (in stark contrast to the many synthetic, non-brewed, soy sauces made in days, not months, with chemicals, defatted soy meal, grains (wheat, rice) and water).

Shoyu is similar to Chinese light soy sauce.

Tamari is a wheat-free soy sauce. Tamari is dark and strong-flavoured and is an excellent alternative for dark soy sauce.

Kecap manis is an Indonesian soy sauce that unlike all other soy sauce, is thick, syrupy and sweet with a complex spiciness (but not hot). Used in marinades, dipping sauces or – my favourite – drizzled over poached eggs.

SPATCHCOCK see POULTRY

SPICE, like dried herb, should be used as close to its date of manufacture as possible. Many people believe a jar of supermarket spice will outlive their grandchildren, when in fact it is probably already past its pungent best. Best of all is to buy whole spices and grind them as you need them. And as the spice snob knows all too well, the best place to buy a particular spice is from a shop based on the cuisine it is used in which ensures a high turnover of that spice. The list below will help you identify which spices are associated with which cuisines so you can source them from a grocer dealing in that produce. It concentrates on indigenous spices with some common spices in the daily use.

Africa allspice, chilli, clove, coriander seed, cumin seed, ginger, pepper

Australia lemon myrtle, Tasmanian mountain pepper, wattle seed, native thyme

Central and Northern Europe aniseed, black pepper, blue fenugreek, caraway seed, celery seed, cinnamon, clove, dill seed, fennel seed, juniper berry, nutmeg, paprika, poppy seed, saffron

South Asia ajowan, black cardamom, black cumin, cardamom, chilli, cinnamon, ginger, turmeric

South-east and east Asia cassia, chilli, clove, cubeb pepper, Indonesian and Vietnamese cinnamon, galangal, garlic, ginger, nutmeg, Sichuan pepper, star anise, turmeric.

Mediterranean region allspice, aniseed, black pepper, cardamom, cinnamon, clove, coriander seed, cumin, fennel, fenugreek, mace, nutmeg, onion seed, saffron, sumac, thyme

West and central Asia asafoetida, black mustard seed, cardamom, chilli, cumin seed, dill seed, fenugreek, garlic, ginger, poppy seed

West India and the Americas allspice, cayenne, celery seed, chilli, clove, filé, paprika, vanilla.

SPICE MIXES AND PASTES Making one's own spice mix is a rewarding culinary challenge that is, unfortunately, rarely undertaken due to the many commercial products available. Recipes for spice mixes can be found in specific cookbooks and on the internet – choose reputable recipes that encourage the use of the freshest possible ingredients. If you're not prepared to make your own, then I recommend pastes available at Indian or Asian food stores or from the local family flogging their wares at the Sunday market.

The aromatics of spice are heightened when exposed to heat. This is why pastes are sautéed to activate them before being added to other ingredients, and whole spices are dry roasted before grinding and mixing into a spice mix.

To dry roast means to cook in a dry pan over a medium heat, remembering to shake or stir the pan. Spices should be dry roasted one at a time as different spices take different lengths of time and you will be in danger of burning some if you cook them all together. Remove from the heat when the spice begins to smoke and transfer to another dish immediately to stop the cooking. Crush whole spices in a mortar and pestle, a food processor, a pepper grinder or a coffee grinder.(After putting spices through a coffee grinder, clean it by grinding a handful of plain rice.)

See also BENGALI FIVE SPICE; GARAM MASALA; KEBSA; MIXED SPICE; PANCH PHORA; QUATRE ÉPICES; RAS EL HANOUT; TOGARASHI.

SPICE PEPPER see SICHUAN PEPPER

SPIRULINA see SEAWEED

SPLIT PEAS These dried peas (green or yellow) are peeled and split in half like split LENTILS and can be used similarly but their cooking times differ: peas are boiled for up to an hour. Used most often in split pea soup, they have an earthy, sweet flavour. To cook, rinse well, then bring to a boil with double the amount of water to peas then simmer until soft (45–60 minutes). They do not maintain their shape when cooked. Split green peas are also known as split dried blue peas and split yellow peas are also known as white peas.

SPRING ONION see ONION

SQUASH is a term used in the US and UK for a vegetable which is divided into two categories: the tough-skinned, orangey-fleshed winter squash (see PUMPKIN) and summer squash, with its thinner skin and lighter flesh and seeds, which includes the likes of yellow and green zucchini and marrow. Some squash grow to the size of a watermelon, which is fine for gardening competitions but bland and fibrous to eat. Large marrows are great for stuffing. **Button squash, pattipan squash, scallopini** and **custard squash** all refer to the same type of summer squash.

SQUID, calamari and **cuttlefish** are all in the same family. Sometimes 'calamari' and 'squid' are used interchangeably, although separately they could be mistaken for one another, line them up and the differences are apparent. Cuttlefish, squid and calamari should be bought whole. Pre-cut calamari or squid rings tend to be cut from a larger specimen, and the larger the creature the tougher it gets.

    Calamari is often mistakenly used to describe cleaned squid and, just to confuse matters, is a term used by Italians and Greeks to describe more than one squid. However, they are indeed different. Calamari as a species are smaller and considered more tender as a food compared to squid. In physical appearance calamari have triangular side fins running the full length of the body. Squid have fins, but these arrow-like and only at the narrow end of the body, not the full length.

    Cuttlefish is a stumpier type of squid, favoured by professional cooks for its stronger flavour, tenderness and its ink.

    Dried squid is enjoyed as a late-night drinking snack. It can also be used as a seasoning, soaked and then shredded before adding to soups, sauces, stir-fries and salads.

STAR ANISE is a star-shaped spice (each star has 8 points) with the distinct flavour and aroma of aniseed or liquorice. It is collected from a small evergreen shrub in Japan yet used significantly in Chinese cuisine. Moderation is the key when using this pungent spice. It is usually added whole to a dish, but each point in the star contains a seed which can be removed and roasted separately then ground. Not to be confused with ANISE.

STAR FRUIT see CARAMBOLA

STEAM This is considered the healthiest way to cook vegetables, as there is no agitation in boiling water and the steam doesn't dilute or remove in great amounts the nutrients within the food being cooked.

Meat, rice and fruit can also be steamed. A liquid, usually water, at boiling point 105°C or higher produces steam which is caught in a lidded receptacle (make sure the food stays out of the water or it will be boiled rather than steamed). Steam burns can be nasty, so be careful when lifting the lid on the steamer, opening it away from the face or arms to allow the severest heat to escape before removing the lid.

STEVIA see 'alternatives to sugar' in SUGAR

STEVIOSIDE see 'alternatives to sugar' in SUGAR

STEW is a slow wet-cooking method whereby food and liquid are cooked in a pot or pan and allowed to simmer for long enough to completely tenderise the food. Although very similar in technique to BRAISING, meat to be stewed is cut smaller, usually diced. Fruits and vegetables can also be stewed but pay close attention to the time required for cooking, as fruit will only take a fraction of the time it takes to stew meat.

STINKYFRUIT see DURIAN

STIR-FRY commonly refers to wok-cooking, although frying in a very hot pan for a very short time can also be referred to as stir-frying. The key to stir-frying is the 'stir' – the food is kept moving at all times.

 Top tips for stir-frying
~ Never overload the wok with food. You'll lose the intense heat and ultimately ending up with a 'stir-braise'. A wok is designed for small amounts of food at a time, especially on domestic hot plates which don't usually produce enough heat for ideal stir-frying
~ A good peanut oil is recommended for stir-frying. Although rice bran oil with its high smoke point is an excellent alternative.
~ Wok implements are vital tools for wok cooking. I prefer the '**hok**': the ladle-shaped, long-handled implement, so I can scoop and turn the food. It is also very handy when it comes to serving, whether soup, noodles or vegetables. The flat, shovel-like lifter is good for moving the food around the wok, ensuring it is cooked quickly.

~ Always heat the wok or pan to very hot before adding the oil, then quickly add the remaining ingredients. If you heat the oil as the wok heats, you'll burn the oil.

~ Some books tell you to heat a wok until 'smoking', then add the oil – right they are.

~ If you have a traditional thin metal Chinese wok, do the following every now and again to help keep the wok sealed and prevent food from sticking. Heat the wok until it's almost white-hot (watch as the bottom of the wok begins to turn white), remove from the heat, cool slightly and wipe with a cloth, return the wok to the heat and again ensure an intense heat is produced before adding oil and the ingredients.

~ If you have an electric wok, a non-stick wok or you're using a pan or skillet, the smoking point is irrelevant. Instead add a few droplets of water and watch as they form small, tight balls that roll around. This is when it is hot enough. Just remember to remove the water before adding oil.

STOCK Good cooks are relentless when talk turns to stocks. You will have heard it before, now hear it again: A good stock is the foundation of good cooking. Fresh chicken stock is heaven, home-made beef or veal stock is a rare treat.

I'm yet to meet someone (other than myself and an avid carnivore friend of mine) who has troubled their stove top with eight hours of simmering bones. The end result is not only great stock, but also a sense of pride and accomplishment. It is accompanied by a god-awful stench throughout the entire house. My family left me for the day and would not return until I could guarantee the odour had gone. My neighbour also mentioned a waft of 'ageing corpses' coming from our direction. How the complaints subsided when French onion soup, sauces and glazes were set before them. I laughed last, until I realised my tea towel collection had been perfumed with 'eau de fonds brun'.

Commercially made liquid stocks are relatively new on the market. Sadly, they are often over-salted and cloudy, with little resemblance to the flavour claimed on their Tetra Pak cartons. Still, they're convenient, and these commercial stocks have made more people aware of the use of stocks in their cooking.

Stock or **bouillon cubes** (sometimes also called **granules** or **base cubes**) have been around much longer, and I always keep a few in the cupboard for times of need. Look for brands that use all-natural ingredients, are free from MSG, gluten and lactose. Interesting to note that a good brand of "chicken" stock I keep in the pantry now has nothing on its ingredients list that resembles poultry, simply a picture of a chicken on the packet. **Powdered stocks** can be used exactly the same as cubes.

✅ **Top tips for making stock**

~ Follow directions for making stock carefully, and don't take shortcuts. Boiling a stock will reintroduce the impurities that floated to the top back into the stock itself, making it go cloudy and soapy tasting. Skimming the top of the stock ensures there are no fats and impurities left to spoil the flavour.

~ **Do not add salt to a stock**. That way you can control the amount of salt in the dish as you prepare it. This gives fresh stock a great advantage over commercial alternatives, which are often too salty and limit the amount of good salts you can add in the cooking.

Beef stock - Fresh, home-made beef or veal stock is always the best option, but it takes time. It takes at least 8 hours to extract all the flavour and gelatinous properties from those thick bones. Escoffier, the all-knowing, brilliant chef of the last century insists that a good estouffade (brown stock) takes at least 12 hours. This to ensure that the mellow characteristics from the "gelatigenous bodies" have been produced, and even then he believes the bones aren't entirely spent. Fresh brown stock can also be reduced to an unctuous glaze, thanks to the collagen in the bones – something cube and Tetra Pak stocks cannot provide.

Chicken stock - Fresh is best, and as it only takes 4 hours, fresh chicken stock is far more achievable than beef for the domestic cook. Chicken stock can be made from the whole bird, often an older fowl, called a BOILER or SOUPER. Chicken necks make for a good stock as well.

Fish stock - Fresh fish stock made at home is a 30-minute job (10 minutes preparation, 20 minutes cooking), so there are no excuses not to make your own. Commercially made cubes (and liquid) stink of something other than fish, and should be used to ward off gremlins, not for cooking. The ingredients for fish stock can be as simple as fish bones, onion, parsley stalks, white wine, lemon juice and water. The best fish bones for stock are sole or whiting. Removing the eyes from the head before making stock is only really necessary if you desperately need a clear stock for something like a consommé. The eyes still contain flavour and gelatinous properties, so a cloudy fish stock is not so bad at all, in most cases. Never boil the stock when making it, especially if needed for a consommé, as the delicate proteins make the stock turn cloudy. And never cook for too long, as that impairs the 20 minutes on a moderate heat is ample time to extract the necessary flavour and gelatine from the delicate fish bones.

Game stock is not available commercially, and is rarely made except in fine restaurants. Game stock is made to be used in a relevant dish of the same meat (e.g. quail, pheasant, partridge, rabbit, hare, venison, kangaroo), in sauces, in a consommé (clear soup) or thick game soup.

Master stock or **superior stock** is an Asian institution. A stock that few outside the Asian community are aware of, yet it's widely enjoyed in combination noodle soup, wonton soup, hot and sour soup, egg flower soup, and many other delicious dishes. It is also used in stir-fry and noodle dishes. I'm taking a chance by saying what's in it, as many chefs have their secret ingredients that make it their own. Basically it is a combination of pork bones, whole boiler chickens, and dried shrimp, squid or scallops (depending on the budget), simmered in water. Ginger, pepper, star anise and lemongrass are some secret ingredients, but many keep it simple with few of these extras. Vegetables are not added; as much as they may impart some flavour, it is believed they absorb valuable meat flavours. These stocks rarely leave the stove top, meat and water are continually added and simmered. I have heard reports of stocks that have been going for years on end.

Vegetable stock can be anything from a carefully boiled-up array of root vegetables to the liquid left over after boiling mixed vegetables for dinner (which can be saved for soups, for making bread or vegan risotto.) Home-made vegetable stock should be made from quality ingredients, not the wilted leftovers fermenting in the bottom of the crisper. Sauté (or roast) the vegetables before adding water to bring out their flavour. The stock will take about 20 minutes to cook if the vegetables are cut small, or up to an hour if they're kept whole. After an hour the vegetables are well and truly spent and any herbs left to steep may turn bitter, so strain everything out. (All the flavour and nutrients are now in the liquid, so eating these soggy leftovers would be the equivalent to tucking into boiled cardboard.) To intensify the flavour, once strained, you can then reduce the stock by half.

 Alternatives to stock

~ **Water** is the obvious choice, but obviously lacks flavour. To compensate, you can add other flavours to the water that are appropriate to your recipe, such as soy sauce, red wine, herb or spice infusions, or garlic. Or, bump up the flavours in the rest of the recipe, for example if you make a risotto with water, use ingredients with strong flavours and finish it with plenty of butter or cheese.

~ There are also some commercial alternatives available: imitation meat stocks in cube or powdered form, and (from health food shops) based powdered beef flavourings.

STONE, as in cherry or olive stone, is called a **seed** in the UK and a **pit** in the US.

STRUCK MEASURE see MEASUREMENTS

SUCANAT see 'alternatives to sugar' in SUGAR

SUCCOTASH is a side dish made from baby lima beans or fresh shelling beans and sweet corn, cooked in butter and water. Fresh succotash made from the fresh scrapings of corn cobs is highly recommended.

SUET is the hard, strong-smelling protective fat collected from around the kidneys of cows and sheep. Used in sweet and savoury pudding, pies and dumplings, for moisture and flavour. Grate or chop finely before adding to the recipe. Fresh suet from the butcher should be treated like all fresh meat and refrigerated or frozen. Packet suet is great for people who can't handle the smell and texture of real suet. The packet stuff has been mixed with flour. Vegetable suet is a solidified vegetable fat sold in 250 g blocks.

SUGAR comes in many forms – dried, powdered, dark sticky liquids – in different grades, and is mostly produced from sugar cane or the white root of sugar beets. (The by-product of sugar cane and sugar beet refining is MOLASSES).

Screened sugars have been through a sifting method to divide the sugar into various sizes for different uses. The result is granulated sugar, such as plain or caster sugar. Different screened sugars are used for commercial products, depending on the granule size required: coarse sugar, Crystal 750, sugar, Non Pareil, fine sugar and extra fine sugar.

Milled sugar refers to powdered sugars such as icing sugar. Most of these contain free-flowing agents, such as starch, tri-calcium phosphate or maltodextrin.

Need I go on about the over-consumption of refined sugars in our diets? Suffice to say that with diabetes an ever-increasing diagnosis in Western society, and obesity on the rise in young children (still), moderation is essential.

⚲ Problem solving
~ **Lumpy sugar?** Pour through a sieve, gently squash in a mortar and pestle or keep to one side and use in hot caramel, toffee, hot beverages or any other dish where free-flowing sugar is not required.

Blended sugar is cane or beet sugar with dextrose (derived from corn) added, which makes for a cheaper product. It is not as sweet as granulated sugar. Because dextrose is hygroscopic (attracts water from the air), using blended sugar in a recipe could alter the end result.

Brown sugar can be light (3.5% molasses) or dark (6.5%), both quite moist. The flavour varies slightly according to the richness of the molasses content. Brown sugar can replace most other brown (especially **Muscovado**) and even white granulated sugar as well as coconut sugar and palm sugar.

SUGAR TEMPERATURES

	°C	°F	USE
small thread	100	212	sugar syrups
large thread	104	219	
small pearl	106	220	
large pearl	109	228	
soft ball	112	234	fudge, fondant
medium ball	114	237	marshmallow, Italian Meringue
firm ball	118	244	caramels
hard ball	120	248	toffee, buttercreams
very hard ball	124	255	Nougat
light crack	135	275	Taffy (US), firm nougat
crack	144	291	pulled sugar
hard crack	152	206	butterscotch, spun sugar, brittle
caramelised sugar	155 - 170	310 - 338	Honeycomb

Caster / castor sugar is the finest of the screened sugars. Most often used in domestic baking and dessert/sweets, because its small granule dissolves quickly. Can be replaced with normal sugar that has been blended until the grains are as fine as possible.

Cinnamon sugar is, as the name suggests, sugar with cinnamon added. To make your own, use seven parts caster sugar to one part ground cinnamon.

Coconut sugar is made from the sap of the coconut tree. (Gathering the sap eventually renders the tree useless for quality coconut production.) The sugar is very dark brown, with less flavour than pure palm sugar – similar in taste to dark-brown sugar which can be used to replace it if necessary. It is sold in a moist block.

Demerara sugar is a light-brown crystal sugar. When made properly, it is only partially refined, which leaves the natural molasses intact, but unfortunately most Demerara sugar available is made from refined white sugar with molasses added. (To find the genuine stuff, look on the packet: there should be no list of ingredients as Demerara sugar is just that, not sugar and molasses.) It can be replaced with light-brown sugar or raw sugar.

Date sugar is made from the sap of the date palm. It adds a delicate flavour to baked goods, beverages and other foods.

Dry fondant sugar, used to make fondant, contains 10% spray-dried glucose.

Evaporated cane sugar juice is one for the vegans. It hasn't gone through the final stages of clarification over charcoaled animal bones that some other sugars are subjected to.

Fondant sugar is slightly different to dry fondant sugar, used in royal icing for cake decorating and fondant making. It is a very fine pre-form of icing sugar (without glucose).

Icing sugar or **pure icing sugar**, known in the US as **confectioners' sugar**, is a milled sugar. Unlike many of the milled sugars, pure icing sugar contains no additives. It can be replaced with a home-made version: blend 1 cup of granulated sugar with 1 tablespoon cornflour until powdery. It can also be called **powdered sugar** and **10 x sugar**.

Muscovado sugar, also known as **Barbados sugar**, is a rich, moist, brown sugar which is less refined than most other brown sugars. Replace with dark brown sugar if necessary.

Okinawa black sugar also known as **Kokuto, Japanese black sugar** and **black sugar,** has been made since the 17th century in the Okinawa prefecture. Made from sugar cane, its rich, intense caramel flavour and trace mineral content, makes this sugar highly desirable. China, Korea and Taiwan also produce their own version of black sugar.

Palm sugar is also know as **jaggery, java sugar** and **gula melaka**. (The latter name also refers to a Malaysian dessert made from tapioca or sago, coconut milk and a palm sugar syrup). This hard block sugar is found in Asian grocers and some supermarkets. Read the ingredients as several brands are made from cane sugar and molasses, not from the sap of the sugar palm. It is available light-coloured and very hard or as a dark, almost black and moister block (which may in fact be coconut sugar – check the label). Palm sugar has a flavour unto itself which other sugars will not bring to the dish.

Panela also known as **rapadura, chancaca** and **piloncillo,** is a brown sugar in rock form, similar to palm sugar. Originating in Central and Latin America. Processed to granular form, Panela is popular in baking as well as being favoured by Baristas.

Pearl sugar is used in the baking industry for decorative purposes. Also known as **decorative sugar** or **sanding sugar,** these are simply lumps of refined sugar particles.

Preserving sugar is designed for jams and preserves. It has large white crystals which dissolve slowly and so do not settle in the bottom of the pan   reducing the need for stirring and the risk of burning. In addition, less froth results in a clearer preserve.

Raw sugar is a semi-refined product similar to **turbinado**. It has a light caramel/molasses flavour. Also called **plantation sugar** and **sugar in the raw**. In Canada, however, 'raw sugar' refers to the product imported simply for refining into other sugars and is therefore not sold to the consumer, as it still contains impurities.

Rock sugar, Chinese rock sugar and **rock candy** are names given to a sugar made from very pure white sugar and comes as large white crystals, either clear or yellow. Not as sweet as granulated sugar, it is used for red roasting and (the yellow variety) as a decorative sugar, as well as in cooking.

Rolled fondant also known as **sugar paste, pastillage** and **roll out icing** is a mix of icing sugar, cornflour and gum arabic. Used in cake decorating as it's easy to mould, shape and colour. Once applied it needs to dry before decorating.

Silk sugar is a new product which, as the name suggests, is as smooth as silk when commercially made into fondant. Not readily available to the public.

Snow sugar or **MR sugar** is a commercially available product favoured by bakers and chefs who have their sweet goods on display. This moisture-resistant product tastes of sugar and looks like icing sugar, but it won't dissolve when dusted over berries or cakes. It cannot be used in the cooking process. Strictly aesthetic.

Soft icing mixture is a milled sugar that is better used for frosting on a cake than in baking, as it contains a starch as a free-flowing agent. See also **icing sugar**, above.

Sugar syrup, known as **simple syrup** in the US, is a syrup of water and sugar, which has been boiled until the sugar dissolves. Used for sweetening bar drinks (cocktails) and as a base for fruit sauces. Usually made with equal parts sugar and water, but can vary depending on the sweetness required (a sweeter mix may be 2 parts sugar to 1 part water).

Turbinado sugar is a light brown crystal sugar similar to **Demerara**. Can use light brown sugar or raw sugar as a substitute.

✪ Alternatives to sugar

~ **In baking**, sugar provides a chemical reaction as well as acting as a sweetener. Be aware of this when substituting with another sweetener in cooking because the alternatives may not provide the bulk and colouring sugar can provide. There are numerous synthetic sweeteners on the market, as well as some good natural sweeteners, which in some cases are many hundreds of times sweeter than sugar. Do your research to establish the benefits and problems of alternatives, depending on your reason for cutting back on sugar. As a note, vegans may choose not to consume white sugars because they can be refined with the use of charcoal made from animal bones.

~ **Agave nectar** is a sweetener extracted from the agave, a large succulent plant with thick fleshy leaves. It is a very thick liquid that goes a long way.

~ **Corn syrup** is available light or dark. The light syrup has been clarified, removing colour and cloudy particles. Dark syrup has had refiners added to produce a stronger-tasting, dark-coloured syrup. Corn syrup is high in fructose, which absorbs and retains moisture well, so using it in baked goods can result in a moist product that stays fresher for longer. Corn syrup can be replaced with other syrups but is not as sweet as, say, honey or maple.

~ **Fructose** is a term for sugar found in honey, corn and certain fruits. The sweetest of the simple sugars, it is almost twice as sweet as sucrose and turns into glucose once ingested. Fructose can be bought in granulated form.

~ **Fruit juice** makes for a good sweetener, but for many diabetics a concentrated fruit juice is still off limits. Fruit crystals, although hard to find, are available.

~ **Glucose powder** is made from grapes or fruit, and is closer to a pure glucose. Both are sold at chemists as dietary supplements, as syrup, powder or tablets. Glucose is much less sweet than sugar, and is valued as an energy booster because it heads straight for the blood stream.

~ **Glucose syrup** is more dextrin than glucose and is made from maize syrup.

~ **Honey** is as much as 60% sweeter than sugar, with a higher caloric count. Honey should never be served to babies, as contaminated honey is the only food product that can cause infant botulism. A true vegan no-no, as it is considered that commercial honey production exploits bees. (Bees naturally produce extra honey for the winter; beekeepers take all the honey, feeding bees a cheap, low-grade corn syrup instead which shortens their life span 2–3 years compared to 6 years for wild bees. Some exclusive keepers rotate honey supplies, ensuring the bees have enough for their winter period, but although honey from these keepers tastes great it has a far smaller yield, is hard to source, expensive and not commercially viable).

~ **Maple crystals** are a wonderful product with a high price tag. Much sweeter than sugar, they have the umami factor: tiny crystals with an excellent maple explosion in the mouth. Finding the product outside Canada and Vermont (US) can be a little frustrating.

~ **Maple syrup** is sweeter and better for you than sugar. Buy organic maple syrup wherever possible, as it doesn't contain the mould inhibitors or formaldehyde that may taint other pure maple syrups. Globally, Canadian maple syrup is famous, however, I'm here to tell you, if you can get your hands on the pure maple syrup from the north, eastern state of Vermont (US), then Canadian will become your favourite back up plan.

~ **Maple -flavoured syrup** is a very cheap imitation of the good stuff. It is a blend of corn syrup (pure sugar) with artificial flavours.

~ **Rice syrup** is only half as sweet as cane sugar, with a similar viscosity to honey. Not recommended as a sugar alternative in cakes and baked goods.

~ **Stevia** is a sweetener made from the South American plant *Stevia rebaudiana 'Bertoni'*. It is a green powder 30 times sweeter than sugar, with no calories and a sweet herby taste. It is not recognised by world health authorities, but it may be that stevia is controversial only because it poses a threat to synthetic brands and the sugar industry. You're most likely to find it as a dietary supplement in health food shops, and stevia cookbooks are available.

~ **Stevioside** is a white powder derived from stevia, but further refined and without the slight herb flavour. It is 300 times sweeter than sugar so should be used sparingly.

~ **Sucanat** is a whole cane sugar which contains the juice of pressed cane sugar with molasses added. Still a sugar as far as diabetics are concerned, it contains a small amount of vitamins, minerals and trace elements which help to reduce the negative effects of long-term white sugar use. Sucanat can be substituted for brown sugar, measure for measure.

~ **Sucrose** is the sugar extracted primarily from sugar cane and sugar beet.

~ **Synthetic (toxic) sweeteners** include many products at your own discretion, and research them before believing they are good at what they do. Neotame, aspartame (NutraSweet, Equal); sucralose - 600 times sweeter than sucrose (Splenda); and acesulfame-k - 200 times sweeter than sucrose (Sunette, Sweet n Safe, SweetOne).

SUGAR SNAP PEA is a pea hybrid, a cross between an English pea and a SNOW PEA. It has a fat edible pod filled with large peas, and can be eaten raw, cooked (steamed or stir-fried) or even pickled.

SUMAC is a tree, whose seed or berry is dried, ground and mixed with salt to produce the spice sumac. This tart, dark-red spice is sprinkled over cooked rice, bread doughs, fish or lamb (before being cooked) and salads. Sumac is found in Middle Eastern grocers, and the dried seeds can also be purchased whole: crush and soak in warm water for about 20 minutes, then strain to produce a juice that is sour enough to be used instead of lemon juice. Note that some wild versions of sumac can be very poisonous.

SUMMER SAVORY see SAVORY

SUMMER SQUASH see SQUASH

SURIMI see CRAB STICKS

SWEAT A method of cooking the male and female of the human species, usually chefs, usually in the middle of summer, and usually in a small kitchen with no air flow. For best results, wrap them in long-sleeved jackets, long pants, thick socks and steel-capped boots, reduce valuable heat loss by covering their heads with a silly-looking toque.
Pressure cook for 12–14 hours until sweating profusely. Best served with a beer! Or, sweating can mean cooking vegetables in a little oil or butter over a medium to low heat, in a covered pot or pan which releases moisture and intensifies the flavour.

SWEDE is also known as **rutabaga, yellow turnip** and **neeps.**

SWEET BELL PEPPER see CAPSICUM

SWEETCORN see CORN

SWISS CHARD see SILVERBEET

SZECHWAN PEPPER see SICHUAN PEPPER

T.

TAHINI / TAHINA is called **sesame paste** in the US. Sesame seeds are hulled, roasted and stone-ground into a wholesome, oily paste. Tahini is used predominantly in Middle Eastern cuisine, in halva, dressings and dips like baba ghannouj (smoky eggplant dip) and humus. A sweetened, dark variety is also available, although the paler variety is superior. It can be found in health food stores supermarkets and most grocery stores. See also SESAME SEED.

TAMARI see SOY SAUCE

TAMARILLO or tree tomato is a fruit the size of a large egg, smooth-skinned, and red, gold or amber in colour. The red variety is very tart, while the gold and amber varieties are milder. Immature, firm fruits can be ripened at room temperature until slightly soft. Although the fruit can be eaten raw (simply cut in half and scoop out the flesh; some people sprinkle it with a touch of sugar), it is more often cooked, stewed or baked. Peel before using: either blanch like a TOMATO or peel with a knife. The juice stains, so take care where you do this. When mixed with other fruits, tamarillos will overpower other flavours. Tamarillos store in the fridge for many weeks, and although the skin may blotch, the pulp will still be edible.

TAMARIND is the fruit of the tamarind tree. It grows in clusters, in hard-shelled pods the size of thin sausages. Crack open the skin to reveal a brown paste surrounding the seeds. The fruit can be eaten fresh, but is often soaked in the same method as the pulp (see below). The seeds and the leaves are also edible, the latter used in curries, relishes and soups. Tamarind is most often used instead of, or as well as, lemon or lime juice in recipes such as Thai curries. Several varieties exist, some are quite sour and others very sweet. Tamarind is sold as a puree in a jar or as a compressed 'cake' of pulp in a sealed packet, either with or without seeds. (Avoid packets that have added salt, as the true flavour of the tamarind is inhibited.) True aficionados will source the whole pods from Asian grocers, either loose or in 500g vacuum-packed packets. Most of us, however, buy puree or pulp, which can be exchanged measure for measure. The puree can be used directly from the jar, while the pulp should be prepared as follows: add hot water to the paste and soak for 10-20 minutes stir and squeeze to dissolve the pulp in the water, then strain out the seeds. Leftover pulp extractions or tamarind water can be frozen. Pour into ice cubes, then transfer to plastic bags once frozen.

TANGELO is said to be the juiciest of all citrus with a very rich flavour. It is a cross between a tangerine (itself a hybrid, see MANDARIN) and POMELO. The most popular commercial variety is the Minneola, a medium to very large, round to bell-shaped fruit with a pronounced neck and very few seeds. Also known as **honeybells.**

TANGERINE see MANDARIN

TAPIOCA see 'cassava flour' in FLOUR

TARAMA translates from the Turkish as 'salted fish roe'. Originally made from salted and dried grey mullet roe, it is now more often produced from the less expensive smoked cod roe. It is the essential ingredient in *taramasalata*, a dip made from tarama, soaked white bread or mashed potato, olive oil and lemon juice.

TARO is an edible tuber that can be used like potato, with a flavour described as a combination of artichoke hearts and chestnuts. The taro family should not be eaten raw. When peeling, I suggest using gloves as the juice from these tubers can cause a skin irritation. Once peeled, keep in cold water until ready to cook, or (an alternative I prefer) cook in the skins then peel. The leaf of the plant can be used like LEAFY GREENS and the young shoots as a vegetable, either roasted or in a stir-fry. *Eddo* and *dasheen* are two varieties of taro whose names seem interchangeable with 'taro' itself. The most common, dasheen, has a shaggy brown skin (similar to a coconut) circled with prominent rings and roughly the size of a turnip. Eddo has a smaller corm that attaches to the larger root. Also known as **yautia** or (in Australia) **yam.**

TARRAGON If your recipe calls for some tarragon, you must be dusting off the French cookbooks. It is also important in the *fines herbes* mix. Use **French tarragon** rather than **Russian tarragon** - the tasteless cousin. Steep leftover fresh tarragon in white vinegar for a classic vinaigrette. It also freezes well (see HERBS for method).

TART see PASTRY

TARTARIC ACID see CREAM OF TARTAR

TEMPEH see 'alternatives' in MEAT

TEMPERATURES Thermometers should be kept upright in a cup in a cupboard or container to avoid damage. To check the accuracy of a candy or sugar thermometer, place it in boiling water for 10 minutes and it should register 100°C. If the reading is out, adjust the temperature required in your recipe accordingly. Accurate oven temperatures are important, especially for baking. See also OVENS and conversions on page 257.

TEMPOYAK is fermented DURIAN, a popular Malaysian side dish.

TEXTURED VEGETABLE PROTEIN (TVP) see 'alternatives to meat' in MEAT

THICKENERS Many different products can be used as thickening agents, depending on the dish.

> **For cold dishes,** see AGAR-AGAR, CARRAGEEN, GELATINE, GELOZONE, ISINGLASS.

> **For sauces, soups and stews,** see BEURRE MANIÉ, LIAISON, PANADA, ROUX and 'how to thicken' in SAUCES. See also PECTIN.

> **Blood** from some animals is used as a thickening agent in certain dishes, black pudding and 'sanguette' (which pretty much fried, coagulated chicken blood). If boiled, blood will clot or separate and lose its effectiveness as a thickener, so avoid heating it for too long or on too high a heat. Always add a little of the sauce to the blood and then stir that mix back into the sauce, heat gently and

serve. Use 250 ml blood to thicken approximately 1 litre of sauce or stock.

Pureed liver can be used as a thickener and is easier to control than blood. Just remember to strain the sauce before serving.

THYME comes in many varieties, all of which can be interchanged successfully, despite obvious differences in pungency. Common thyme and lemon thyme suit most foods. I find myself drying the bunch as soon as it gets home – using it and hanging it up at the same time.

TISANE Originally, tisane simply meant 'barley water' but today it more often refers to herbal infusions. Tea is a more common word for all infusions whether made from tea leaves or herbal or fruit mixes, while most tisanes are made from medicinal plants.

TOGARASHI or **seven-flavour spice**, is a popular Japanese spice mix used as a condiment to sprinkle over hot pots and noodle dishes, or for sukiyaki, or as a seasoning. The seven flavours are ground chilli, poppy seeds, sansho pepper, black sesame seeds, white sesame seeds, rape seeds and ground tangerine peel. The amount of chilli can be varied according to taste.

TOMATILLO, also known as **husk tomato**, is a type of CAPE GOOSEBERRY. It is a small green or green-purple fruit (the size of a large cherry tomato) surrounded by an enlarged calyx or husk which should be removed before cooking. As the fruit ripens, it fills the husk and can split it open by harvest time. Tomatillos are an important ingredient in fresh and cooked green salsas and other Latin American dishes. The freshness and greenness of the husk are the key qualities. The fruit should be firm and bright-green to provide the right colour and acidic flavour.

TOMATO

 Top tips for tomatoes
    ~ Fragrance is a better indicator of a good tomato than colour; use your nose to smell the stem end. The stem should retain the

garden aroma of the plant itself. If it doesn't, your tomato will lack flavour.

~ Keep tomatoes on the window sill to ripen, then store at room temperature. If tomatoes are fully ripe or starting to soften, use them immediately or move them to the fridge. Refrigeration will stop the flavour from developing, so only refrigerate after they are fully ripe.

~ The best knife for cutting tomatoes has a serrated edge, about 15-cm long, with finer teeth than a bread knife.

~ Add to a leafy salad at the last minute to prevent the acid and weight of the tomatoes from breaking down the lettuce.

~ To avoid soggy sandwiches, place each slice of tomato on a piece of paper towelling before it goes in the sandwich to absorb excess water.

~ The acid in fresh or canned tomatoes will strip an iron pan of its natural non-stick coating, leaving it susceptible to rusting – choose something like stainless steel for cooking.

~ Tomato 'water', the clearish liquid that escapes from a sliced tomato, can be used as a low-acidity stand-in for lemon juice. Try it for marinating raw fish.

~ To peel a tomato, score the skin very lightly with the point of a sharp knife. Then blanch for 10–15 seconds, no more. Any book that calls for 30–60 seconds in boiling water is having a laugh – the longer the tomato cooks, the more flesh will be ripped off when you peel the tomato. Don't drop the tomatoes in iced water after blanching, as this will dilute the flavour.

~ Unripe, green tomatoes can be dipped in polenta and fried.

~ Rehydrate dried tomatoes (those not sold in oil) in hot water for 15 minutes. Drain and then marinate in olive oil, chopped herbs and balsamic or white wine vinegar (1 part vinegar to 5 parts oil). Store inan airtight container in the refrigerator.

Beefsteak tomatoes are bright-red and flat-ribbed with solid, juicy flesh. Good for slicing.

Cherry tomatoes, teardrop tomatoes and **grape tomatoes** are, respectively, small and round, teardrop or oblong in shape. They are red or yellow, ideal for salads or mixed into a pasta at the very last minute.

Heirloom tomato also **Heritage tomato** (UK) is defined as an open-pollinated, non-hybrid heirloom cultivar of tomato. Sweeter, full flavoured an in a variety of shapes, sizes and colours, heirlooms are far superior to anything found in the supermarket. There are over 10, 000 cultivars of tomato. Here is not the place to discuss those. However, I do encourage a trip to a local farmers market to discover what varietals are being sold.

Purple tomatoes from South America are very tasty raw, but can be cooked.

Roma tomatoes are also known as **plum tomatoes, sauce tomatoes** and **egg tomatoes**. This medium-sized, oblong tomato is ideal for soup, pasta sauce, drying, roasting and salad, as it has few seeds.

Tiger tomatoes are novel and very tasty raw.

Yellow tomatoes can be pear-shaped, round or oblong and suit all dishes, pickling, roasting and eating fresh.

TONKA BEAN is a sweet, aromatic seed (rather than a bean) used in foods such as ice-creams, custards, cakes and biscuits, although it can have a wonderful influence over savoury food if used correctly. It is rare these days as it has been suspected of having carcinogenic and poisonous properties. If a recipe calls for tonka beans, try substituting them with vanilla bean (see VANILLA).

TREACLE see MOLASSES

TREE MELON see PEPINO

TREE TOMATO see TAMARILLO

TREX see 'vegetable fat' in FAT

TRUFFLE is a highly prized fungus that can be eaten raw (thinly shaved or grated) or cooked (usually sautéed, mixed in a farce or pasta filling and in cream sauces). The price of truffles can range from $US300 per kg to $US4000 per kg. Traditionally sourced from France and Italy, truffles are now successfully grown in other parts of the world, including China, New Zealand, Australia and the US.

TUBER Any underground plant stem that can usually be cooked in the same way as a potato. Tubers that are often seen only in FLOUR form, yet are equally good as a vegetable, are arrowroot, cassava (tapioca root), Japanese artichoke, malanga, taro and water chestnuts. *Tuber* can alsorefer to the genus *Tuber* of which the fruiting body of the **ascomycete fungus** (TRUFFLE) is a species of.

TURKEY like Santa Claus, is recognised only once a year in many countries, with the exception of the US. Turkey is processed from 4 weeks to 10 months old. If cooked properly, turkey yields succulent, tasty white meat, just as good hot as it is cold. The problem lies in the fact that unlike, say, roast lamb, that gets a workout several times a year, turkey is rarely cooked, and so the inexperienced cook is scared into overcooking it, thereby rendering the meat drier than a salted pretzel. Turkey, like chicken, prefers gentle cooking and its juices will run clear when cooked. Here's a very rough guide to times for the first-time turkey roaster: try 30–35 minutes per kilo (no stuffing) or 40–45 minute per kg (with stuffing) at 170°C. See POULTRY for general information and further cooking tips.

TURMERIC is a rhizome, a member of the ginger family originating from India and other south Asian countries. Often used in its dried, powdered form, turmeric is excellent when raw and grated, as well as pickled.

TURNIP-ROOTED VEGETABLE see CELERIAC

TVP (TEXTURED VEGETABLE PROTEIN) see 'alternatives to meat' in MEAT

U.

UBE is a type of tropical purple yam from the Philippines. With a slightly sweet, vanilla flavour, it's ideal for desserts and sweets.

UGLI FRUIT is a hybrid of grapefruit, orange and tangerine. It tastes similar to grapefruit but it's sweeter. The outer skin is a distinctive mottled green and yellow which peels away easily to reveal easily segmented pulp with few seeds. Properly pronounced 'HOO Glee' but most Westerners name it for its looks: 'ugly'.

UGNI FRUIT This is the fruit of the evergreen shrub, *Ugni molinae*, a native to Chile, Argentina and southern Mexico. It is also known as the **Chilean guava, New Zealand cranberry** (when grown in New Zealand), or **Tazziberry**. It is a petite purple, red, or white berry used in sweet dishes, jams and to make the traditional Chilean liqueur Murtado.

UMAMI is the fifth taste. Where once there was salty, sweet, bitter and sour, all easily detected by certain areas of the tongue, there also lurked this extra taste sensation, the wow factor. It has been written about many times, as far back as 1825 when the French gastronome Brillat-Savarin used the word 'osmosone' to describe the sensation. The Japanese word is hard to translate directly, and it is said to involve all the senses, not just a singular taste. Food writers have variously described it as a rich, savoury taste, a perception of thickness and mouthfulness, well-rounded, full-bodied or even yummy. Other appropriate words might be 'savoury', 'meaty', 'deliciousness' or 'pungent'. An excellent example of umami is in a piece of good parmesan cheese. The little white flecks or crystals are a natural MSG produced by the cheese and an important chemical for the umami effect: the small tasty 'explosions' on the tongue when you eat parmesan. Other foods with umami are naturally brewed soy sauce and fish sauce. The crudest form of umami is synthetic MONOSODIUM GLUTAMATE used to give food the extra lift and enhanced flavour – steroids for food, if you will.

UME A fruit sometimes called the **Japanese plum, Japanese apricot, Chinese plum** or **plum blossom**. Ume is a member of the plum/prune family *Prunus mume,* yet is more closely related to the apricot. Ume is used in jams, sauces, juices and liquor. It is very common in Chinese,

Vietnamese, Korean and Japanese cuisines. **Umeshu** is the liqueur made form steeping the plums in alcohol and sugar.

UMEBOSHI literally translates as 'dried ume'. The fruit is pickled (brined in 20% salt) and then dried. Eating umeboshi in Japan is the equivalent of the English expression "an apple a day".

UNAGI is Japanese for eel.

UNI see URCHIN

URCHIN also **sea urchin.** Urchin comes from the middle English word for "hedgehog" due to the spiked resemblance. The edible part of the sea urchin are the gonads, often simply called the coral or roe. Considered a delicacy in some countries, especially Japan where it is known as UNI, eaten raw.

VACHERIN see MERINGUE

VANILLA is available as pods or beans, as well as extracted in liquid forms. The lion's share of the world's vanilla comes from the bourbon vanilla plant (nothing to do with alcohol), grown in Madagascar, Mexico, Indonesia and Tahiti.

Vanilla bean also known as **vanilla pod** is expensive for a reason. It's hand-pollinated then hand-picked. Each bush produces about 40–50 beans, which can only be picked when the bean is dark, plump and almost splitting open. This means the bush needs going over daily until all are picked. The bean is then fermented for 4 weeks. The crystallised vanillin coating on the pod is called the 'givre' (French for 'frost'). The more visible the givre, the better quality the bean. Once removed from its packet, vanilla beans dry quickly so I recommend storing beans in a jar of sugar until needed.(The sugar will take on the perfume of the vanilla). Slice the bean lengthways and then infuse in milk, cream or syrup for custard, pastry cream, ice cream and fruit or sugar syrups. Sometimes the tiny black specks or seeds within are scraped out and added to the recipe separately. Don't throw the pod away after use as it still has some residual flavour. Rinse it quickly, pat dry and store in sugar. It is still good enough for another infusion, albeit a little diluted and without the trademark black seeds. Pure vanilla extract is made from beans that have been steeped in alcohol. The extract has an alcohol content of at least 35% (by law). It is rich and syrupy and dark brown in colour. Be prepared to pay handsomely for a small bottle of this extract and use sparingly (more sparingly than essence). Vanilla essence is a watered down version of vanilla extract – the affordable domestic vanilla. A thin, medium-brown liquid bulked out with corn or sugar syrup, it has a higher alcohol content. Imitation vanilla is a synthetic, chemical attempt at recreating the flavour and smell of vanilla: highly disappointing compared to the real thing.

VEAL is a meat that not many outside Europe have embraced. Italians are the largest consumers of veal per capita, and produce excellent quality. Many people object to eating veal because of the much publicised inhumane treatment of the young calves, but this differs from country to country. Although there was a time when young calves were bled daily to produce white meat, this barbaric practice was stopped. The practice that replaced it was for calves to be held from a few days after birth in individual cages that restrict movement and fed on a diet of milk supplement until they reach slaughter weight. European law has now made veal production far more humane but the US is yet to abolish old rearing habits. Bobby veal receives its name from a time when these very young calves would fetch a bob each. Bobby veal in the US and Australia is reminiscent of the veal found in European countries: pink, wobbly and tender meat. Milk-fed veal is older, 8–12 weeks, and more common. Some try to pass off young beef as veal, but the difference is obvious: it shows none of the colour and texture characteristics of true veal. As Italy is the leader in consumption it seems only natural to listen to their cooks when it comes to handling and cooking veal, so start with recipes in your Italian recipe books. One thing to remember is that veal is an underdeveloped protein, in other words, delicate. Overcooking, or cooking too fast on a high heat will damage these proteins, dry and toughen the meat. So cooking methods for beef and lamb can be applied to veal, the temperature at which it is cooked should therefore be monitored.

VEGETABLE Botanically, vegetable matter is classified as any part of a plant that is not involved in reproduction. Most of us think of them as the edible leaves, stems, roots, tubers, seeds and flowers of certain plants. Some foods that are actually fruits are classified as vegetables. Capsicum, eggplant, tomato, pumpkin, squash, zucchini, cucumber, chilli, tomatoes, avocado and choko are all fruit because they all harbour seeds. The one fruit that doesn't? Mushrooms.

Vegetables, like fruit, continue to live and mature after they are picked, i.e. they absorb oxygen, give off carbon dioxide, tend to become warmer, with changes in flavour, appearance and texture. We can think of vegetables in nine main vegetable groups: bulbs (leek, onions, garlic, etc.), flower vegetables (broccoli, cauliflower), fungi, leaf vegetables (cabbage, lettuce, endive, parsley, watercress), pulses/legumes (peanuts, peas, beans, lentils), root vegetables (carrots, parsnips, swede, salsify), stem vegetables (fennel, asparagus, celery) and tubers (potatoes, yams, Jerusalem artichoke, sweet potato).

VEGETABLE OYSTER see SALSIFY

VEGETABLE PEAR see CHOKO

VEGETABLE SPAGHETTI is a member of the SQUASH family. These large squash, the size of an ostrich egg reveal the meaning behind their name once opened: almost the entire contents hold spaghetti-like flesh. Its flavour is quite bland (like the insides of a zucchini) and can be boiled for a short time in plenty of water. Also known as vegetable squash or spaghetti squash.

VENISON most commonly refers to the meat from deer. It is a dark-red, tender meat with little fat, which is good to remember when cooking – for example, it is often LARDED before roasting and should be rubbed with oil before grilling or frying. Marinating can enhance its gamey flavour, but is not necessary. A basic marinade is red wine, crushed juniper berries, pepper, bay leaves and olive oil. Venison should be grilled or pan-fried rare to medium rare (much past this point and the meat begins to dry out) so if rare meat is not your thing, try braising, stewing or casseroling instead. Choose the same cuts for different cooking methods as you would beef, veal and lamb. See also CERVENA.

VERJUICE is made from unfermented green or unripe fruit, predominantly grapes. This sour liquid is similar to vinegar but not as harsh. Used in medieval and Renaissance times, verjuice is making a welcome comeback. It is great for deglazing pans, in sauces and in dressings. Verjuice can be difficult to source on the supermarket shelf, so look for it in specialty food stores, food halls and markets.

VINAIGRETTE see DRESSINGS

VINEGAR The basic principle of how vinegar is made is relatively simple: natural sugars (whatever the source) are fermented to alcohol, followed by a second fermentation into vinegar, with both stages affected by micro-organisms. Vinegar lasts a long time. After sitting several months, opened vinegar may change colour, go cloudy or form sediment, but the product is fine to use. However, if a recipe calls for a particular vinegar, ask yourself before you buy it how often and how much it will be used. There's not much point in having great quantities of flavoured vinegars if only a splash is used on occasion.

✅ **Top tips for vinegar**

~ For a soft-pink colour, fill a bottle with washed chive blossoms and cover with white wine vinegar. Allow to sit for 8–10 days (no longer or the herbs will become bitter), strain and bottle, to use in salad dressings. This can work with purple basil or African blue basil, too.

Balsamic vinegar This Italian staple can be so good it can be drunk like a port or mixed with fruit. The aged balsamic vinegars are the good ones; beware of those that list sugar as an ingredient, as the sugar acts as a colouring agent, whereas good balsamic relies on ageing and refining to define the flavour and quality. Balsamic vinegar is not classed as a wine vinegar, as it is made from specific varieties of grape must (what's left after the juice has been extracted from the grape) not wine.

Fruit vinegar can be flavoured with raspberry, apple cider, blackcurrant, blueberry, date, pineapple and mango, to name just a few. Fruit vinegars are great in salad dressings, marinades and sauces. It is simple enough to make them at home if you can find a good recipe.

Herb vinegar can be easily made at home, and it's an especially good way to use up a leftover bunch of HERBS. Warm the vinegar (wine, rice or cider), then add a few sprigs of the herb (don't add too many herbs, as the vinegar will lose its ability to preserve them), seal tightly and let stand. Discard the herbs after a couple of weeks, as they turn bitter.

Malt vinegar is crucial as an accompaniment for English fish and chips and is a favourite for pickling vegetables. Quality malt vinegar is made from barley, malt and yeast, with a natural dark-caramel colour, while poor quality malt vinegar is made from acetic acid, water and caramel colouring. Malt vinegar is prepared differently to fruit vinegars –similar to the preparation of beer – and then aged.

Rice vinegar (or **rice wine vinegar,** although it's not made from rice wine) is a milder, sweeter, less acidic white vinegar than most Western vinegars.This mildness is characteristic of all the rice vinegars.

Red rice vinegar is salty compared to other vinegars, used in sweet and sour dishes and dipping sauce. Black rice vinegar is a popular vinegar for use in dipping sauce as well as in stir-fries and shark fin soup. The best quality Japanese rice vinegar, used in sushi rice, is made from unpolished glutinous rice.

Sherry vinegar is to Spain what balsamic is to Italy. Also known as **Xeres vinegar**, it is excellent in sauces to accompany meats, the aged version is smooth and distinctive, and lends itself well to salad dressings and use with eggs.

White vinegar is plain and nasty, good for acidulating water and as a cleaning agent. Wine vinegar includes white wine vinegar, red wine vinegar, champagne vinegar and sherry vinegar. Quality wine vinegars require time and patience, good wine and good barrels.

White wine vinegar makes a great base for home-made flavoured vinegars (fruit and herb), as well as mayonnaise and hollandaise. **Red wine vinegar** is used for a salad dressings and to deglaze pans for meat sauces.

✪ Alternatives to vinegar

~ **Lemon juice** or **lime juice** make an excellent natural substitute for vinegar. Although it does come in only one flavour – lemon – it will replace vinegar in mayonnaise, dressings, sauces and dips,marinades and on fish and chips.

~ **Sorrel leaves** put through a juicer produce a bright green and very sour liquid, with lemon flavour.

~ **Tamarind juice** see TAMARIND

~ **Verjuice** can serve as a substitute for vinegar in many dishes but, like lemon juice, it is limited in its flavour. If a recipe calls for balsamic, sherry or another aromatic vinegar, then verjuice will not deliver near equal results.

~ **Wine or fortified wine** in rare cases for cooking will satisfy a recipe that needs vinegar.

W.

WAKAME see SEAWEED

WASABI is also known as **Japanese horseradish** because the flavour of fresh horseradish resembles the hot bite delivered by wasabi. Other than that they are not related. Fresh wasabi has a unique spicy heat about it, which doesn't linger in the mouth like chilli. Because true wasabi is difficult to grow and in short supply, an imitation wasabi (not made from the wasabi root) is used extensively in homes and restaurants. It is not as smooth or refreshing a flavour as true wasabi. Sold as wasabi powder and prepared wasabi (paste) these imitations are made from horseradish powder or paste and mustard powder as well as artificial colours (blue#1 and turmeric), sorbitol, citric acid, karaya gum, Xanthan gum, guar gum and artificial flavours. Wasabi is used as a condiment, served with sushi and sashimi and noodle dishes.

The fresh leaves and petioles of wasabi are also edible fresh (salads, wraps, sushi) or dried and used as a wasabi flavouring in other processed foods. These are quite mild compared to the rhizome. The root is scrubbed (like ginger) then grated finely; Japanese chefs use a shark-skin grater to produce a velvety smooth paste. Sometimes the wasabi is lightly diluted with light soy sauce and used for dipping called 'wasabi-joyu'.

WASHING UP is usually considered a chore and not a privilege, but it ought to be seen as the enjoyable last phase in the eating experience. Or so I keep telling my kids.

Problem solving
~ **Smelly jar?** Half fill with water and 1–2 tablespoons of bicarbonate of soda, shake well and let stand for an hour.

~ **Melted cheese stuck to dishes?** Remove melted cheese from plates or equipment with a scraper or paper towelling. Rinse under cold water as washing under hot water continues to soften and cook the cheese, making it near impossible to remove from scourers, brushes and dish cloths

~ **Egg stuck to the dishes?** Immediately wash with cold water any utensils, equipment, cutlery and crockery that have come into contact with egg. Leaving egg to dry and crust on anything, including the kitchen bench, results in unnecessarily hard work. Washing in hot water only continues the cooking process, making cleaning even more laborious.

~ **Aluminium pots with stains or dark rims?** Probably caused by boiling salted water. Can be lightened by simmering 1 tablespoon of cream of tartar in water.

~ **Hard-to-clean aluminium pot?** Boiling apple peel in an aluminium pot makes cleaning them easier.

~ **Cleaning iron pans or skillets** - Simply wipe out with a paper towel. Synthetic detergents and even soap break down the natural non-stick properties of cast iron. To avoid rust, always store with the lid off so moisture doesn't collect in the pan. To season a new pan, rub with oil inside and out and then bake in a hot oven (250°C) for 2 hours. Allow to cool and wipe over with paper towel.

~ **Plastic or glassware stuck together?** Add cold water to the top one and submerge the bottom one in hot water. (The water should be neither ice cold nor boiling; tap water temperature will suffice.)

~ **Smoking grill top or BBQ grill?** Rub with half a swede on a regular basis. Swede is a root vegetable similar to turnip.

~ **Food burnt to the base of a pot or saucepan?** Below are four methods to try:

1). Add water and a strong detergent, then boil for 10–15 minutes.
2). Sprinkle the burnt area with salt and heat on the stove top. This may help the burnt surface to break or flake away with the salt.
3). Add water and half an onion and bring to the boil.
4.) If it happens to be your favourite pot, or a lucky one, take it to a 'metal finisher', where they will add chemicals not readily available and too dangerous for the general public to use.

WATERMELON are part of the cucumber family originating in Africa. With over 1000 varietals in varying in shape (round or elongated), rind colour and pattern, flesh colour (pink, red or yellow), and whether they have seeds or more popularly - without seeds.

WAX JAMBU also known as **Java apple**, is native to Malaysia and Indonesia. A small, pear-shaped fruit with a waxy skin and a crisp, juicy flesh, it is subtly sweet and resembles and APPLE. Wax jambu are commonly eaten fresh, although some inferior varieties are bland and eaten with a sprinkle of sugar. Available throughout Asia, but difficult to source elsewhere.

WHITEBARK RASPBERRY also known as **Western raspberry, blue raspberry** and **blackcap raspberry.** Whitebark raspberry gets its name form the thick, white waxy coating as they grow. The flesh has a blue/black or deep purple colour. Interesting to note that foods that are artificially coloured bright blue are based on the whitebark raspberry and labelled as "raspberry" flavoured, done so to differentiate from "cherry, watermelon and strawberry flavoured foods, often coloured red.

WHITE CHOCOLATE see CHOCOLATE

WHITE CURRANT see CURRANT

WHITE RADISH see DAIKON

WHITE TURMERIC see ZEDOA

WILD RICE see RICE

WINDSOR BEAN see 'broad beans' in BEAN

WINE BERRY native to Chine, Japan and Korea now growing wild in other regions worldwide. A member of the rose family with very similar qualities to raspberries.

WINTER SAVORY see SAVORY

WINTER SQUASH see PUMPKIN; SQUASH

WITCHETTY GRUB see XYLEUTES

WITLOF is known as **chicory** or **chicory heads** in the UK and **Belgian endive** in the US. It is sometimes also called **French endive** or **Belgian chicory.** It has a small, creamy-coloured, cylindrical head with slightly bitter leaves which are a very pale green at the tip. Witlof is grown in complete darkness to prevent it from turning green. The leaves can be separated and tossed in salad, whole or sliced. It also braises well (45 minutes) and can be steamed or sautéed.

WOLFBERRY most commonly known as **Goji** or **gojiberry.**

WOMBOK or **wong bok** is also known as **Chinese cabbage, napa cabbage, Chinese leaves** and **Peking cabbage.**

and small white seeds. The flesh can be eaten out of hand and can be sweet or sour.

WOOD APPLE is a native fruit of India, Sri Lanka and Bangladesh, also known as bael, stone apple and elephant apple. Wood apple is not remotely related to the apple family, rather it is a softball sized fruit with a very hard rind which can be difficult to crack open, it appears greenish-brown in colour from outside and contains sticky brown pulp.

X.

XANTHAN GUM see 'alternatives' in GLUTEN

XO is a spicy sauce seafood-based sauce that is made in Hong Kong. The sauce is a blend of dried scallops, chili peppers, ham, and dried garlic. Its unique flavour has made it a staple in many Chinese regions.

XOCOLATI is also known as Mexican hot chocolate. See CHOCOLATE.

XOCONOSTLE or **opuntia** which is **prickly pear,** the fruit of which must be peeled very carefully to remove the small spikes on the outer skin before use. Also known as **cactus fruit, cactus fig** and **Indian fig.**

XYLEUTES is the genus of moth from which comes the very edible **witchetty grub (witjuti)**, savoured by indigenous Australians. Eaten raw (except the head) or roasted. Some noted Australian chefs venturing into indigenous ingredients or colloquially 'bush tucker' (the use of native ingredients as food) will use these grubs in sauces, soups, salads or as finger food. Do they taste like chicken? Not unless you think chicken has a nutty flavour with a soft centre.

XYLITOL is a sugar substitute made from the extracted fibres of plants like corn husks.

Y.

YABBY see CRAYFISH

YAM is a word used in Africa, Asia, Australia, Caribbean and South America to encompass a range of botanically different tubers such as taro and sweet potato as well as the true yam. All edible yams must be cooked (boiled, steamed, roasted, baked or fried) to break down the toxic substance called dioscorine, which can taste bitter or make people violently ill, depending on the species.

Once cooked they are very starchy with little flavour. The development of several cultivars of sweet potato, a much tastier staple, has meant the yam has taken a back seat in mainstream cooking. The New Zealand yam is from a different family: a small dark-orange tuber with a sweet, tangy

YANGMEI is a delicate fruit, extremely common in China and is frequently eaten raw and used in creating alcoholic drinks. Somewhat expensive due to its perishable nature and needing to be chilled from harvest, it is rarely seen outside of China for this reason. About the size of a cherry with a flavour similar to strawberry.

YEAST is used primarily for making bread dough rise. A fungus that is all around and inside us, it multiplies rapidly in the right conditions, consuming sugar and emitting carbon dioxide and alcohol. When using yeast it is important to follow the recipe particularly in regard to the temperatures of the ingredients. Excess heat and excess salt can both kill yeast and prevent the dough from rising.

 Top tips for yeast

~ Always follow the quantities specified in a recipe: more yeast does not mean a greater yield.

~ Naturally, old yeast loses its leavening properties. If you are using old yeast, you could try doubling the resting time but don't be tempted to double the quantity. Then go out and buy more fresh yeast.

~ If you need to slow the rate at which your dough is proving, place it in the fridge, where it will continue to rise, just much more slowly. Even a dough left overnight retains a good leavening ability. (For tips on freezing dough see BREAD.)

~ Fresh yeast cannot be substituted measure for measure with dried yeast. A firm equivalent is hard to provide but, as a guide, for every 7 g packet of dried yeast, use 15 g fresh yeast.

~ It is said that less yeast and longer rising produce a better-developed flavour.

~ A brick (500 g) of fresh compressed yeast can be broken down into manageable portions. The best way to do this is with a wire cheese cutter, then wrap in plastic and store in an airtight container in the freezer for about 3 months.

Brewer's yeast can be bought either 'activated' or 'deactivated'. Activated brewer's yeast is used for beer and wine making; deactivated is used for nutritional purposes (see 'nutritional yeast', below).

Yeast extracts – which are not extracts at all – are made from brewer's yeast that has been treated to remove bitterness. The salty, viscous result is an edible spread. It has been stated by food writers in the US that Vegemite, Promite or Marmite are used as 'a spread like peanut butter'. In fact, they are spread as you would butter, that is, thinly: one reason why Vegemite has not taken off in the US.

Dried yeast (active dry yeast in the US) is sold as dried granules that must be completely dissolved (hydrated) in warm liquid for the yeast to work. This yeast can be stored in the fridge to extend its shelf life. Dried yeast is twice as strong fresh yeast weight for weight. The strength of dried yeast means it should not be used in baked goods that call for a lot of yeast as the flavour will be overpowering.

Fresh yeast, is also known as **compressed fresh yeast, cake yeast, baker's yeast** or **active fresh yeast**. The best place to buy fresh yeast is your local baker. Buying from a supermarket is not recommended, as the product does not rotate quickly enough, which means you get an older yeast in large blocks. The local baker can sell you smaller amounts. (It would be considerate to ring ahead so the yeast can be cut, measured and set aside, as most bakers have gone home by the time you get there and the service staff may not know where to find it or how to deal with it.) Fresh yeast is an activated yeast and should not be consumed raw as it will continue to grow in the intestine and absorb valuable nutrients from the body. Store in the fridge or freezer (defrost before use) to prolong its life.

Instant yeast (fast-rising yeast, rapid-rise yeast or **bread machine yeast** in the US) has a smaller granule than dried yeast, so it does not need to be dissolved in warm liquid, simply mix straight into the dried ingredients. Store in the fridge once opened.

Nutritional yeast is different from the yeast used for bread. It is found in health stores, usually as a big yellowish flakes or finer granules. Nutritional yeast is a brewer's yeast, only it has been deactivated so as not to produce alcohol or bubbles. It is used by vegans in cooking as a cheese substitute (for flavour without texture). Buy the lemon/yellow-coloured one, not the brown one, which is bitter.

Wild yeast occurs naturally in the air and water and is the cause of any food with a sugar content turning sour. The fermentation of fruit is the action of wild yeast, as is the distinct sour flavour that gives a 'fizzy' sensation on the tongue on leftover roasted vegetables that have been sitting in the fridge. Wild yeast can be cultivated in a starter dough for bread making, particularly artisan breads (hand-crafted using a starter) like sourdough, ciabatta and French breads.

YOGHURT is the controlled fermentation of milk (usually cow's or goat's milk, but also sheep, buffalo, camel, yak, mare and soy) by two bacteria, Lactobacillus bulgaricus and Streptococcus thermophilus. It can be sweetened or unsweetened, set or stirred. Stirred yoghurt is fermented in a mixing container before being stirred and packaged, while set yoghurt is fermented and set in individual containers. With its sour tang, unsweetened yoghurt can lift an ordinary meal to new heights. Used as an accompaniment to fruit, salads, in sauces, desserts, or simply on its own.

Greek yoghurt is richer and thicker than normal yoghurt with a higher fat content (8–10%compared to 3–4%). This richness is achieved by first boiling the milk (cow's or goat's) to reduce water content.

European-style yoghurt is similar to Greek, only made elsewhere...in Europe.

 Top tips for yoghurt

~ To thin yoghurt for a dressing, first stir or whisk the yoghurt before adding other ingredients.

~ To thicken yoghurt naturally, place in a sieve or strainer lined with cheesecloth or muslin for anywhere from 1–24 hours depending how thick you need it. See also LABNA.

~ To prevent curdling, try whisking the yoghurt until smooth and then adding to the hot dish slowly. Adding a small amount of starch (corn, wheat, potato or rice) to the yoghurt will also work (1 teaspoon for every 250 g or ml yoghurt).

 Alternatives to yoghurt

~ **Soy yoghurt** is made in the same manner as dairy yoghurt but with soy milk. As too is **coconut yoghurt**. Readily available in supermarkets and health food shops.

YUBA is the skin that collects at the top of a vat of congealing soy milk, used in the making of bean curd skin noodles (see NOODLES) and yuba sheets, thin sheets of bean curd skin that can be rehydrated and wrapped around other foods or deep fried and broken up then sprinkled on salads or vegetables.

YUCA not to be confused with yucca (a different species of plant). Yuca is more commonly known as **cassava** and used in much the same way as yams, sweet potato and potato. Yuca is further processed to produce **tapioca flour.**

YURINE is a lily root/bulb or bud that is peeled and sliced for use in

Japanese soup.

YUZU is a citrus fruit the size of a MANDARIN but with more seeds, the sourness and skin colour of a lemon and the smell of a lime. Used in cooking rather than eating straight because of its high acid content, the shredded peel is sprinkled over Japanese simmered dishes, and the juice is combined with ponzu in a Japanese version of the French bouillabaisse (seafood pot soup). Also known as **citron** or **cedro**. If not available, try using equal parts lemon and lime juice.

Z.

ZA'ATAR , the Arabic word for wild thyme, is both a herb and a spice mix used in Middle Eastern cooking. It is sprinkled on bread before baking, on soups or seafood, barbecued mutton and grilled meats. It is a blend of sumac, sesame seeds and the herb za'atar, and can be bought ready-made in Middle Eastern and Lebanese produce shops.

ZAPOTE see SAPOTE

ZEDOARY is a rhizome related to TURMERIC, sometimes known as white turmeric. It is primarily used in Thailand where the young rhizome is eaten as an aromatic but bitter vegetable. The dried spice is mixed with other spices in small amounts in curries, mostly in Indian and Indonesian cuisine. The rhizome smells like turmeric and mango, it is orange in the centre, and has a spicy ginger-like flavour with a bitter aftertaste.

ZHE FRUIT from south east Asian, related to the mulberry and goes by the names **cudrang, kujibbong, mandarin melon berry, silkworm thorn, zhe** or **che.**

ZIG ZAG VINE a tropical indigenous fruit of Eastern Australia and Papua New Guinea. Eaten fresh with an almost orange sherbet flavour.

ZIZIPHUS MAURITIANA is a tropical fruit originating from South East Asian, eaten raw, pickled or as a jam, as well as preserved in salt solution or sun dried. Also known as **Chinese date, Indian Jujube, Chinese apple** and **Dunks.**

ZOMI see PALM OIL

ZUCCHINI is a highly perishable summer SQUASH. Refrigerated, zucchinis will last about four days before the rot begins to set in. The larger they get, the tougher and more bitter they become. The blossoms of the young plant can be eaten, often stuffed or fried. Also known as **courgette** and sometimes **Italian marrow squash**.

WEIGHT CONVERSION (IMPERIAL TO METRIC)

IMPERIAL WEIGHT	EXACT METRIC EQUIVALENT	METRIC APPROXIMATION	ALSO KNOW AS
¼ oz	7 g	5 g	2 dram
½ oz	14.1 g	15 g	
1 oz	28.3 g	30 g	8 drams
2 oz	56.6 g	55 g	
3 oz	84.9 g	85 g	
4 oz	113.2 g	115 g	¼ lb
5 oz	141.5 g	140 g	
6 oz	169.8 g	170 g	
7 oz	198.1 g	200 g	
8 oz	227 g	230 g	½ lb
9 oz	255.3 g	250 g	¼ kg
10 oz	283 g	280 g	
11 oz	311.3 g	310 g	
12 oz	340 g	340g	
13 oz	368.6 g	370g	
14 oz	396.6 g	400g	
15 oz	424 g	425 g	
16 oz	454 g	450 g	1 lb
17 oz	482.3 g	480 g	1 lb, ½ kg
2 lb	898 g	900 g	1 kg

COMMONLY USED ABBREVIATIONS

°C	degrees Celsius (centigrade)
°F	degrees Fahrenheit
C	cup
cl	centilitre
cm	centimetre
D	dessert spoo
dl	decilitre
dr	dram (drachm)
fl oz	fluid ounce
g	gram (gramme)
gal	gallon
in	inch
kg	kilogram
L	litre
l	litre
lb	pound
mg	milligram
min	minim
ml	millilitre

COMMONLY USED ABBREVIATIONS

mm	millimetre
oz	ounce
pt	pint
qt	quart
T	tablespoon
tsp	teaspoon
tbsp	tablespoon

OVEN TEMPERATURES

CELSIUS	FAHRENHEIT	GAS MARK	DEFINITION
100	200	¼	VERY COOL
110	225	¼	VERY COOL
120	240	½	COOL/SLOW
130	250	1	COOL/SLOW
140	275	2	COOL/SLOW
150	300	3	COOL/SLOW
170	325	4	MODERATE
180	350	5	MODERATE
190	375	6	MODERATE
200	400	7	HOT
220	425	8	HOT
230	450	9	VERY HOT
240	475	10	VERY HOT
250	500	10	VERY HOT

CELSIUS / FAHRENHEIT CONVERSION

°C	°F	°C	°F	°C	°F
-18	0	85	185	175	347
0	32	90	194	180	356
5	41	95	203	185	365
10	50	100	212	190	374
15	59	105	221	195	383
20	68	110	230	200	392
25	77	115	239	205	401
30	86	120	248	210	410
35	95	125	257	215	419
40	104	130	266	220	428
45	113	135	275	225	437
50	122	140	284	230	446
55	131	145	293	235	455
60	140	150	302	240	464
65	149	155	311	245	473
70	158	160	320	250	482
75	167	165	329	255	491
80	176	170	338	260	500

LIQUID VOLUME CONVERSION (METRIC TO IMPERIAL)

METRIC VOLUME	EXACT IMPERIAL EQUIVALENT	US CUSTOMARY	ALSO KNOWN AS
1 ml	0.0338 fl oz		1 cc, 16 minims, 20 drops
3.7 ml	0.1251 fl oz		1 fl dram, 60minims
5 ml	0.1691 fl oz		1 tsp, 60 drops thin liquid
10 ml	0.3381 fl oz		1 dessert spoon (D) 1 cl
15 ml	0.5072 fl oz		1 tablespoon (T)
20 ml	0.6762 fl oz		¼ dl, 8 fl drams
25 ml	0.8453 fl oz		2 tablespoon (T)
30 ml	1.0143 fl oz	1 fl oz	2 tablespoon (T)
50 ml	1.76 fl oz	2 fl oz	½ dl, 1 jigger
75 ml	2.66 fl oz	2 ½ fl oz	¾ dl
100 ml	3.52 fl oz	3 ½ fl oz	1 dl
120 ml	4.06 fl oz	4 fl oz	1 gill (US), (118.2ml) 32 drams
125 ml	4.40 fl oz	4 ½ fl oz	¼ pint, ½ cup
150ml	5.28 fl oz	5 fl oz	1 gill (UK), (142ml)

VOLUME CONVERSION (METRIC TO IMPERIAL)

METRIC VOLUME	EXACT IMPERIAL EQUIVALENT	US CUSTOMARY	ALSO KNOWN AS
200 ml	6.6 fl oz	6.3 fl oz	
236ml	8.33 fl oz	8 fl oz	1 cup (US), ½ pint (US)
250 ml	8.81 fl oz	9 fl oz	¼ litre, 1 cup (UK), 16 tablespoons
275ml	9.67 fl oz	9 ½ fl oz	½ pint (UK)
475 ml	15.99 fl oz	16 fl oz	1 pint (US)
500 ml	17.63 fl oz	18 fl oz	½ litre
570ml	20.27 fl oz	20 fl oz	1 pint (UK), 4 gills
1 litre	35.26 fl oz	35 fl oz	1000ml, 1 qt, 2 pints (US) 4 cups (UK)
1.1 litres	37.18 fl oz	37 fl oz	1100ml, 1 dry qt
3.8 litres	128.44 fl oz	128 fl oz	1 gallon (US), 4 quarts, 16 cups
4.5 litres	158.67 fl oz	160 fl oz	1 gallon (UK)
34 litre	1149.2 fl oz	1150 fl oz	1 firken

LESS COMMON MEASUREMENTS

A10	commercial food can (3kg)
A12	commercial food can (4.2kg)
Baker's dozen	13
Bush / Bushel (US Imperial dry measure	8 gallons (4 pecks, 35Litre dry)
3 bushels	1 sack
deck	10 bunches
dram (fluid)	3.7 ml
gill (UK)	137.7 ml
gill (US)	118.3 ml
gallon (UK)	4.546 L
Gallon (US)	3.785 L
Head	1 only (used for vegetables such as cauliflower and cabbage)
No. 1 can (US)	310 g, 11 oz
No.2 can (US)	560 g/ 600ml / 20 oz
No. 2½ can (US)	850 g/ 840 ml /28 oz
No. 303 can (US)	450g / 480 ml / 16 oz
Peck (US imperial dry measure)	8 quarts (8.8 L dry)
pint (UK)	568.3 ml
pint (US)	473.2 ml
5 quarters	1 load (ld)
12 sacks	1 chaldron

COMMON DIMENSIONS OF COOKING EQUIPMENT / BAKING EQUIPMENT

The conversions given are based on what recipe books commonly call for when specifying items such as cake pans, frying pans and cutters. They are not exact conversions. For example, 30 centimetres is not exactly 12 inches, but a cookbook will usually ask for a 30 cm / 12 in diameter tin or pan.

1 cm	½ inch
2.5 cm	1 in
4 cm	1 ½ in
5 cm	2 in
8 cm	3 in
10 cm	4 in
12 cm	5 iin
20 cm	8 in
23 cm	9 in
28cm	11 in
30 cm	12 in
33 cm	13 in (1 foot)
45 cm	18 in
60 cm	24 in

EQUIVALENT QUANTITIES FOR SOME COMMON FOODS

Weights are equivalent to 1 cup (250 ml) of the product
+ means just over the weight specified
- means just under the weight specified

INGREDIENT	g / kg	oz / lbs
blueberries, fresh/raw	100g	4oz
breakfast cereals, Bran Flakes	37 g	1 ½ oz
breakfast cereals, Cornflakes	25 g	1 oz
breakfast cereals, crushed flakes	75 g	3 oz
breakfast cereals, Rice Bubbles/Crispies	25 g	1 oz
breakfast cereals, Puffed Rice	-25 g	-1 oz
bread, fresh/stale, broken into pieces	50 g	2 oz
breadcrumbs, fresh	50 g	2 oz
breadcrumbs, dry	90 g	3½ oz
broccoli florets, fresh/raw	175 g	6 oz
Brussel sprouts, fresh/raw	100 g	4 oz
bulgar wheat, raw	225 g	8 oz
bulgar wheat, cooked	250 g	9 oz
butter	225 g	8 oz
cabbage, raw, chopped	100 g	4 oz
cabbage, cooked, chopped	225 g	8 oz
candied fruit	225 g	8 oz
candied peel	75 g	3 oz
capsicum, chopped	175 g	6 oz
carrots, cooked/raw, chopped	150 g	+5 oz
carrots, raw, julienne/grated	50 g	2 oz
cashew nuts, whole/chopped	150g	+5 oz
cauliflower florets, fresh/cooked	325 g	-12 oz
celeriac, raw, chopped	150 g	+5 oz
celeriac, cooked, chopped/mashed	200 g	7 oz
celery, raw, chopped	100 g	4 oz
celery, cooked, chopped	225 g	8 oz
cheese, hard, grated	100 g	4 oz

INGREDIENT	g / kg	oz / lbs
cheese, hard, cubed	125 g	-5 oz
cheese, cottage or cream	225 g	8 oz
cheese, soft, grated	100 g	8 oz
cherries, fresh, pitted	225 g	4 oz
chicken, cooked, shredded (meat only)	125 g	8 oz
chocolate, grated	125 g	- 5 oz
chocolate chips	175 g	- 5 oz
citrus fruit, segments/large pieces (flesh only)	225 g	8 oz
cocoa powder	100 g	4 oz
coconut, flaked/grated	75 g	3 oz
cod, flaked (flesh only)	200 g	7 oz
coriander, chopped	50 g	2 oz
corn kernels, fresh	175 g	6 oz
corn, tinned	250 g	9 oz
cornflour	125 g	- 5 oz
cornmeal	150 g	+ 5 oz
corn syrup	300 g	11 oz
crackers, broken	175 g	6 oz
cranberries, fresh/raw	100 g	4 oz
cucumber, raw, chopped	150 g	+ 5 oz
currants (e.g. black or red), fresh	100 g	4 oz
currants, dried	150 g	+ 5 oz
dates, whole	225 g	8 oz
dates, pitted, chopped	175 g	6 oz
eggplant, raw, chopped	250 g	9 oz
eggs, hard boiled, chopped	225 g	8 oz
figs, chopped	150 g	+ 5 oz
flour, white, rye, barley	+100 g	+ 4 oz
flour, wholewheat	150 g	- 5 oz
flour, chickpea	75 g	3 oz

INGREDIENT	g / kg	oz / lbs
flour, cornflour	125g	- 5 oz
flour, potato	150 g	5 oz
flour, rice	150 g	+ 5 oz
flour, tapioca	125 g	5 oz
frozen vegetables, chopped	150 g	+ 5 oz
garlic flakes	140 g	5 oz
ginger, fresh, chopped	100 g	4 oz
grapefruit, segments/large pieces (flesh only)	225 g	8 oz
grapes, whole	+100 g	+ 4 oz
grapes, halved, pitted	175 g	6 oz
greens, raw, chopped	100 g	6 oz
greens, cooked, chopped	225 g	8 oz
haddock, flesh only, flaked	200 g	7 oz
ham, cooked, chopped	150 g	+ 5 oz
hazelnuts, whole	150 g	+ 5 oz
hazelnuts, chopped	175 g	6 oz
jam	325 g	- 12 oz
lard	225 g	8 oz
lentils, uncooked	200 g	7 oz
lentils, cooked	75 g	3 oz
lettuce, chopped	75 g	3oz
margarine	225 g	8 oz
meat (red), minced	225 g	8 oz
meat (red), cooked, chopped	1 50 g	+ 5 oz
milk powder	125 g	- 5 oz
mincemeat	225 g	8 oz
mint, fresh, chopped	+ 25 g	+ 1 oz

INGREDIENT	g / kg	oz / lbs
molasses	325 g	- 12 oz
mushrooms, fresh, whole	125 g	5 oz
mushrooms, fresh, chopped mushrooms, fresh,	100 g	4 oz
sliced	+ 75 g	+ 3 oz
nectarines, fresh, peeled and sliced noodles,	225 g	8 oz
uncooked	75 g	3 oz
noodles, cooked	150 g	+ 5 oz
nuts see *individual nuts*		
oatmeal	-100 g	- 4 oz
okra, raw	100 g	4 oz
onion, raw, sliced	100 g	4 oz
onion, raw, chopped	150 g	+5 oz
oranges, segments or large pieces (flesh only)		
oysters, without shell	225 g	8 oz
	225 g	8 oz
parsley, fresh, coarsely chopped	25 g	1 oz
pasta, short cut, uncooked	100 g	4 oz
pasta, short cut, cooked	200 g	7 oz
peaches, fresh, sliced	225 g	8 oz
peanut butter	250 g	9 oz
peanuts, shelled	150 g	+ 5 oz
peanuts, chopped	125 g	- 5 oz
pearl barley	200 g	7 oz
pears, fresh, peeled and sliced	225 g	8 oz
pears, tinned, drained and chopped	+ 175 g	+ 6 oz
peas (green), shelled, fresh or frozen	150g	+ 5 oz
peas, split, uncooked	225 g	8 oz
peas, split, cooked	100g	4 oz

INGREDIENT	g / kg	oz / lbs
pecan nuts, shelled, halved	100 g	4 oz
pecan nuts, shelled, chopped	125 g	- 5 oz
pineapple, fresh, skinned, chopped pineapple,	200 g	7 oz
crushed	225 g	8 oz
pistachio nuts, whole	150 g	+ 5 oz
pistachio nuts, chopped	100 g	4 oz
plums, fresh, stoned	175 g	6 oz
poppy seeds	125 g	- 5 oz
potatoes, raw, chopped	175 g	6 oz
potatoes, cooked, chopped or mashed prunes,	225 g	8 oz
dried	175 g	6 oz
prunes, cooked, stoned	125g	- 5 oz
pumpkin, cooked, chopped	150 g	+ 5 oz
pumpkin, cooked, mashed	225 g	8 oz
quince, fresh, stoned	175 g	6 oz
raisins, dried	150 g	+ 5 oz
raisins, cooked	200 g	7 oz
raspberries, fresh	125 g	- 5 oz
rhubarb, fresh, raw, chopped	100 g	4 oz
rhubarb, cooked, fresh or tinned and drained	200 g	7 oz
rice, raw	225 g	8 oz
rice, cooked	250 g	9 oz
rolled oats, uncooked	100 g	4 oz
salmon, tinned, drained, flaked	225 g	8 oz
sauerkraut	150 g	+ 5 oz
semolina, dry	200 g	7 oz
shallots, raw, sliced	100 g	4 oz
shallots, raw, chopped	150 g	+ 5 oz
shortening	225 g	8 oz
soybeans, cooked	75 g	3 oz

INGREDIENT	g / kg	oz / lbs
spaghetti, uncooked	100 g	4 oz
spaghetti, cooked	50 g	- 2 oz
spinach, cooked (450 g raw weight) spinach,	225 g	8 oz
raw	75 g	- 3 oz
squash (summer), cooked, chopped squash	125 g	-5 oz
(winter), cooked, mashed strawberries, fresh,	450 g	16 oz
halved/sliced	200 g	7 oz
suet, shredded	125 g	- 5 oz
sugar, granulated, caster or superfine sugar,	225 g	8 oz
brown	200 g	7 oz
sugar, icing	125 g	- 5 oz
sultanas	150 g	+ 5 oz
swede, raw, chopped	150 g	+ 5 oz
swede, cooked, chopped or mashed sweet	200 g	7 oz
potatoes, raw, chopped	150 g	+ 5 oz
sweet potatoes, cooked, mashed	200 g	7 oz
tapioca, dry	150 g	+5 oz
tomatoes, fresh, chopped	200 g	7 oz
tomatoes, tinned	225 g	8 oz
tomato paste or sauce	225g	8 oz
tuna, flaked (flesh only)	225g	8 oz
turkey, cooked, shredded (meat only)	125 g	- 5 oz
turnips, raw, chopped	150 g	+ 5 oz
turnips, cooked, chopped or mashed	200 g	7 oz
walnuts, shelled, halved	100 g	4 oz
walnuts, shelled, chopped	125 g	- 5 oz
yoghurt	250 g	9 oz
zucchini, sliced	150 g	+ 5 oz
zucchini, chopped	175 g	6 0z

ADDITIVES

This list of additives is designed as a quick reference to the main food additives ever present in packaged foods. If you still have concerns you can have a checklist sent to you from your country's governing food authority that deals with additives, genetically modified foods, labelling, irradiation, food standards and safety.

Some additives are not labelled, and this is legal when an ingredient within a processed food itself contains additives. Confusing? Yes, but the simple answer is to contact the manufacturer for this ingredient information. Otherwise send for a complete 'code breaker' from your national food authority.

Food additives are an important component in the preservation of our food, ensuring longevity and ease of use. Additives are also used to improve the taste and appearance of the food. However, with the good comes the bad, and some additives do have an adverse effect on some people. Most intolerances are blamed on the additive, when in fact the intolerance may be attributable to a naturally occurring food component such as amines, glutamates and salicylates. In either case people with allergies want to know what it is they are consuming, others simply don't like the amount of added extras thrown into a tasty snack.

The varied functions of food additives are: colouring agents, flavouring, colour retention salicylates.agents, preservatives, flavour enhancers, mineral salts, food acids, humectants, emulsifiers, food acids, anti-caking agents, stabilisers, thickeners, vegetable gums, propellants, glazing agents and flour treatment agents.

There are so many food additives out there, with equally confusing names, that code numbers have been added to simplify their identification. This list (sourced from the Australian and New Zealand Food Authority) is an international list, with the codes being universal, but keep in mind it is not the most extensive list, and each country may allow and use additives that are not used and accepted in other countries. A letter in front of the numbers simply denotes a country for example 'E100' is still turmeric, but found on packages in the UK.

The following list shows code number, prescribed name and use. Additive numbers are in **bold-face type**, followed by the name in <u>Roman</u>, then the use in *italic*.

100 curcumin *colouring* **100** turmeric *colouring* **101** riboflavin *colouring* **101** riboflavin 5' phosphate sodium *colouring* **102** tartrazine *colouring* **103** alkanet *colouring* **104** quinoline yellow CI 47005 *colouring* **110** sunset yellow FCF *colouring* **120** carmines *colouring* **120** cochineal CI 75470 *colouring* **122** azorubine *colouring* **123** amaranth *colouring* **124** ponceau 4R *colouring* **127** erythrosine *colouring* **129** allura red AC CI 16035 *colouring* **132** indigotine *colouring* **133** brilliant blue FCF *colouring* **140** chlorophyll *colouring* **141** chlorophyll-copper complex **colouring 142** food green S *colouring* **150** caramel *colouring* **151** brilliant black BN *colouring* **153** activated vegetable carbon *colouring* **153** carbon blacks *colouring* **155** brown HT *colouring* **160** carotene, others **colouring 160a** beta-carotene *colouring* 160b annatto extracts *colouring* **160e** beta-apo-8' carotenal *colouring* **160f** E-apo-8' carotenoic acid methyl or ethyl ester *colouring* **161** xanthophylls *colouring* **162** beet red *colouring* **163** anthocyanins *colouring* **170** calcium carbonate mineral salt, *colouring* **171** titanium dioxide *colouring* **172** ironoxide, red, black, yellow *colouring* **174** silver *colouring* **181** tannic acid *colouring* **200** sorbic acid *preservative* **201** sodium sorbate *preservative* **202** potassium sorbate *preservative* **203** calcium sorbate *preservative* **210** benzoic acid *preservative* **211** sodium benzoate *preservative* **212** potassium benzoate *preservative* **213** calcium benzoate *preservative* **216** propylparaben *preservative* **218** methylparaben *preservative* **220** sulphur dioxide *preservative* **221** sodium sulphite *preservative* **222** sodium bisulphite *preservative* **223** sodium metabisulphite *preservative* **224** potassium metabisulphite *preservative* **225** potassium sulphite *preservative* **228** potassium bisulphite *preservative* **234** nisin *preservative* **235** natamycin *preservative* **242** dimethyl dicarbonate *preservative* **249** potassium nitrite *preservative, colour fixative* **250** sodium nitrite *preservative, colour fixative* **251** sodium nitrate *preservative, colour fixative* **252** potassium nitrate *preservative, colour fixative* **260** acetic acid, glacial *food acid* **261** potassium acetate *food acid*

262 sodium acetate *food acid* **262** sodium diacetate *food acid* **263** sodium acetate *food acid* **264** ammonium acetate *food acid* **270** lactic acid *food acid* **280** propionic acid *preservative* **281** sodium propionate *preservative* **282** calcium propionate *preservative* **283** potassium propionate *preservative* **290** carbon dioxide *propellant* **296** malic acid *food acid antioxidant* **297** fumaric acid *food acid* **300** ascorbic acid *antioxidant* **301** sodium ascorbate *antioxidant* **302** calcium ascorbate *antioxidant* **303** potassium ascorbate *antioxidant* **304** ascorbyl palmitate *antioxidant* **306** tocopherols concentrate, *mixed antioxidant* **307** dl-a-tocopherol *antioxidant* **308** g-tocopherol *antioxidant* **309** d-tocopherol *antioxidant* **310** propyl gallate *antioxidant* **311** octyl gallate *antioxidant* **312** sodecyl gallate *antioxidant* **315** erythorbic acid *antioxidant* **316** sodium erythorbate *antioxidant* **319** tert-butylhydroquinone *antioxidant* **320** butylated hydroxyanisole *antioxidant* **321** butylated hydroxytoluene *antioxidant* **322** lecithin antioxidant, *emulsifier* **325** sodium lactate *food acid* **326** potassium lactate *food acid* **327** calcium lactate *food acid* **328** ammonium lactate *food acid* **329** magnesium lactate *food acid* **330** citric acid *food acid* **331** sodium acid citrate *food acid* **331** sodium citrate *food acid* **331** sodium dihydrogen citrate *food acid* **332** potassium citrates *food acid* **333** calcium citrate *food acid* **334** tartaric acid*food acid* **335** sodium tartrate *food acid* **336** potassium acid tartrate *food acid* **336** potassium tartrate *food acid* **337** potassium sodium tartrate *food acid* **338** phosphoric acid *food acid* **339** sodium phosphates *mineral salt* **340** potassium phosphates *mineral salt* **341** calcium phosphates *mineral salt* **342** ammonium phosphates *mineral salt* **343** magnesium phosphates *mineral salt* **349** ammonium malate *food acid* **350** dl-sodium malates *food acid* **351** potassium malate *food acid* **352** dl-calcium malate *food acid* **353** metatartaric acid *food acid* **354** calcium tartrate *food acid* **355** adipic acid *food acid* **357** potassium adipate *food acid* **365** sodium fumarate *food acid* **366** potassium fumarate *food acid* **367** potassium fumarate *food acid* **368** ammonium fumarate *food acid* **375** niacin colour *retention agent* **380** ammonium citrate *food acid* **380** triammonium citrate *food acid* **381** ferric ammonium citrate *food acid* **385** calcium disodium ethylenediaminetetraacetate (EDTA) *preservative* **400** alginic acid *thickener, vegetable gum*

401 sodiumalginate *thickener, vegetable gum* **402** potassium alginate *thickener, vegetable gum* **403** ammonium alginate *thickener, vegetable gum* **404** calcium alginate *thickener, vegetable gum* **405** propylene glycol alginate *thickener, vegetable gum* **406** agar *thickener, vegetable gum* **407** Carrageenan *thickener, vegetable gum* **407a** processed eucheuma seaweed *thickener, vegetable gum* **409** arabinogalactan *thickener, vegetable gum* **410** locust bean gum *thickener, vegetable gum* **412** Guar gum *thickener, vegetable gum* **413** tragacanth *thickener, vegetable gum* **414** acacia *thickener, vegetable gum* **415** Xanthan gum *thickener, vegetablegum* **416** Karaya gum *thickener, vegetable gum* **418** gellan gum *thickener, vegetable gum* **420** sorbitol *humectant* **421** mannitol *humectant* **422** glycerin *humectant* **433** polysorbate 80 *emulsifier* **435** polysorbate 60 *emulsifier* **436** polysorbate 65 *emulsifier* **440** pectin *vegetable gum* **442** ammonium salts of phosphatidic acid *emulsifier* **444** sucrose acetate isobutyrate emulsifier, *stabiliser* **450** potassium pyrophosphate *mineral salts* **450** sodium acid pyrophosphate *mineral salt* **450** sodium pyrophosphate *mineral salt* **451** sodium tripolyphosphate *mineral salt* **452** potassium tripolyphosphate *mineral salt* **452** sodium metaphosphate, *insoluble mineral salt* **452** sodium polyphosphates, *glassy mineral salt* **452** potassium polymetaphosphate *mineral salt* **460** cellulose microcrystalline, *powdered anti-caking agent* **461** methylcellulose *thickener, vegetable gum* **464** hydroxypropyl methylcellulose *thickener, vegetable gum* **465** methyl ethyl cellulose *thickener, vegetable gum* **466** sodium carboxymethylcellulose *thickener, vegetable gum* **470** magnesium stearate *emulsifier, stabiliser* **471** mono- di-glycerides of fatty acids *emulsifier* **472a** acetic and fatty acid esters of glycerol *emulsifier* **472b** lactic and fatty acid esters of glycerol *emulsifier* **472c** citric and fatty acid esters of glycerol *emulsifier* **472d** tartaric and fatty acid esters of glycerol *emulsifier* **472e** diacetyltartaric and fatty acid esters of glycerol *emulsifier* **473** sucrose esters of fatty *emulsifier* **475** polyglycerol esters of fatty acids *emulsifier* **476** polyglycerol esters of interesterified ricinoleic acid *emulsifier* **477** propylene glycol mono- and di-esters *emulsifier* **480** dioctyl sodium sulphosuccinate *emulsifier* **481** sodium oleyl lactylate *emulsifier* **481** sodium stearoyl lactylate *emulsifier*

482 calcium oleyl lactylate *emulsifier* **482** calcium stearoyl lactylate *emulsifier* **491** sorbitan monostearate *emulsifier* **492** sorbitan tristearate *emulsifier* **500** sodium bicarbonate *mineral salt* **500** sodium carbonate *mineral salt* **501** potassium carbonates *mineral salt* **503** ammonium bicarbonate *mineral salt* **503** ammonium carbonate *mineral salt* **504** magnesium carbonate *anti-caking agent, mineral salt* **507** hydrochloric acid *acidity regulator* **508** potassium chloride *mineral salt* **509** calcium chloride *mineral salt* **510** ammonium chloride *mineral salt* **511** magnesium chloride *mineral salt* **512** stannous chloride *colour retention agent* **514** sodium sulphate *mineral salt* **515** potassium sulphate *mineral salt* **516** calcium sulphate f*lour treatment agent, mineral salt* **518** magnesium sulphate *mineral salt* **519** cupric sulphate *mineral salt* **526** calcium hydroxide *mineral salt 529* calcium oxide *mineral salt* **535** sodium ferrocyanide *anti-caking agent* **536** potassium ferrocyanide *anti-caking agent* **541** sodium aluminium phosphate, *acidic acidity regulator, emulsifier* **542** bone phosphate *anti-caking agent* **551** silicon dioxide *anti-caking agent* **552** calcium silicate *anti-caking agent* **553** talc *anti-caking agent* **554** sodium aluminosilicate *anti-caking agent* **556** calcium aluminium silicate *anti-caking agent* **558** bentonite *anti-caking agent* **559** kaolin *anti-caking agent* **570** stearic acid *anti-caking agent* **575** gluconod-lactone *acidity regulator* **577** potassium gluconate *stabiliser* **578** calcium gluconate *acidity regulator* **579** ferrous gluconate *colour retention agent* **620** l-glutamic acid f*lavour enhancer* **621** monosodium l-glutamate *flavour enhancer* **622** monopotassium l-glutamate *flavour enhancer* **623** calcium di-l-glutamate *flavour enhancer* **624** monoammonium l-glutamate *flavour enhancer* **625** *magnesium di-l-glutamatelavour enhancer* **627** disodium guanylate *flavour enhancer* **631** disodium inosinate *flavour enhancer* **635** disodium ribonucleotides *flavour enhancer* **636** maltol *flavour enhancer* **637** ethyl maltol *flavour enhancer* **640** glycine *flavour enhancer* **641** l-leucine *flavour enhancer* **900** dimethylpolysiloxane *emulsifier, antifoaming agent, anti- caking agent* **901** beeswax, *white and yellow glazing agent* **903** carnauba wax *glazing agent* **904** shellac, *bleached glazing agent* **905b** petrolatum *glazing agent* **905a** mineral oil, *white glazing agent* **914** oxidised polyethylene *Humectant*

920 l-cysteine monohydrochloride *flour treatment agent* **925** chlorine *flour treatment agent* **926** chlorine dioxide *flour treatment agency* **928** benzoyl peroxide *flour treatment agent* **941** nitrogen *propellant* **942** nitrous oxide *propellant* **950** acesulphame potassium *artificial sweetening substance* **951** aspartame *artificial sweetening substance* **952** sodium cyclamate *artificial sweetening substance* **952** cyclamic acid *artificial sweetening substance* **952** calcium cyclamate *artificial sweetening substance* **953** isomalt *humectant* **954** sodium saccharin *artificial sweetening substance* **954** saccharin *artificial sweetening substance* **954** calcium saccharin *artificial sweetening substance* **955** sucralose *artificial sweetening substance* **956** alitame *artificial sweetening substance* **957** thaumatin *flavour enhancer, artificial sweetening substance* **965** maltitol and maltitol syrup *humectant, stabiliser* **966** actitol *humectant* **967** xylitol *humectant, stabiliser* **1001** choline salts and esters *emulsifier* **1100** amylases *flour treatment agent* **1101** proteases papain, bromelain, ficin *flour treatment agent, stabiliser, flavour enhancer* **1102** glucose oxidase *antioxidant* **1104** lipases *flavour enhancer* **1105** lysozyme *preservative* **1200** polydextrose *humectant* **1201** polyvinylpyrrolidone *stabiliser, clarifying agent, dispersing agent* **1202** polyvinylpolypyrrolidone *colour stabiliser* **1400** dextrin *roasted starch thickener, vegetable gum* **1401** acid *treated starch thickener, vegetable gum* **1402** alkaline *treated starch thickener, vegetable gum* **1401** acid *reated starch thickener, vegetable gum* **1402** alkaline *treated starch thickener, vegetable gum* **1403** bleached starch *thickener, vegetable gum* **1404** oxidised starch *thickener, vegetable gum* **1405** enzyme-treated starches *thickener, vegetable gum* **1410** monostarch phosphate *thickener, vegetable gum* **1412** distarch phosphate *thickener, vegetable gum* **1413** phosphated distarch phosphate *thickener, vegetable gum* **1414** acetylated distarch phosphate *thickener, vegetable gum* **1420** starch acetate esterified with acetic anhydride *thickener, vegetable gum* **1421** starch acetateesterified with vinyl acetate *thickener, vegetable gum* **1422** acetylated distarch adipate *thickener, vegetable gum* **1440** hydroxypropyl starch *thickener, vegetable gum* **1442** hydroxypropyl distarch phosphate *thickener, vegetable gum* **1450** starch sodium octenylsuccinate *thickener, vegetable gum*

1505 triethyl citrate *thickener, vegetable gum* **1518** triacetin *humectant* **1520** propylene glycol *humectant* **1521** polyethylene glycol 8000 *antifoaming agent*

BIBLIOGRAPY

Adria, Ferran (2008), *A Day at elBulli,* London, Phaidon Press Limited

Alexander, Stephanie (1996), *The Cook's Companion,* Sydney: Penguin Books Australia Ltd.

Bear, Marina and John with Zeryck, Tanya (1998), *How to Repair Food,* Berkeley, California: Ten Speed Press.

Barbot, Pascal and Rohat, Cristophe and Masui, Chiriro, (2012) *Astrance, A Cook's Book.* France, Editions, du Chene

Beeton, Isabella (1981), *Mrs Beeton's Cookery Book*, Dee Why West, NSW: Rigby Publishers.

Berriedale-Johnson, Michelle (1998), *Cooking for Diabetics,* London: Hermes House.

Blumenthal, Heston (2011), *Heston Blumenthal at Home,* Great Britain, Bloomsbury Publishing Pty ltd

Boxer, Arabella and Innes, Jocasta and Parry-Crooke, Charlotte and Esson, Lewis (1984), *The Encyclopedia of Herbs and Spices*, London: Octopus Books Ltd.

Bras, Michel, (2008), *Essential Cuisine,* France. Editions du Rouergue

Brown, Colin (1985), *The Game Cookbook*, North Ryde, NSW: Methuen Australia Pty Ltd.

Campbell, Susan (1985), *The Cook's Companion,* London: Chancellor Press.

Coffey, Lynette (1991), *Wheatless Cooking*, Ringwood, Victoria: Penguin Books Australia Ltd.

Cummings, Joe (2000), *World Food Thailand,* Hawthorn, Victoria: Lonely Planet Publications Pty Ltd.

Davidson, Alan (1999), *The Oxford Companion to Food*, New York: Oxford University Press.

Dye, Molly (2001), *Domestic Bliss*, Sydney: Nation Wide News Pty Ltd.

Escoffier, Auguste (1979), *The Complete Guide to the Art of Modern Cookery,* London: William Heinemann Ltd.

Escoffier, Auguste (1941), *The Escoffier Cookbook, A Guide to the Fine Art of Cookery,* New York: Crown Publishers.

Evans, Matthew and Cossi, Gabriella (2000), *World Food Italy,* Hawthorn, Victoria: Lonely Planet Publications Pty Ltd.

Fernandez-Armesto, Felipe (2001), *Food: A History,* London: Macmillan

Geddes, Bruce (2001), *World Food Caribbean,* Footscray, Victoria: Lonely Planet Publications Pty Ltd.

Geddes, Bruce (2000), *World Food Mexico*, Hawthorn, Victoria: Victoria: Lonely Planet Publications Pty Ltd.

Gilmore, Peter (2018), *From the Earth,* Richmond, Victoria, Australia. Hardie Grant Books (Melbourne).

Hughes, Martin with Mookherjee, Sheema and Delacy, Richard (2001), *World Food India*, Footscray, Victoria: Lonely Planet Publications Pty Ltd.

Hughes, Martin (2000), *World Food Ireland*, Hawthorn, Victoria: Lonely Planet Publications Pty Ltd.

Johnson, Pableaux with O'Brian, Charmaine (2000), *World Food, New Orleans*, Footscray, Victoria: Lonely Planet Publications Pty Ltd.

Keller, Thomas (2008), *Under Pressure,* New York, NY, USA. Artisan

Levy Beranbaum, Rose (2003), *The Bread Bible,* New York, NY, USA, W. W. Norton & Company, Inc.

Lo, Kenneth (1979), T*he Complete Encyclopaedia of Chinese Cooking,* London: Octopus Books Ltd.

Low, Tim (1989), *Bush Tucker*, North Ryde, NSW: Angus and Robertson Publishers.

Madison, Deborah ((1997), *Vegetarian Cooking for Everyone,* New York: Broadway Books.

Manley, Lynton G. (1986), *Sauces for Courses*, Victoria: Edward Arnold Australia Pty Ltd.

Mariani, John (1994), T*he Dictionary of American Food and Drink*, 2nd rev edn, New York: Hearst.

Montagné, Prosper and Gottschalk, Dr (1961), *Larousse Gastronomique*, London: Hamlyn.

Morton, Julia F (1976), *Herbs and Spices,* New York: Golden Press.

Niland, Josh (2019), *The Whole Fish Cookbook,* Sydney, NSW: Hardie Grant.

Niland, Josh (2021), *Take One Fish,* Sydney, NSW: Hardie Grant.

Norman, Jill (1990), *The Complete Book of Spices,* London: Dorling Kindersley.

Oliver, Jamie (2001), *Happy Days with the Naked Chef,* London: Penguin Books Ltd.

Purnell, Dawn (1998), T*he Australian Kitchen Companion,* Smithfield, NSW: Gary Allen Pty Ltd

Roden, Claudia (1989), *Mediterranean Cookery,* London: BBC Books. Root, Waverley, (1980), Food, New York:

Root, Waverley, (1980), *Food,* New York: Simon & Schuster.

Roux, Michel and Roux, Albert (1986), *The Roux Brothers on Patisserie,* London: Macdonald & Co Ltd.

Slater, Nigel (2009), *Tender, Volume 1,* Great Britain, Harper Collins Publisher

Stamets, Paul (2019), *Fantastic Fungi,* San Rafael, California, USA. Earth Aware Editions.

Sterling, Richard (2000), *World Food Spain,* Hawthorn, Victoria: Lonely Planet Publications Pty Ltd.

Sterling, Richard (2000), *World Food Vietnam,* Hawthorn, Victoria: Lonely Planet Publications Pty Ltd.

Sterling, Richard and Chong, Elizabeth and Qin, Lushan Charles, (2001), *World Food Hong Kong,* Footscray, Victoria: Lonely Planet Publications Pty Ltd.

Stobart, Tom (1999), *The Cook's Encyclopaedia,* London: Grub Street.

Style, Sue (1992), *A Taste of Switzerland,* London: Pavilion Books.

Szathmary, Louis (1974), *American Gastronomy,* Chicago: Henry Regnery.

Taylor, Sally (1986), *Eating for Healthy Living,* Sydney: Golden Press.

Telford, Anthony (2003), *The Kitchen Hand,* Crows Nest, NSW. Allen & Unwin

Telford, Anthony (2009), *The Basics, a really useful cookbook,* Crows Nest, NSW. Allen & Unwin

This, Herve (2002), *Molecular gastronomy,* New York, USA.
    Columbia University Press
Thompson, David (2002), *Thai Food,* Camberwell, Victoria:
    Penguin Books Australia Ltd.
Ude, Louis Ustache (1828), *The French Cook*, repr. New
    York: Arco (1978).
Valent, Dani and Masters, Jim & Perihan (2000), *World Food Turkey,*
Hawthorn, Victoria: Lonely Planet Publications Pty Ltd.
Verrall, William (1988), *A Complete System of Cookery*, ed
    Ann Haly, Lewes: Southover.
Werle, Loukie (1997), *Australasian Ingredients*, Rushcutters
    Bay, NSW: Gore & Osment Publications Pty Ltd.
Wheeler, Alwyne (1979), *Fishes of the World: An Illustrated
    Dictionary*, London: Ferndale.
Willan, Anne (1977), *Great Cooks and Their Recipes: From
    Taillevent to Escoffier*, London: Elm Tree.

ACKNOWLEDGEMENTS

Thank you to anyone who used their time
to make money
and then used some of that money
to buy my book.

I appreciate you.